AF803106

Intellectual Property in Russia

Intellectual property (IP) rights are essential for a firm's competitive edge and success and form significant assets for many firms. The authors of this book argue that IP is a complex phenomenon, which inevitably requires both economic and legal considerations because the lack of understanding of the mechanisms for the protection and preservation of IP can undermine any of the potential economic benefits.

The book outlines the opportunities that can be derived from the use of IP in business and also identifies the rules necessary for their implementation. It offers comprehensive, systemic research of IP based on the most up-to-date legislation and cases of IP use in Russia. Such an approach will allow readers to fully understand the peculiarities of IP as a special phenomenon of the Russian market. There is a good balance between theoretical knowledge and practical implementation, and the plain language and unique approach to structuring information make the book accessible and easy to understand. It contains a special glossary of terms to facilitate the understanding of the material presented in the book.

Although the book looks specifically at the Russian case, it will have international appeal since IP, by its very nature, has become a transnational phenomenon. Moreover, the international regulatory framework provides for the similarity of legal regulation of IP. The book will find an audience among researchers concerned with the economics and law of IP, as well as policymakers and practitioners involved in business IP.

Natalia M. Udalova is a Senior Lecturer in the Civil Law and Civil Process Department at The National Research University, Higher School of Economics, Nizhny Novgorod, Russia.

Anna S. Vlasova is a Candidate of Juridical Sciences, an Associate Professor in the Civil Law and Civil Process Department at The National Research University, Higher School of Economics, Nizhny Novgorod, Russia.

Routledge Studies in the Economics of Business and Industry

An Economic Theory of Managerial Firms
Strategic Delegation in Oligopoly
Luca Lambertini

Economics of the Indian Steel Industry
Susmita Dasgupta

The Globalisation of Indian Business
Cross Border Mergers and Acquisitions in Indian Manufacturing
Beena Saraswathy

Economics and Management in the Biopharmaceutical Industry in the USA
Evolution and Strategic Change
Rachel Kim

Shipbuilding in the United Kingdom
A History of the British Shipbuilders Corporation
Hugh Murphy

Intellectual Property in Russia
Natalia M. Udalova and Anna S. Vlasova

A Market Process Theory of the Firm
An Alternative to the Neoclassical Model
Mateusz Machaj

For more information about this series, please visit www.routledge.com/Routledge-Studies-in-the-Economics-of-Business-and-Industry/book-series/RSEBI

Intellectual Property in Russia

Natalia M. Udalova
and Anna S. Vlasova

Routledge
Taylor & Francis Group
LONDON AND NEW YORK

First published 2021
by Routledge
2 Park Square, Milton Park, Abingdon, Oxon OX14 4RN

and by Routledge
605 Third Avenue, New York, NY 10158

Routledge is an imprint of the Taylor & Francis Group, an informa business

© 2021 Natalia M. Udalova and Anna S. Vlasova

The right of Natalia M. Udalova and Anna S. Vlasova to be identified as authors of this work has been asserted by them in accordance with sections 77 and 78 of the Copyright, Designs and Patents Act 1988.

All rights reserved. No part of this book may be reprinted or reproduced or utilised in any form or by any electronic, mechanical, or other means, now known or hereafter invented, including photocopying and recording, or in any information storage or retrieval system, without permission in writing from the publishers.

Trademark notice: Product or corporate names may be trademarks or registered trademarks, and are used only for identification and explanation without intent to infringe.

British Library Cataloguing-in-Publication Data
A catalogue record for this book is available from the British Library

Library of Congress Cataloging-in-Publication Data
A catalog record has been requested for this book

ISBN: 978-0-367-56563-3 (hbk)
ISBN: 978-0-367-56564-0 (pbk)
ISBN: 978-1-003-09837-9 (ebk)

Typeset in Bembo
by Deanta Global Publishing Services, Chennai, India

Dedicated to my dear parents, Irina and Sergei. With love and respect.

Anna

Dedicated to my wonderful and beloved parents – Irina and Mikhail.

Natalia

Contents

About the Authors

Anna S. Vlasova is a Candidate of Juridical Sciences (the equivalent of a PhD, in Russia) and Associate Professor at the Civil Law and Civil Process Department of the National Research University Higher School of Economics, Nizhny Novgorod, Russia. Her sphere of scientific interests includes civil law, corporate law, business law, tax law and legal linguistics. Anna has experience in advising businesses on various legal issues and currently teaches business and corporate law. Anna is the author of scientific publications on business and corporate law issues in leading Russian journals.

Natalia M. Udalova is a Senior Lecturer in the Civil Law and Civil Process Department of the National Research University Higher School of Economics, Nizhny Novgorod, Russia. Natalia is the author of scientific publications dedicated to various issues of civil law. Her sphere of scientific interest includes civil law, business law, contract law and IP law. Natalia has law, economic and management degrees. In addition, Natalya has more than 10 years of law practice in the bar association. She teaches IP in Russian and in English. Her publication list includes an IP textbook written specifically for this course and scientific articles on business and corporate law issues in leading Russian journals.

Preface

The importance of intellectual property (IP) in modern world cannot be overemphasized. Intellectual property has become an integral part of day-to-day life. Undoubtedly, even in earlier times, people faced intellectual property on a daily basis, but its real value began to be recognized relatively recently, and upon realized, the attitude towards it began to change rapidly. Nowadays, intellectual property is considered to be an extremely important asset that plays a significant role.

The business community also recognizes the benefits and opportunities that arise from the correct use of IP. Proper use of intellectual property gives business persons competitive advantages, which can contribute to the development of their business and strengthen its market position. But sometimes, business persons make improper use of intellectual property, and this also requires attention.

At the same time, determining the areas of work that involve intellectual property, both economic parameters and legal regulations, must be taken into consideration, because a lack of understanding of the mechanisms of the use, transfer, protection, etc., of intellectual property can eliminate all potential economic benefits.

The extensive and sufficiently developed international regulatory framework provides for the uniformity of IP legal regulation. Nevertheless, although IP cannot be strictly limited to the national legislation, issues related to its daily use are largely determined by the area (and the corresponding legislation) within which it is implemented. The IP objects are used everywhere and each country has its own regulation. Russia is no exception.

Since the legal regulation of IP in the Russian Federation is based on international legal treaties and conventions, it has much in common with that of other countries, i.e., members of the relevant treaties. But different countries have different solutions to the same issues. Metaphorically speaking, we have an identical foundation but different buildings constructed on it.

Therefore, it is useful to examine foreign practices. The focus on Russian practice gives an opportunity to discover something new. And furthermore, Russian practice is used as a base for speaking about universal phenomena.

Moreover, nowadays there are a lot of foreign IP subject matters circulating in the Russian market. According to statistics,[1] foreign applicants from different countries are interested in obtaining legal protection for their results of intellectual activity. That's why knowledge on IP in Russia seems to be attractive to different people. And this book is the first step towards attaining this knowledge.

Truly speaking, the foreign experience in the field of IP can be useful not only for practice, scientific research and improving legal regulation, but also for replenishing knowledge, which is necessary for the development of an open-minded specialist.

Thus, the purpose of this book is to describe intellectual property in the sphere of business as well as to identify the rules regulating it, based on the experience of Russia's legal system. It covers the following issues: the concept and types of IP, intellectual property rights, legal regulation for IP in the Russian Federation, public authorities and other organizations functioning in the field of IP, the creation of IP – including the creation by employees – IP registration, IP in corporate relations, IP commercialization, IP management, transfer of IP rights, IP protection, etc. The authors attempt to examine the theoretical aspects of the procedures and to show the specific nature of their implementation.

The book represents comprehensive systemic research of intellectual property based on laws, scientific research and cases of IP use in Russia. Such an approach will allow a complete understanding of the peculiarities of IP as a special phenomenon in business.

The book will be useful to scientists, practicing lawyers, students and anyone interested in the specifics of intellectual property in business.

Anna Sergeevna Vlasova
Candidate of Juridical Sciences, Associate Professor, Civil Law and Civil Process Department
National Research University Higher School of Economics, Nizhny Novgorod, Russia

Natalia Mikhailovna Udalova
Senior Lecturer, Civil Law and Civil Process Department
National Research University Higher School of Economics, Nizhny Novgorod, Russia

Note

1 Annual Report of Federal Service for Intellectual Property (Rospatent) 2019 (https://rospatent.gov.ru/en/reports2019)

Acknowledgements

The authors thank everyone, without whose assistance the appearance of this book would not have become possible.

We express our appreciation to the editorial staff of Routledge (Taylor & Francis) for the opportunity to write this book. We personally thank Kristina Abbotts, Christiana Mandizha, Alexandra Atkinson, Sushmitha Ramesh, Bríana Walsh.

We are grateful to our families for their support.

Anna Vlasova
Natalia Udalova

Part One

General provisions on intellectual property

1 The concept and types of intellectual property

Despite the fact that the term "intellectual property" (IP) has become widely used, disputes over the appropriateness of its application still exist. On the one hand, the conventionality of this concept is pointed out; on the other hand, it is considered as a real legal category (The Fifth Session of the Supreme Soviet of the USSR, 1991, p. 11; Litovkin et al., 2008, p. 35).

It should be noted that the term "property" in the expression "intellectual property", translated from English into Russian, means ownership, and not property itself, i.e., objects of rights. Victor A. Dozortsev pointed out this problem and explained that ownership has a narrower meaning than property (Dozortsev, 2003). The Constitutional Court of the Russian Federation also noted that the protected results of intellectual activity are objects of civil rights, i.e., they are property (Ruling of the Constitutional Court of the Russian Federation of December 4, 2007, on case No. 066-O-P).

It seems that criticism of the term "intellectual property" in Russia is mainly due to whether the concept of ownership can be applied to intellectual objects.

The definition of the ownership concept is not normatively fixed in Russian legislation. It is considered more as an economic category, while in the context of the law, attention is paid to the right of ownership, which, as follows from Article 209 of the Civil Code of the Russian Federation[1] (the Civil Code), includes the rights of possession, use and disposal.

In this regard, the question arises of whether the indicated triad can be applied to intellectual objects, too, although they are incorporeal and intangible. Despite the presence of supporters of such an application, the position of their opponents is more common. For example, the impossibility of possessing such an object due to its immateriality (Litovkin et al., 2008) is highlighted, although, in practice, the conclusion of agreements on joint possession takes place, for example, an agreement on joint possession of trademarks (Ruling of the Presidium of the Intellectual Property Court of October 2, 2015, on case No. SIP-248/2014). In addition, the Civil Code provides a direct indication that it is not the object of intellectual rights itself that can be disposed of but rather the exclusive right to it (Article 1229). Thus, only the right of use applies to the object of IP rights.

It should be noted that all reasoning about IP as a category is important not only as a theoretical concept but also in practice. For example, there is a question of whether revendication can be applied to IP (the action of claiming back an IP subject matter from someone else's illegal possession). Opponents talk about the inability to use proprietary methods in the sphere of IP protection (Gavrilov, 2019), but there is also an opposite point of view (Sagdeeva, 2019). It is noteworthy that in judicial practice, there were attempts to implement this method of protecting IP right, but the courts insisted on its inapplicability (Resolution of the Federal State Commercial Court of Moscow Circuit of December 15, 2010, on case No. A40-166028/09-15-778; Resolution of the Thirteenth State Commercial Court of Appeal of March 11, 2010, on case No. A56-55994/2008).

Article 1227 of the Civil Code explicitly states that the provisions of Section II of the Civil Code, "The Right of Ownership and Other Property Rights", do not apply to intellectual rights unless otherwise established by the rules of the Civil Code. Thus, IP is normatively distinguished from the right of ownership and other property rights.

In accordance with Article 1225 of the Civil Code, IP includes the results of intellectual activity and the means of individualization of legal entities, goods, works, services and enterprises equated to them, which are provided with legal protection, namely:

1. works of science, literature and art;
2. programs for electronic data processing machines (computer programs);
3. databases;
4. performance;
5. phonograms;
6. over-the-air and cable transmission of radio and TV programs (broadcasting and cable broadcasting);
7. inventions;
8. utility models;
9. industrial designs;
10. selective breeding achievements;
11. topographies of integrated circuits;
12. production secrets (know-how);
13. company names;
14. trademarks and service marks;
15. geographical indications;
16. appellations of origin of goods;
17. commercial names.

The Supreme Court also explains that in accordance with the provisions of Part IV of the Civil Code, the term "intellectual property" covers only the results of intellectual activity and the means of individualization equated to them, but not the rights to them (Article 1225 of the Civil Code)(Resolution of the Plenum of the Supreme Court of the Russian Federation No. 10 of April 23, 2019, "On the Application of Part IV of the Civil Code of the Russian Federation"; hereinafter Resolution of the Plenum of the Supreme Court No. 10).

However, some scholars consider IP as a set of rights (Sergeev, 2018). Moreover, in accordance with "GOST R 55386-2012. The National Standard of the Russian Federation. Intellectual Property. Terms and Definitions",[2] approved and enacted by Order of the Federal Agency on Technical Regulating and Metrology (Rosstandart) No. 2087-st of December 27, 2012 (hereinafter GOST R 55386-2012), IP is a set of rights to the protected results of intellectual activity in industrial, scientific, literary and artistic fields as well as the means of individualization equated to them (intellectual rights) related to:

- artistic, literary, scientific and other works;
- programs for electronic data processing machines and databases;
- artists' performances, sound recordings, phonograms, radio, television and cable broadcasting;
- inventions in all areas of human activity;
- selective breeding achievements;
- utility models;
- industrial designs;
- production secrets (know-how);
- topographies of integrated circuits;
- trademarks and service marks, company names, appellations of origin of goods, commercial names;
- scientific discoveries;
- protection against unfair competition.

It is noteworthy that this example also demonstrates a broader understanding of IP in comparison with the normatively defined one.

Despite the ambiguous attitude towards the term "intellectual property", it seems that this concept is a fairly comprehensive generic concept used to arrange the regulation of a significant number of objects that imply the emergence of so-called exclusive rights.

Such a generalization of objects that are different in their essence is necessary to ensure the principle of regulatory saving, which creates the possibility of achieving effective legal regulation at the lowest cost through the rational use of the funds available. The Civil Code, for this purpose, separates the so-called general part and a number of specialized parts of the peculiarities of the specific results of intellectual activity and the means of individualization of legal entities, goods, works, services and enterprises.

Since the above list of IP subject matter is exhaustive, it cannot be broadly interpreted. In other words, without changing the law, it is impossible to put a completely new, unnamed IP subject matter under legal protection.

However, as noted by Novoselova and Rozhkova (2014), the principle of an open list applies to works of science, literature and art. According to this principle, they can include both objects specified in the Civil Code and those not named in this regulatory legal act. And indeed, there is no mention of an exhaustive list of copyright objects in clause 1 of Article 1259 of the Civil Code.

Accordingly, a copyright object could be any work, including those not directly identified as such in the Civil Code. This is justified by the pronounced creative nature of the corresponding activity, the result of which a work of science, literature and art could be created. The formation of an exhaustive list does not meet the goals of the copyright object's legislative regulation.

It is worth noting that besides not having an exhaustive list of such works, there are no clear criteria for the allocation of them either. The law books drew attention to this issue long ago.

In particular, as noted by Vladimir Ya. Ionas 1972 (Ionas, 1972, pp. 7–8), on the one hand, many civil law scholars supported the idea that the definition of "a work" is not a task of civil law, since it should be determined by special sciences: the theories of literature, art and science. At the same time, a different position was gradually formed, where the definition of "a work" is a civil law matter. For example, as noted by Vladimir I. Serebrovsky, "a work" can be defined as a set of ideas, thoughts and images. In his opinion, as the result of the author's creative activity, the "work" is expressed in a material form that is perceptible to human senses and can be reproduced (Serebrovsky, 1956, p. 32).

As seen, the creativity aspect is critically important in the context of producing a work of art, literature or science.

Therefore, as noted in clause 80 of the Resolution of the Plenum of the Supreme Court No. 10, when deciding whether to consider a specific result of intellectual activity a copyright object, the courts should consider that such a result must be achieved through creative activity. In this case, the question arises: creativity is necessary for the result of intellectual activity to be considered a work, but of what does it actually consist?

Questions on the essence of creativity have arisen before, and they are still being discussed.

Gabriel F. Shereshenevich, who defended his PhD dissertation on copyright at Kazan University in 1891, pointed out that the main immediate goal of spiritual creative activity is to strive to consolidate in colours, words and tones those images and ideas that creative people have in their mind in a form that is still unclear, unfinished (Shereshenevich, 2017, p. 8).

Olympiad S. Ioffe noted that creativity can be defined as an intellectual activity that ends with the act of creating a work, as a result of which new concepts, images and (or) forms of their embodiment appear, which are an ideal reflection of objective reality (Ioffe, 1965, p. 5).

So, as Vladimir I. Serebrovsky justly pointed out, in a literary work, spiritual creativity is expressed verbally, in scientific work, verbally, too, and also through various calculations, tables, formulas, diagrams, etc., and in works of art, it finds its reflection in sounds, paints, volumetric design, etc. (Serebrovsky, 1956, p. 32).

In modern legal literature, the term "spiritual creativity" has been replaced with "creativity" and "creative activity", which is in line with the normative regulation.

When characterizing creativity in the modern world, some scholars stick to the position that such intellectual activity is based on existing works, their elements and parts, and changing these works at the behest of one's imagination, giving new importance, sound and meaning to the existing work. This is due, in particular, to the fact that "one should experiment with the form, but not with the content" (Semenova, 2018).

In Russian legal doctrine, "creativity" is defined in its narrow sense as the creation of new cultural or material values. The basis for this is, for example, Article 3 of the Fundamentals of the Legislation of the Russian Federation on Culture (Law of the Russian Federation No. 3612-1 of October 9, 1992), according to which creative activity is the creation of cultural values and their interpretation. At the same time, in a broad sense, creativity is understood as the creation of something that did not exist before and previously unknown combination of the "already known elements" (Gongalo, 2018).

Olga V. Bogdanova considers creativity to be a result of an individual's intellectual, spiritual and mental activity. At the same time, according to the author, such activity is not only aimed at creating a thing that is an object of property rights (Bogdanova, 2017).

Nowadays, creativity can be described in different ways. Nevertheless, it is a kind of intellectual and spiritual activity of an individual, as the result of which IP subject matter, including copyright, may appear, rather than something else. It is the understanding of creativity formed in earlier legal literature sources that allow us to look at creativity from the perspective necessary for understanding IP. However, the question arises as to how such an intellectual process shall be delimited from mechanical, routine or uncreative activity. What should be the criteria for such a distinction?

It seems that discussions of the essence of creativity keep going due to the uncertainty of this phenomenon, as well as due to the dynamics of social relations, economic and social development, the emergence of new forms of creative activity and its results. And despite the fact that creativity, in this case, is not a legal matter, but is interesting in connection with its result and its use (Ioffe, 1965, p. 5), understanding the essence of creativity is critically important in order to determine the possibility of the legal protection of the results of intellectual activity.

It seems that it was the difficulty in identifying creativity and the creative process that served as the basis for forming the following position. In Russia, the results of intellectual activity are assumed to be achieved in a creative way until it has been proven otherwise. Thus, there is a presumption of creativity when a work is being produced. In addition, the lack of novelty, uniqueness and (or) originality of the result of intellectual activity cannot indicate that such a result was not achieved from creative activity and, therefore, is not an object of copyright (clause 80 of Resolution of the Plenum of the Supreme Court No. 10).

Currently, the creative nature of creating a work does not depend on whether the work is created by the author with their own hand or using technical means. At the same time, the results that are achieved with the help of technical means only and in the complete absence of human creative activity (for example, photographing and filming with a video surveillance camera operating in automatic mode, used to record administrative offences) are not copyright objects.

It should be noted that the objects of copyright that receive appropriate protection, by virtue of paragraph 5 of Article 1259 of the Civil Code, do not include:

- ideas;
- concepts;
- principles;
- methods;
- processes;
- systems;
- ways of doing something;
- solutions to technical, organizational or other problems;
- discoveries;
- facts;
- programming languages;
- geological information about the subsoil.

Thus, a chess game or teaching methods are not protected by copyright.

In each specific case, the question of the creative nature of the work, and, accordingly, the relevance of the result of intellectual activity to copyright objects is resolved by the courts independently, focusing on the above-mentioned regulations and clarifications of the Supreme Court of the Russian Federation, and relying on the judge's inner conviction.

For example, when the State Commercial Court of the Sverdlovsk Region had to resolve such a dispute, it proceeded from the fact that the controversial photographs (of the case) are the result of the creative work of its author, due to their high social, artistic and cultural value. This was indicated by the particular angle of shooting, the remoteness of the camera lens from the object of shooting, colour rendering and other artistic techniques; the above translates to unique (without intentional copying) content of the people depicted therein in a specific way (Decision of the State Commercial Court of the Sverdlovsk Region of April 9, 2014, on case No. A60-48473/2013).

In another case, the following results of intellectual activity were recognized as creative works due to their creative nature: regulations on the distinctive and constructive features of the network of game development rooms, design projects of game rooms, printing and content of the website. As a result, the courts concluded that they were illegally used by another business entity in its business activity by opening game rooms and creating a website. The Intellectual Property Court noted that, referring to the lack of creative nature in the objects used, the defendant did not give specific arguments regarding which elements of these objects related to ideas, concepts, principles, methods, processes, systems and solutions of technical, organizational or other tasks (Ruling of the Supreme Court of the Russian Federation of September 8, 2020, on case No. A27-10300/2019).

In another case, the Supreme Court of the Russian Federation upheld the position of the lower courts, refusing to satisfy the claims placed by the plaintiff. The courts of the first instance and appeal courts proceeded from the lack of evidence of the defendant's violation of the plaintiff's exclusive right to the disputed composite works, having established that the structural model, concept, organizational solution as well as the words "didactic material", "colouring" and "application" in the titles of publications and the subject matter of the drawings are not protected by copyright. The layout solutions for the covers of the plaintiff's works and the selection of drawings were not new or original and could not be perceived as made in a creative way (Ruling of the Supreme Court of the Russian Federation of May 14, 2018, on case No. A40-207329/2015).

There is one more example of a lack of creativity. The court of general jurisdiction did not uphold a claim to recognise the author of photographic images reproduced in a book because the images were made by a scanning microscope (Ruling of the Constitutional Court of the Russian Federation No. 918-O of April 23, 2020).

Nevertheless, despite the absence of an exhaustive list of the analyzed copyright objects, possible examples of such objects will be mentioned in this chapter.

According to Article 1259 of the Civil Code, items classified as creative works may be works of science, literature or art, regardless of the merits and purpose of the work, as well as the method of their expression. They include:

- literary works;
- dramatic and musical-dramatic works, scripts;
- choreographic works and pantomimes;
- musical works with or without lyrics;
- audiovisual works;
- painting, sculpture, graphics, design, graphic stories, comics and other works of fine art;
- works of decorative and applied art and scenographic art;
- works of architecture, urban planning and garden design, including in the form of projects, drawings, images and models;
- photographic works and works obtained by methods similar to photography;

- geographical and other maps, plans, sketches and plastic works related to geography and other sciences.

In accordance with clause 2 of this article, the so-called "derivative works" are classified as objects of copyright. These are works based on other work (translation, modification), film adaptation, arrangement and staging. In addition, composite works (works that result from a creative selection or arrangement of previously existing materials) will also be protected as a subject matter of IP.

The so-called "complex objects" must be distinguished from the composite works. Composite works are, among other things, collections, anthologies, encyclopaedias, internet sites, atlases and databases (clause 2 of Article 1259 of the Civil Code). This list is not limited. A complex object consists of several protected results of intellectual activity.

The legal regulations for complex objects apply to the completed work as a whole, meaning that the impossibility of using at least one of its components will lead to the loss of the creator's intention attached to the complex object and will entail the impossibility of its further application (clause 17 of the "Review of Judicial Practice on Cases Related to the Resolution of Disputes about Protection of Intellectual Rights", approved by the Presidium of the Supreme Court of the Russian Federation of September 23, 2015; hereinafter Review of Intellectual Property Judicial Practice, 2015). This determines certain peculiarities of the implementation of intellectual rights associated with a complex object. In particular, the author of any work included in a complex object does not have the right to revoke it, regardless of who owns the intellectual rights to the complex object itself. Article 1240 of the Civil Code contains an exhaustive list of complex objects: films, other audiovisual works, theatrical performances, multimedia products and databases.

Unfinished works will also be the subject matter of IP. Of course, the completeness or incompleteness of a work can only be judged by its author since only this person is familiar with the idea of the work. Nevertheless, given the constant development of copyright relations, the following explanation of the Supreme Court of the Russian Federation is very significant.

Parts of a work (clause 7 of Article 1259 of the Civil Code) will also be protected, subject to the following conditions put together:

- this part of a work retains its recognizability as a part of a particular work when used separately from the work as a whole;
- by themselves, such parts of a work, separated from the work as a whole, can be recognized as an independent result that is made by the author in a creative way and expressed in a material form.

Parts of a work may include, among other things, the title of the work, its characters, excerpts of text (paragraphs, chapters, etc.), excerpts of an audiovisual work (including its individual frames), preparatory materials obtained during the development of a computer program and audiovisual displays generated by it. Protection of part of a work as an independent result of intellectual activity shall be carried out only if such a part is used independently from the work as a whole (clause 81 of the Resolution of the Plenum of the Supreme Court No. 10).

According to the explanation of the Supreme Court of the Russian Federation, a character is a set of descriptions and (or) images of one or another person described in the work in a form (or forms) inherent to the work: in writing, orally, as an image, a sound or video recording and in a volumetric form, etc. Not every person in the work can be called a character in the above sense, but a character only exists as an independent result of intellectual activity. At the same time, it is important whether a specific person from the work has sufficient individualizing characteristics.

In particular, it matters whether the work defines the following aspects about the person described:

- appearance;
- character;
- distinctive features (e.g., movements, voice, facial expressions, speech characteristics);
- other features that make the person recognizable even when used separately from the entire work.

In the context of the above, the case mentioned below may be interesting. A legal dispute arose, part of which was the resolution of whether it was legally possible to use a character. As follows from the content of judicial acts, the exclusive right to the audiovisual works (animated films) united by the common name "Mowgli", consisting of the following works, *Raksha* (1967), *Abduction* (1968), *Akela's Last Hunt* (1969), *Battle* (1970) and *Return to the People* (1971), belongs to the Gosfilmofond (state film archive) of Russia as a legal successor of the Soyuzmultfilm film studio. The Soyuzmultfilm film studio had the copyright for the Mowgli films based on the provisions of Part 1, Article 486 of the Civil Code of the Russian Soviet Federative Socialist Republic (RSFSR) of June 11, 1964 (hereinafter Civil Code of the RSFSR; previously, organizations could be authors, see section "Creation and registration of IP").

The AST publishing house has an exclusive sub-licence for using the films from the Soyuzmultfilm collection for reproduction until August 1, 2014, and for distribution util December 1, 2014. In accordance with clause 1.2.4 of the sub-licence, the AST publishing house acquired the right to use films united by the general name "Mowgli", including in such ways as processing films into works of fine art (drawings) and using them in a reworked form for preparation, publication and distribution of printed materials.

In February 2014, the SAMOVAR publishing house, without obtaining permission from the AST publishing house, published *Mowgli* by Rudyard Kipling, using the characters of the mentioned audiovisual works to design the book cover and illustrations in a modified form. The SAMOVAR publishing house obtained permission from the heir of Aleksandr V. Vinokurov. This artist created the images of the characters used in the audiovisual works that became the subject of controversy. The artist used (creatively reworked) images of the animated film's characters to create illustrations for the book. The AST publishing house went to court, believing that the SAMOVAR publishing house violated its rights as the holder of the exclusive licence for the use of the audiovisual works by using the films' characters in a revised form (drawings) in the new printed version of *Mowgli*.

Satisfying the claims in part, the court, guided by the previous legislation of the RSFSR, as well as the Civil Code, proceeded from the fact that the copyright for animated films created before August 3, 1993, including the rights to the characters, belonged to the company that carried out the filming, that is the film studio. Individuals who took part in creating the animated films during the specified period do not have exclusive rights to the animated films and their characters. Consequently, the exclusive rights to the films and their characters could not be transferred to the heir of Aleksandr V. Vinokurov (the creator of the contested characters), and, thus, the heir cannot transfer them to another person.

The applicants' argument that the defendant used only sketches and drawings developed by the artist for creating the characters, but did not use the characters themselves, was a subject of consideration of the Intellectual Property Court and was rejected with reference to clause 82 of the Resolution of the Plenum of the Supreme Court No. 10. The court noted that the drawings and sketches were made by the artist precisely for the purpose of creating the visual image of the characters, in connection with which, after the embodiment of such drawings and sketches in the characters of the audiovisual work, the use of drawings and sketches themselves separately from the use of the character shall not be possible (Ruling of the Supreme Court of the Russian Federation of October 24, 2019, on case No. A40-133098/2015).

It is not only reproducing a character in a book, as in the example described, that is considered an unacceptable use of a character, but also to sell various products with the image of the character. It should be noted that such litigation is widespread in Russia nowadays.

The following litigation example seems to be an excellent illustration. A claim was made in relation to an individual entrepreneur to get compensation for the violation of the exclusive rights to the characters of the animated series *Masha and the Bear*. The plaintiff pointed out the violation of the exclusive rights to the following characters: Masha, He-Bear, She-Bear, Hare and Wolf. The courts ruled in favour of the plaintiff's claims, proceeding from the fact that the characters of the animated series Masha and the Bear are copyright objects and the distribution of any products containing images of the characters of the work without the permission of the copyright holder is illegal. It was found that there were sale offers and actual sales of goods with the images of the named characters (a sticker book and a bookmark) by the individual entrepreneur. The amount of compensation to be paid was determined by the court based on the principles of reasonability, fairness and proportionality of compensation to the consequences of the violation (Resolution of the Intellectual Property Court of August 20, 2014, on case No. A50-23306/2013).

In contrast to the character, the protection of the work title is more controversial. The legal literature expresses different positions regarding the protectability of the title, the requirements for the title to be recognized as an object of copyright and more (Vitko, 2020).

For example, it was established in court that the title of an audiovisual work *Igry Bogov* (Games of the Gods "in English") is not an independent copyright object. At the same time, the plaintiff presented a linguistic study that concluded that the title of *Igry Bogov* is the result of independent creative activity. However, according to the court, there were no issues requiring expert knowledge in the dispute. In this regard, the court assessed the expert opinion along with other evidence in the case and did not agree with the conclusion. The court noted that, according to the defendants' evidence, the Russian Wikipedia (http://ru.wikipedia.org) website mentions an *Igry Bogov* film directed by Mark Tarteltaub based on the novel of the same name by Marie Philips. The phrase "*Igry Bogov*" is also used in the titles of books by the following authors: Alexander Anisimov (2000), Natalia Malevana (2013), Vladimir Kryshtalev (2010) and Alexander Zolotko (2006). The specified phrase is also used as the name of a sports program about basketball transmitted by the RBK channel (a TV channel in Russia). Thus, the court recognized the phrase as frequently used (Resolution of the Ninth Commercial Court of Appeal of April 1, 2014, on case No. A40-111951/13).

It should be pointed out that the issue of the protection of rights to the work title arises more and more often due to the commercialization of titles. It has to do with registering a trademark or a service mark that coincides with the title. The court practice in this case varies. The decision on the possibility of registering the trademark (service mark) that reproduces the work title in one way or another, most often, depends on the popularity of the title (see below on the trademark (service mark) requirements).

An example of such contradictions between the copyright holder of the work and its title and the person who registered the trademark is the court case challenging Rospatent's non-normative act that denied satisfying the copyright holder's objections to the granting of legal protection to the trademark *NU, POGODI!* (roughly translated as "WELL, JUST YOU WAIT!").

This is the name of a very famous animated series in Russia. It was created by the Soyuzmultfilm film studio in 1969–1993. At the time of litigation, the rights to it belonged, as explained by the court, to the Federal State Unitary Enterprise Creative-Production Association Film Studio Soyuzmultfilm. However, the trademark was registered by another entity.

In order to restore the rights and legitimate interests of the applicant, the Intellectual Property Court considered it possible to invalidate the provision of legal protection to said trademark and obliged Rospatent to make the corresponding entry in the State Register of Trademarks and Service Marks

(Decision of the Intellectual Property Court of October 3, 2019, on case No. SIP-453/2019). The court did not doubt the popularity of the work title. Therefore, the copyright holder was able to challenge the grant of protection to the trademark, *NU, POGODI!*

However, the situation is not always so favourable for the copyright holder. Thus, the fact of the publication of a literary work without evidence of the acquisition of the corresponding material by any significant number of consumers of goods and services (or other evidence of consumer awareness of the work) does not indicate the popularity of the work (and accordingly, the existence of any associative links in relation to this work) (Decision of the Intellectual Property Court of October 3, 2019, on case No. SIP-313/2019).

Thus, despite the fact that the work title is protected in Russia as an object of copyright, the possibility of exercising the corresponding rights to it is not unconditional.

The described practice illustrates the need for a detailed study, firstly, of the IP legislation, and, secondly, the information about the author, right holder, transferred rights, etc. Both the legal and economic consequences of the violation of the relevant rights, the lack of proper permissions to use either the entire work or its characters, title and other components shall be considered. Possible risks should be assessed in case of the protection of rights by the right holder and authorized persons (for more details on the protection of rights, see Protection of intellectual property rights).

The work is recognized as such, regardless of the fact of its publication. The only thing that is important is that the work should be expressed in a material form, including:

- written form,
- verbal form (in the form of public speeches, public performances and other similar forms),
- form of an image,
- form of a sound or video recording,
- three-dimensional form.

The registration of the work or its compliance with any other formalities is not required under Russian law (clauses 3–4 of Article 1259 of the Civil Code).

In practice, there are situations when it is difficult to distinguish one work from another. Such a case took place in relation to a textbook on sociology, whose author transferred the full exclusive rights to the textbook to two different publishing houses (for the rights to IP, see the next section of the book). However, the court found that these publishers have rights to different works. Despite the fact that both of the books published by the houses are on sociology, and there are similarities in the textual part of the works, the textbooks have different purposes. In particular, the court took into account the author's explanation that the creation of two different works on the topic of sociology began at the same time, in the summer of 2009. He said that the works (textbooks on sociology) are different in their purpose and their content. The court noted that one textbook was prepared for students, graduate students and teachers of social faculties (that is, it is a specialized book), while another textbook was prepared for students of technical higher educational institutions. Since the works are addressed to different readers, they, in the courts' opinion, cannot be the same (Resolution of the Intellectual Property Court of March 29, 2019, on case No. A40-138728/2017).

Computer programs play a significant role in modern activities. In accordance with clause 1 of Article 1259 of the Civil Code, they are copyright objects and are protected as literary works. A computer program is a collection of data and commands presented in a material form intended for the operation of computers to achieve certain results; preparatory materials obtained in the course of developing a computer program and the audiovisual displays generated by it are included too (Article 1261 of the Civil Code). If and when the exclusive right to the computer program is still valid, the copyright holder can register it at his or her own will (for more information, see section "Creation and registration of IP") (for computer programs, see also section "IP in digital economy").

As previously noted, a database is also considered as a work by Russian copyright law. It can be classified as both a composite work and a complex IP object. A database is a set of independent materials (articles, calculations, regulations, court decisions and other similar materials) presented in a material form, systematized in such a way that these materials could be found and processed using a computer (clause 2 of Article 1260 of the Civil Code). A database, as well as a computer program, can be subject to registration at the copyright holder's will (for more information on registration issues, see section "Creation and registration of IP") (for more information on database, see also section "IP in digital economy").

The next category of IP subject matter is the so-called "objects of related rights". Objects of related rights include (Article 1304 of the Civil Code):

- performances,
- phonograms,
- transmission of broadcasts from broadcasting or cablecasting organizations,
- databases regarding their protection against unauthorized extraction and the reuse of their constituents,
- works of science, literature and art in the public domain regarding the protection of the Publisher's rights.

A performance includes:

- performances by performing artists and conductors, if these performances are expressed in a form that allows their reproduction and distribution by technical means;
- stage setting by production designers, if these settings are expressed in a form that allows their recurrent public performance while maintaining

the recognizable settings, as well as in a form that allows reproduction and distribution by technical means.

Despite the fact that copyright and related rights are proven to be closely connected, related rights are independent of the copyright on works of science, literature and art used to create objects of related rights; copyright, however, must be respected (Article 1303 of the Civil Code). It is pointed out that related rights objects of this type are the only ones based on creativity, while other objects result from organizational and technical activities (Eremenko, 2012).

The definition of phonograms is given in Article 1304 of the Civil Code. These are any purely aural recordings of performances or other sounds or their displays, with the exception of the sound recordings included in an audio-visual work. Meanwhile, the display of sounds implies its digital representation, which can be turned into an ear-perceptible form with the help of appropriate technical means (Article 1305 of the Civil Code). The rights to a phonogram belong to its producer: a person who has taken the initiative and responsibility for the first fixation of the performance of sounds or other sounds or representations of these sounds (Article 1322 of the Civil Code).

With respect to broadcasts from broadcasting or cablecasting organizations of radio and TV programs, the corresponding rights arise in favour of a broadcasting and cable broadcasting organization (a legal entity that independently determines the content of radio and television broadcasts (a set of sounds and (or) images or their displays) and carries out broadcasting or cablecasting on their own or with the help of third parties) (Article 1239 of the Civil Code).

The Law of the Russian Federation No. 2124-1 of December 27, 1991, "On the Mass Media", regulates aspects of such organization's activities in which a broadcaster means a Russian legal entity that forms a TV channel or radio channel and distributes it in accordance with the established procedure on the basis of a licence for television broadcasting and (or) radio broadcasting (Article 2 of the mentioned law).

The issuance of a corresponding licence is within the competence of the Federal Service for Supervision of Communications, Information Technology and Mass Media (Roskomnadzor), which also forms and maintains the register of licences for television and radio broadcasting. The official website of this state body has a search engine to navigate the register (by the licensee and by licence number) (https://rkn.gov.ru/mass-communications/reestr/teleradio/).

Databases are also an object of related rights in terms of their protection from unauthorized extraction and reuse of the materials that make up their content (for database, see also section "IP in digital economy"). In this case, the rights of the manufacturer, the person responsible for the creation of the database, and the work on the collection, processing and arrangement of its constituent materials are protected. The exclusive right to extract materials from the database and subsequently use them in any form and in any way arises if the creation of the database requires significant financial, material, organizational or other costs. It should be noted that the presumption of the materiality of the costs for creating a database is provided for by law, on the condition that the database in question contains at least 10,000 independent information elements (materials) that make up its content. This presumption is rebuttable and must be contested by a person proving otherwise (Resolution of the Thirteenth State Commercial Court of Appeal of May 29, 2020, on case No. A56-37859/2019).

As mentioned earlier, the database is also subject to copyright. Marina A. Rozhkova proposes differentiating databases into creative (its formation requires creativity) and investment-based (its creation implies significant financial investments), noting that a database can combine both creativity and investment (Rozhkova, 2019). Vladimir A. Korneev and Maria A. Kolsdorf explain that the structure of a database will be protected by copyright, while related rights are applied to the content materials (Korneev & Kolsdorf, 2019).

As an object of related rights, works of science, literature and art, published after their transfer to the public domain, are also protected regarding Publishers' rights protection.

A Publisher is a person who lawfully made public or organized the publication of a work of science, literature or art that had not been previously made public and passed into the public domain (Article 1337 of the Civil Code). Only a natural person can be a Publisher; that is why scholars consider if it is reasonable to exclude a legal entity (Stepanov, 2009). Publication can take place only if it does not contradict the author's will, which is expressed by them in writing (in a will, letters, diaries, etc.) By virtue of a special instruction of the Civil Code, the rights of a Publisher do not arise with respect to works that are located in state and municipal archives.

On the basis of Article 1349 of the Civil Code, the objects of patent rights include:

- the results of intellectual activity in the scientific and technical sphere that meet the requirements established by the Civil Code for inventions and utility models, and
- the results of intellectual activity in the field of design that meet the requirements set by the Civil Code for industrial designs.

In Russia, the following objects cannot be recognized as objects of patent rights:

1 methods of cloning a person and his or her clone,
2 methods for modifying the genetic integrity of human germline cells,
3 the use of human embryos for industrial and commercial purposes,
4 the results of intellectual activity, which, on the basis of the above-mentioned article of the Civil Code, may be recognized as inventions, utility models or industrial designs but contradict public interests and the principles of humanity and morality.

Based on clause 1 of Article 1350 of the Civil Code, a technical solution is protected in any area as an invention if it is:

- a product (in particular, a device, substance, microorganism strain, plant or animal cell culture); or
- a method (the process of performing actions on a material object with the help of material means), including the use of a product or a method for a specific purpose.

An invention is granted legal protection if it is new, has an inventive step and is industrially applicable (clause 1 of Article 1350 of the Civil Code). An invention is new if it is not known from prior art. The invention has an inventive step if a specialist in the field considers it an adequate distance beyond or above current technology. Current technology for an invention includes any information that became publicly available in the world prior to the priority date of the invention.

When determining the novelty of an invention, current technology also includes, subject to their earlier priority:

- all requests filed in the Russian Federation by other persons for the grant of patents for inventions, utility models and industrial designs, to which any person can have access;
- inventions, utility models and industrial designs patented in the Russian Federation.

These requirements are significant and should be taken into account by the applicant if one wishes to obtain a patent for an invention. If they have not been considered and the necessary analysis has not been carried out, then the applicant increases the risk of a patent being refused.

An example is the situation reflected in the Decision of the Intellectual Property Court of July 22, 2020, on case No. SIP-1064/2019. A request was filed for a patent for the invention *Sposob provedeniya forumov, tok-shou, konferentsiy i kompleks ustroystv dlya ikh osushchestvleniya (varianty)* (in English, as method of holding forums, talk shows, conferences and the set of tools for their implementation (options). The patent was refused because Rospatent thought that the invention did not correspond with the inventive step patentability condition because it is created by combining information known from patent documents, as well as a professional's general knowledge.

However, if the invention patent has been issued, but the patented object does not meet the requirements for novelty and an inventive step, this is not a favourable situation for the patent holder, either. In this case, there is the risk of patent invalidation. For example, a patent of the Russian Federation for the invention *Sposob ucheta markiruemoy produktsii* (translated into English as method of accounting for labelled products) was issued. Later, another business entity applied to Rospatent with an objection to the patent. The objection was motivated, among other things, by the non-compliance of the decision on the contested patent with the novelty and inventive step conditions. In support of the objection filed, it is indicated that the method of accounting for labelled products does not imply the interaction between any material objects. It was pointed out that the resulting effect is achieved because a certain order of work is observed based on the agreement between work participants or the rules. In addition, it was stated that there was a direct mention of the method to be patented on a website. Based on the objection consideration results, Rospatent established that the achieved technical result for the contested invention consists of increasing the reliability of the information on the movement of the labelled production units from the manufacturer to the consumer through internal accounting of labelled products. At the same time, this result is achieved only due to the effective organization of the accounting process for labelled products within the company, where, by agreement, it was decided to put an individual code corresponding to federal special labelling on each unit of products for the subsequent accounting of the federal special labelling and the number of products in the package. Rospatent concluded that the technical result under the contested patent is achieved through the agreement at the company and is of a non-technical nature, and therefore the object under the contested patent cannot be classified as an invention. Due to the above, Rospatent decided to satisfy the objection. The patent for the invention was declared totally invalid (Decision of the Intellectual Property Court of December 6, 2019, on case No. SIP-587/2019).

It should be borne in mind that an attempt to patent an invention that does not meet the requirement of novelty and inventive step entails costs that are not only directly related to the patenting but to the possible need to challenge Rospatent's decision, too.

Based on the provisions of the Civil Code, an invention is industrially applicable if it could be used in industry, agriculture, healthcare, other sectors of the economy or in the social sphere. When examining the possibility of using an invention, the description of the invention in the request as of the filing date (if on this date the request contained claims, in the description or the claims section) is checked to see if it indicates its purpose. In addition, the indicated documents and drawings attached to the request are checked to see if they provide any means and methods used to describe the invention in various items of the claims. In the absence of this information in said documents, it is permissible that the means and methods were described in a source that became publicly available before the priority date of the invention. It should be ensured that the indicated purpose is achievable if implementing the invention according to any of the claims.

If experimental data can only prove the possibility of creating the invention and achieving the specified purpose, examples of its implementation accompanied by the corresponding data are checked for inclusion in the invention description. The examples given are also checked to see if they are sufficient so that the conclusion on the compliance with the specified requirement can be applied to particular manifestations of the feature covered by the concept provided in the claims.

If it is established that all of these requirements are met, Rospatent shall recognize the invention as complying with the industrial applicability condition. Failure to fulfil even one of these requirements assumes that the invention does not meet the industrial applicability condition.

In this case, a request is sent to the applicant, which provides all the arguments and suggests that the applicant should respond to these arguments"and correct the claims (if the examination so decides that the indicated conclusion may be changed when the request documents are amended). In this case, the request may contain specific recommendations for the claim's correction.

Verification of novelty and an inventive step shall not be carried out if it is established that the invention does not comply with the industrial applicability condition. (Order of Rospatent No. 236 of December 27, 2018, "On Approval of the Guidelines for the Implementation of Administrative Procedures when Registering an Invention and Issuing Patent for an Invention, its Duplicate").

The following example can illustrate this situation. A patent request was filed with Rospatent for an invention called *Pervyy sposob Yur'eva formirovaniya sil i/ili momentov vnutri zamknutoy izmenyaemoy mnogomassovoy sistemy dlya ee lineynogo i/ili uglovogo peremeshcheniya v prostranstve bez vzaimodeystviya s vneshney sredoy i ustroystvo ego osushchestvleniya* (in English, Yuryev's first method of forming forces and/or momentums inside a closed variable multi-mass system for its linear and/or angular movement in space without interaction with the external environment and a device for its implementation). Rospatent refused the patent for the invention, based on the results of the substantive examination, claiming it was due to the inconsistency of the given technical solution with the industrial applicability condition. The court supported Rospatent's decision, according to which the invention did not comply with this patentability condition, indicating that the implementation of the claimed method with the special device would not ensure the achievement of the invention's purpose due to a direct contradiction with Newton's first and third laws, the law of momentum conservation and the law of conservation of angular momentum, respectively. The court noted that the experiment demonstrated by the applicant in Rospatent and the device operation examples did not prove the possibility of moving the closed variable multi-mass system as a whole under the action of internal forces without any interaction with the external environment. The notified authority concluded that the claimed invention does not comply with the industrial applicability condition based on general scientific knowledge. At the same time, the court rejected the applicant's argument about the non-refutation of both the novelty and the inventive step of the claimed method and the device for implementing the method (Ruling of the Supreme Court of the Russian Federation of October 24, 2018, on case No. SIP-476/2017).

Thus, as noted by Alexander K. Yurchenko, an invention can be defined as a creative solution to a practical (utilitarian) problem, and inventive creativity is not limited to a knowledge of technical capabilities (Yurchenko, 1963, pp. 14, 17).

A technical solution related to a device is protected as a utility model. If a technical solution cannot be recognized as a device, then the utility model patent on it is not issued.

For example, a joint-stock company (JSC)[3] applied to Rospatent for a patent on a utility model called *Sistema avtomaticheskogo opredeleniya narusheniy pravil parkovki* (in English, System for automatic detection of parking violations). However, Rospatent concluded that the declared solution is not a device as per the provisions of clause 1 of Article 1351 of the Civil Code. Based on the provisions of clause 2 of Article 1379 of the Civil Code, the authority suggested that the JSC should use the right to transform the utility model application into an invention application. Considering that the JSC failed to use this right, Rospatent decided not to grant the patent on the named utility model. The courts concluded that the decision of Rospatent was well-grounded (Ruling of the Supreme Court of September 23, 2015, on case No. SIP-926/2014).

One more example of a no-device situation can be provided. Another company applied to Rospatent for a patent on a utility model, *Ustanovka dlya polucheniya vspenennykh granul* (in English, installation for the production of foamed granules). Based on the application examination results, the company was denied the patent because the above solution is not a device but a set of devices that do not have structural unity. That is, the utility model type of legal protection cannot be granted in accordance with clause 1 of Article 1351 of the Civil Code. Rospatent's position was later supported by the courts (Ruling of the Supreme Court of April 9, 2018, on case No. SIP-425/2017).

Thus, when filling out an application, it is necessary to clearly understand which object of patent rights the applicant is dealing with. It is important to have an answer to the question of whether the invented technical solution can, in fact, be classified as a device. It is necessary to study the existing requirements, determine the risk of non-recognition of the object as a utility model and consider the procedure for further actions. It should be pointed out that the study of judicial and administrative practice is essential for the economic entity to make appropriate decisions.

It should also be borne in mind that in accordance with subclause 3, clause 2 of Article 1376 of the Civil Code, the utility model claim should refer to one technical solution. In other words, it should include one set of essential features necessary to achieve a technical result. In this regard, the utility model claim should not include alternative features or include several sets of essential features, each of which is crucial for the achievement of different technical results (clause 121 of Resolution of the Plenum of the Supreme Court No. 10).

This type of IP subject matter is granted legal protection if it is new and industrially applicable.

The utility model is new if the totality of its essential features is not known from prior art. In relation to the utility model, prior art includes any information that has become publicly available in the world prior to the utility model's priority date. Prior art also includes (subject to earlier priority) every application for the patent of an invention, utility model or industrial design that is submitted within the Russian Federation by other persons and with which any person has the right to get acquainted in accordance with the Civil Code, and also inventions and utility models already patented in the Russian Federation. As explained in judicial practice, the novelty of the utility model, as a condition of its patentability, is directly related to the establishment of essential features that characterize the utility model as a technical solution and contribute to the achievement of a certain technical result (Decision of the Supreme State Commercial Court of the Russian Federation of December 13, 2012, on case No. VAS-13348/12).

The disclosure of the utility model information by the author of the utility model, the applicant or any person who received this information directly or indirectly from them (including after exhibiting the utility model), the result of which information about the essence of the utility model became publicly available, is not a circumstance preventing the recognition of the patentability of the utility model, provided that the application for the issue of the patent on the utility model is filed with Rospatent within six months from the date of the information disclosure. The applicant has the burden of proving that there were circumstances in which the disclosure of information did not preclude the utility model's patentability.

A utility model, as well as an invention, is industrially applicable if it can be used in industry, agriculture, healthcare, other sectors of the economy or in the social sphere.

When drawing up the application to Rospatent to obtain a patent on an invention or utility model, the applicant should consider if the object belongs to the following categories:

1 discoveries;
2 scientific theories and mathematical methods;
3 solutions concerning only the appearance of products and aimed at satisfying aesthetic needs;
4 rules and methods in games, intellectual or economic activities;
5 computer programs;
6 solutions consisting only in the presentation of information.

This is important because clause 5 of Article 1350 and clause 5 of Article 1351 of the Civil Code expressly indicate that all the above are not inventions or utility models.

Moreover, the specified list is not exclusive. For instance, objects not directly listed above are not inventions if they do not meet the definition of an invention, given in clause 1 of Article 1350 of the Civil Code (clause 118 of Resolution of the Plenum of the Supreme Court No. 10).

For example, a patent application was filed for a group of inventions, *Sposob Ismailovoy N.V. obucheniya chteniyu i uchebnoe posobie dlya ego osushchestvleniya* (in English, N.V. Ismailova's method for teaching reading and a textbook for its implementation). Rospatent concluded that the developed training program is a method of intellectual activity, and by virtue of clause 5 of Article 1350 of the Civil Code, cannot be classified as an invention since this solution is not of a technical nature. As a consequence, the solution cannot be recognized as subject to protection as an invention (Resolution of the Presidium of the Intellectual Property Court of April 2, 2018, on case No. SIP-482/2017). However, it should be noted that the listed objects cannot be categorized as inventions only when the application for the granting of the invention patent concerns these objects as such (clause 5 of Article 1350 of the Civil Code).

These provisions regarding the impossibility of recognizing objects as inventions also apply to the utility models (clause 5 of Article 1351 of the Civil Code).

The invention or utility model type of legal protection shall not be granted to (clause 6 of Article 1350, clause 6 of Article 1351 of the Civil Code):

1 plant varieties, animal breeds and biological methods for their production, i.e., methods completely consisting of cross-breeding and selection, except for microbiological methods and products obtained by such methods;
2 topographies of integrated circuits.

Unlike inventions or utility models, appearance solutions for industrial or handicraft products are protected as an industrial design (clause 1 of Article 1352 of the Civil Code). The industrial design is granted legal protection if, judging by its essential features, it is new and original.

The essential features of the industrial design include those that determine the aesthetic features of the appearance of the product, in particular, the shape, configuration, ornament, combination of colours, lines, product contours and texture of the product material. Features that are solely due to the technical function of the product are not protected as an industrial design.

An industrial design is new if the totality of its essential features, which are reflected in the images of the product appearance, is not known from the information that had become generally available in the world before its priority date.

An industrial design is original if its essential features are determined by the creative nature of the product's particular qualities. The information that had become publicly available in the world before its priority date should not reveal another appearance solution for a product used for a similar purpose and with the same general impression on the informed consumer as the one produced by the industrial design reflected in the images of the product appearance.

It should be noted that the informed consumer is a hypothetical person who will use the product the industrial design embodies if he or she shows an interest in products of the same or similar purpose and, as a result, is aware of the kind of appearance and features such products usually have.

When comparing the general impressions produced by the claimed industrial design and the one opposed to it, information about known solutions that determine the appearance of products used for the same or similar purpose (the analogue series) shall be taken into account. In addition, the limitations on the authors developing appearance solutions for the product intended for this purpose shall be considered, too, especially those associated with the technical function of the product or its element and the standardized requirements for the product, if any (the designer's degree of freedom) (clause 75 of the "Rules for the Preparation, Submission and Consideration of the Documents that are Obligatory to Initiate Legally Significant Actions for the State Registration of Industrial Designs; Types of Documents", adopted by Order of the Ministry of Economic Development of the Russian Federation No. 695 of September 30, 2015; hereinafter Rules for the State Registration of Industrial Designs).

When establishing the novelty and the originality of an industrial design (should earlier priority be the case), all applications for inventions, utility models, industrial designs and applications for the state registration of trademarks and service marks, which are filed in the Russian Federation and available to the public, shall also be considered.

If information about the industrial design was disclosed by its author, applicant or any person who received this information directly or indirectly from them, then, unlike in the case of a utility model, the period within which the application should be submitted to Rospatent is 12 months from the date of the information disclosure.

By virtue of clause 5 of Article 1352 of the Civil Code, the industrial design type of legal protection shall not be provided for the solutions, all features of which derive exclusively from the technical function of the product and the solutions that can mislead consumers of the product.

The next group of IP subject matter is comprised of the so-called means of individualization of legal entities, goods, works, services and enterprises.

This group of objects includes:

- company name of a legal entity – a commercial organization,
- commercial name,
- trademark and service mark,
- geographical indication and appellation of origin of goods.

In accordance with clauses 1 and 2 of Article 1473 of the Civil Code, a legal entity, being a commercial organization, takes part in civil circulation under its company name, which is determined by its constituent documents and is included in the Unified State Register of Legal Entities (USRLE) upon being registered as a legal entity. The company name is not just an IP subject matter; it is a means of identifying a legal entity, allowing it to be distinguished from other legal entities. Therefore, the Russian normative regulation and the way it is implemented aim to maintain a commercial organization's company name's uniqueness.

Clause 3 of Article 1474 of the Civil Code indicates that a legal entity shall not be allowed to use a company name identical to the company name of another legal entity or similar to it to the point of confusion. The prohibition shall be applied if the specified legal entities carry out similar activities and the company name of the second legal entity was included in the USRLE earlier than the company name of the first legal entity (some features of the practice are discussed in section "IP in corporate relations"). Looking ahead, it should be emphasized that the company name is also a corporate asset of a commercial, corporate organization. This is why the description of this IP subject matter was included, as noted in section "IP in corporate relations".

The commercial name should be distinguished from the company name. In accordance with Article 1538 of the Civil Code, legal entities engaged in business activity (including non-profit organizations whose constituent documents grant them the right to carry out such activities in accordance with the law), as well as individual entrepreneurs, can use commercial names that are not company names and are not subject to mandatory inclusion in the constituent documents and the USRLE for the individualization of their trade, industry and other enterprises.

It should be pointed out that the term "enterprise" in Russia can be used in various contexts. For instance, a unitary enterprise is an organizational and legal form of a legal entity in Russia; it can be state or municipal, and in this case, it is a subject of law (also, see section "IP in corporate relations"). However, with regard to the commercial name, we do not imply this one meaning of "enterprise". It is about an enterprise as an object of rights.

An enterprise as an object of rights is a property complex used for doing business. The enterprise as a whole, being a property complex, is recognized as real estate. The enterprise as a whole or a part of it can be an object of sale and purchase, pledge, lease and other deals related to the establishment, modification and termination of property rights. The structure of the enterprise as a property complex includes all types of property intended for its activities comprising land, buildings, structures, equipment, inventory, raw materials, products, rights of claim, debts, as well as the rights to the signs that individualize the enterprise, its products, work and services (commercial name, trademarks, service marks) and other exclusive rights unless otherwise provided by law or contract (Article 132 of the Civil Code).

The right holder can use the commercial name to individualize one or more enterprises. At the same time, two or more commercial names cannot be simultaneously used to individualize one enterprise (clause 2 of Article 1538 of the Civil Code).

As can be seen from the above, while non-profit organizations do not have a company name, they can be owners of the right to a commercial name. However, taking into account the legislative regulation of their activities in Russia, such organizations shall have the right to carry out income-generating activities in accordance with their charters, and such activity shall serve to achieve the goals for which they were created and correspond to such goals (clause 4 of Article 50 of the Civil Code). In addition, it should be borne in mind that some types of non-profit organizations in Russia have limited rights to business activity. For example, a self-regulatory organization does not have the right to business activity at all (clause 1 of Article 14 of Federal Law No. 315-FZ of December 1, 2007, "On Self-Regulatory Organizations").

As noted by the Supreme Court of the Russian Federation in clause 177 of the Resolution of the Plenum of No. 10, both verbal and pictorial or combined signs are subject to protection as a commercial name. However, such a sign shall meet the following regulatory conditions:

- it must be sufficiently distinctive,
- its use by the right holder for the individualization of the enterprise must be known within a certain territory.

In this regard, the right to a commercial name does not arise earlier than the moment of its first use for an enterprise's individualization (for example, a store, a restaurant, etc.).

Since the current legislation does not provide for the registration of a commercial name, the existence of the above conditions can be established only when implementing laws (in a judicial or administrative order) on the basis of the documents confirming the actual use of the commercial names.

In this regard, the situation described in a Rospatent Information Letter of January 30, 2009, "On Registration of Commercial Names", is worth mentioning (published in "Patents and Licences", No. 3, March 2009).

The state authority drew attention to the fact that a patent attorney used a newly launched website to advertise his services that consisted of entering commercial names into the "Register of Russian Commercial Names" for a fixed fee. Rospatent pointed out that the information on this site was not based on the norms of the current legislation. In particular, the message posted on the website reads that the "Register of Russian Commercial Names" was created in order to facilitate the fixation of the rights to commercial names existing in Russia, promote their protection and confirm the use of the commercial names. This site also states that the entry of the commercial name to the register would confirm the time when the right to the commercial name arose.

It must be noted that there is no special state register for commercial names. That is why it is difficult to assess the consequences of the proposed non-state registration. It would not result in the emergence of an exclusive right and would barely play the role of irrebutable proof of its belonging to a particular right holder.

Moreover, the practice, including judicial practice, is evidence that it is the normative conditions of the commercial name that were indicated earlier, and not abstract registration, that matter.

The following case is an interesting example.

As can be seen from the judicial acts based on the results of the case consideration, a limited liability company[4] (LLC), *Apteka ot Sklada* (in English, pharmacy from warehouse) applied to the antimonopoly authority, indicating that the actions of Doctor Chekhov LLC constitute a case of unfair competition. The antimonopoly authority decided that the actions of Doctor Chekhov had to be recognized as an act of unfair competition as Doctor Chekhov used a company name of *Apteka ot Sklada* in the external design of its pharmacies located in the city of Kazan. By order of the Department of Federal Antimonopoly Service (FAS) (for more details, see section "The state regulation of IP"), Doctor Chekhov was obliged to stop these violations. Disagreeing with FAS's decision regarding non-normative acts, Doctor Chekhov applied to the state commercial court. The courts of first and appellate instances examined and evaluated the evidence presented in the case materials and concluded that there were grounds to consider the above non-normative acts illegal. The courts proceeded from the fact that the documents presented in the case materials confirm that Doctor Chekhov and persons belonging to the same business group had used the *Apteka ot Sklada* commercial name in the certain area a year before the registration of *Apteka ot Sklada* LLC. So, the emergence of the exclusive right to the commercial name in other territory is not required. But the Court of cassation recognized this conclusion as an erroneous one. (Ruling of the Supreme Court of December 23, 2019, on case No. A65-4722/2016).

Please, LLC in turn, had to put considerable effort into proving the priority date of its commercial name within a particular area.

The situation is as follows.

NEMS, LLC became the right holder of a trademark – a graphic image in the form of a red square, in the upper part of which there are eight white squares of the same size. The trademark was registered in March 2016 with the priority date of July 31, 2014. On December 28, 2017, Gigvi filed an objection to Rospatent against the granting of legal protection for this trademark. Proving its point, Gigvi indicated that since October 11, 2012, it had owned a commercial name similar to the point of confusion with the disputed trademark, which had become known within the Konkovo district and the Severnoye Chertanovo micro-district of Moscow, and had been used to individualize its store. This applies, among other things, to the individualization of the online store (http://gigwi.ru/ru), the warehouse and the showroom. The commercial name had been used earlier than the priority date of said trademark to introduce pet goods manufactured by a Chinese company into civil circulation in the territory of the Russian Federation and sold in large pet goods networks of the Russian Federation.

Gigvi also noted that since 2012 it had repeatedly participated in international exhibitions and the All-Russia Forum. Therefore, due to the popularity of its goods, the consumer has formed a stable connection between goods marked with a similar commercial name and its manufacturer. In this regard, the registration of the contested trademark can mislead the consumer about the manufacturer of the goods.

Gigvi indicated that since the beginning of the use of its commercial name, it had been actively engaged in commercial activities related specifically to pet products. Gigvi submitted the following sources of information to confirm this circumstance:

- contracts for participation in exhibitions with attachments;
- photographs of exhibition stands and awards;
- printouts of information about participation in the Pet Vet Russia Expo from the zoorussia.ru website;
- sales invoices, payment orders for promotional materials and packaging materials;
- "Toys for Pets" price list;
- "Minimarket" advertising booklet;
- printed pages from *Zoobusiness in Russia* magazine;
- other documents.

As a result of the case consideration, confusion was established between the commercial name used by Gigvi since 2012 and the mentioned trademark, which has a later priority date. In addition, the state authority concluded that the trademark and the commercial name are used for similar goods and services. Therefore, Rospatent (upon rehearing Gigvi's appeal), by the decision of October 30, 2018, recognized the granting of legal protection to the disputed trademark as invalid for a part of the goods and services (Decision of the Intellectual Property Court of August 22, 2019, on case No. SIP-797/2018; Ruling of the Supreme Court of April 16, 2020, on case No. SIP-797/2018).

This indicates the importance of the availability of evidence to support the position and prove the existence of the right to the commercial name, which is known within a certain area.

However, in Russian practice, not only the question of being recognizable within a particular geographical area is of great importance. Sufficient distinctiveness of the commercial name also affects the rights of the business entity.

For example, *Berezhnaya Apteka Aprel*, LLC (gentle pharmacy April) believed that it was the right holder of the commercial name *Aptechnyj Sklad* (pharmacy warehouse). Therefore, this company applied to FAS, claiming the illegal use of the *Aptechnyj Sklad* commercial name being similar to the point of confusion by a number of Stavropol pharmacy companies in the course of their business. However, FAS refused to initiate the antimonopoly violation case by pointing out that the *Aptechnyj Sklad* commercial name used by the company does not have sufficient distinctive features and is generally used ("pharmacy", "pharmacy warehouse"). At the same time, FAS, having established that the company's business is related to pharmaceutical activities (except for wholesale trade), concluded that the *Aptechnyj Sklad* commercial name used by the applicant could mislead the consumer about the seller and their prices for products since it does not reflect the company's actual activities.

Considering the decision of the antimonopoly authority illegal, the company turned to the state commercial court. The courts of the first instance and appellate instance concluded that FAS had grounds for refusing to initiate a case on violation of the antimonopoly law and the circuit court (cassation instance) agreed with them. The courts took into consideration, however, that FAS later addressed the company with a warning to terminate its activities that contain signs of violation of the antimonopoly legislation related to the use of the *Aptechnyj Sklad* commercial name, since that can mislead consumers (Ruling of the Supreme Court of the Russian Federation of April 19, 2018, on case No. A63-2313/2017).

A commercial name is often used when doing business, and certain conditions that it meets are normatively established.

It is important to mention that a recognizable commercial name can be considered as a strong competitive advantage. That is why the use of such a name by any other person, undoubtedly, can harm the reputation of the right holder of the commercial name, mislead consumers and cause losses. All this destabilizes civil turnover.

It is also worth noting that one's business plan shall not be based on unfair behaviour, e.g., using someone else's commercial name in any form. A business entity can protect the rights to its commercial name so that an unfair entrepreneur can incur significant costs by acting in bad faith.

The legal regime of a trademark (service mark) differs from that of a commercial name.

In accordance with Article 1477 of the Civil Code, a trademark is a sign that serves to individualize the goods of legal entities or individual entrepreneurs. In this case, a service mark is a sign that serves to individualize the work performed by legal entities or individual entrepreneurs or the services they provide. The Civil Code rules on trademarks apply accordingly to service marks. Therefore, the further use of the term "trademark" is reasonable and implies the applicability of the described material to service marks. These marks are subject to state registration in the territory of the Russian Federation, upon which a certificate is issued (for more details on the registration, see section "Creation and registration of IP").

Verbal, pictorial, volumetric and other signs or combinations thereof may be registered as trademarks. A trademark can be registered in any colour or colour combination (Article 1482 of the Civil Code).

However, when creating a trademark, it is important to comply with the requirements for its distinctiveness, and the same is required for commercial names. There are a number of regulatory rules for a trademark regarding its elements, which are key for its state registration (see also section "Creation and registration of IP").

The following example can illustrate the implementation of the normative approach to trademarks.

Jaguar Land Rover Limited decided to register the volumetric sign as a trademark for the following products:

- cars, spare parts and accessories for cars,
- games and toys, scale models of vehicles and models, models (toys) related to cars sold individually or in sets; toy vehicles.

The application stated that

> the sign is a three-dimensional image of the exterior of a motor vehicle manufactured by the applicant, the hallmark of which is the original and spectacular V-shaped silhouette of the car body, formed by a sloping "floating" roof, rising line of the front door glass and a narrow rear window, which creates an overall feeling of speed.

Rospatent refused to register the sign as the trademark. The decision was substantiated by the fact that the sign submitted for registration as a trademark does not prove quite distinctive due to the dominance of an unprotected element, while the applicant has not proved the distinctive character of the sign.

The authority found that the object to be registered as a trademark is a volumetric sign representing a three-dimensional image of a car demonstrated by the general view as well as other perspectives of the sign (front view, rear view, general rear view, side view, top view). The declared sign, according to Rospatent, is a realistic image of the product itself. This is a specific serial model of a compact SUV (the crossover), called the Range Rover Evoque, the legal protection of which is sought not in relation to a specific car model but for a generic concept of goods of this type. In this case, an unprotected element of the sign is the realistic image of the car, consisting of all the structural elements inherent in this vehicle, while the body shape that determines this type of car is in this case also known in civil circulation and corresponds to "crossover" cars. Comparing the sign's body shape for registration and other modern crossover cars of such brands as KIA Sportage, Jeep Compass, Honda CR-V and Mitsubishi ASX, Rospatent concluded that, all in all, this body shape is typical for this type of car.

At the same time, the administrative authority drew attention to the fact that the listed features could be important from the point of view of cars' industrial design. The courts upheld Rospatent's position (Decision of the Intellectual Property Court of December 17, 2019, on case No. SIP-428/2019).

Another example of the controversial character of distinctiveness is an attempt by ADVERSUS, LLC to register the Coffee Cola combined sign as a trademark. Rospatent denied the registration of the specified sign as a trademark. This decision by Rospatent was motivated by the fact that this sign includes two verbal elements, which, when translated from English into Russian, have the following meanings:

- Coffee (in Russian, *кофе*) – a drink made from seeds (grains, fruits of the tropical coffee tree; https://www.babla.ru/английский-русский/cofee);
- Cola (in Russian, *кола*) – a tonic drink from the seeds of the tropical cola tree (https://translate.academic.ru).

Rospatent took into account the semantics of the named words and concluded that these words in relation to such goods as non-alcoholic drinks;

non-alcoholic coffee-flavoured drinks characterize those goods, indicating their type and composition.

The court of first instance agreed with Rospatent's conclusion that, taking into account the semantics of the words "coffee" and "cola" in relation to these goods, the disputed sign, without additional reasoning or speculation, is associated with the drink containing coffee and cola; in general, it is descriptive, it indicates the type and properties (content) of non-alcoholic coffee-containing beverages, in respect of which legal protection of the trademark is sought, and, therefore, is not distinctive.

At the same time, considering the mutual arrangement of the coffee and cola elements in the sign, the court of first instance also stated that they are visually divided into two separate words with dominant positions and independent semantics.

The business entity submitted documents that, in its opinion, confirmed the distinctive character of the sign in question, which it had acquired as a result of its active, intensive use. The court examined the documents. However, the court indicated that the design of the sign that was created was not attached to the agreement for the Coffee Cola trademark logo design of January 15, 2013, and the contract for the provision of advertising services of January 1, 2013, did not contain an indication of what goods were to be advertised and under what sign. All the evidence meant the claimed sign was not allowed to be correlated with the sign developed under the former contract and with the sign advertised under the latter contract. The court of first instance also noted that the case file did not contain documents confirming the above agreements' actual execution.

In addition, the court of first instance recognized as justified Rospatent's conclusion that advertising printed materials (leaflets, brochures, information magazines of the Victoria supermarket for April 2016 and the MAGNIT hypermarket for 2016, No. 7), as well as photographs of the goods, contained information on products marked with the sign significantly different from the one declared for registration in terms of its compositional and graphic design.

As the cassation instance, the Intellectual Property Court supported these conclusions (Resolution of the Presidium of the Intellectual Property Court of November 11, 2018, on case No. SIP-156/2018).

Thus, the distinctiveness of a trademark is critical. The trademark serves as a means of individualization of manufactured goods, allows the buyer to identify marked goods with a specific manufacturer and provides an idea of the quality of a product (Resolution of the Federal State Commercial Court of the West Siberian Circuit of July 16, 2009, on case No. A75-6721/2008). Trademark preparation is a creative process, but creativity does not replace the need to comply with the legally established requirements.

Therefore, when planning the creation and creating a trademark, it should be borne in mind that it is not only ideas about the desired trademark that are important. It is necessary to navigate both the regulatory requirements for trademarks and the practice of implementing the legislation. This will help to minimize unnecessary costs and avoid or properly prepare for litigation.

Attention should be paid to the special trademark regime in Russia that is established for well-known trademarks. A person who considers their trademark to be well-known in the Russian Federation has the right to submit an application to Rospatent, which may recognize it as such, if this trademark, as a result of its intensive use, on the date indicated in the application, is widely known in Russia among consumers in relation to the applicant's goods. This extends both to trademarks protected in the territory of the Russian Federation on the basis of its state registration or in accordance with an international treaty and to a sign used as a trademark without having legal protection in the territory of the Russian Federation. The trademark and the sign used as a trademark cannot be recognized as well-known if they become widely known after the priority date of another person's trademark that looks identical or similar to the point of confusion and that is intended for similar goods.

As indicated in clause 3.2 of Ruling No. 2145-O of the Constitutional Court of the Russian Federation of September 19, 2019, being a well-known trademark (sign used as a trademark) is a fact of objective reality and the procedure for recognizing such a trademark (sign) as a well-known trademark is intended to confirm or refute this fact, and not to ensure its occurrence.

In this regard, it is worth mentioning the following court case: PALDO Co. Ltd. requested invalidation of Rospatent's decision to refuse to recognize the "DOSHIRAK" sign as a well-known trademark in the Russian Federation and the imposed obligation to provide legal protection to the goods, instant noodles. The judicial act analyzed Rospatent's position as regards well-known trademarks (signs). According to Rospatent, the necessary condition for their recognition as well-known trademarks in the Russian Federation is meeting the following requirements:

- this trademark (sign) has become widely known because of the activities of the applicant themselves;
- the trademark (sign) used to individualize some goods should be clearly associated with such goods as originating from the specific source, meaning as produced or distributed by the applicant, that is, a particular person.

Based on this position, the fact that the declared sign has acquired wide popularity among consumers of certain types of goods/services is not enough to recognize it as a well-known trademark.

The court concluded that the criteria applied by Rospatent are based on a misinterpretation of the law since the norms of international and national legislation do not connect the recognition of a trademark as well-known with the condition that the applicant (as a particular person) should be known to the consumers of the goods or services marked with the trademark. Consumer awareness consists in the fact that the products come from the same source, but the consumer does not need to identify the product with the applicant. Therefore, a well-known trademark appears as the result of the use of the sign, including by a group of persons, but is not determined by the consumers' knowledge of a particular person from this group. A different approach, as noted by the court, is inconsistent with the normatively established function of the trademark as the sign that serves to individualize goods, but not the persons producing these goods (Resolution of the Presidium of the Intellectual Property Court of October 23, 2020, on case No. SIP-1099/2019).

A well-known trademark is granted legal protection provided for trademarks by the Russian legislation; it is valid indefinitely.

One more feature of the regime under consideration must be pointed out, too. The legal protection of a well-known trademark also applies to goods that are not homogeneous with those in respect of which it is recognized as well-known if the use of this trademark by another person in relation to these goods is associated by consumers with the owner of the exclusive right to the well-known trademark and can infringe such copyright holder's legitimate interests (Article 1508 of the Civil Code).

Thus, the recognition of a trademark (sign) as well-known has obvious advantages. One should consider this possibility when doing business.

The geographical indication, which is granted legal protection, is a sign that identifies a product that comes from a certain geographical area and the quality, reputation or other characteristics of which are largely related to its geographical origin (product characteristics). At least one of the production stages that play a significant role in the formation of the product characteristics should be carried out in the indicated geographical area.

The appellation of origin of goods, which is granted legal protection, is a sign that consists of the modern or historical, official or unofficial, full or abbreviated name of a country, urban or rural settlement, locality or other geographical areas, including such name or the derivative of such name, and has become known as a result of its use in relation to the goods, the special features of which are exclusively determined by natural conditions and (or) human factor typical of this geographical object. All stages of the production of goods that play a significant role in the formation of their special properties should be carried out within the geographical area.

The stages and boundaries of the production of the good and special properties of the goods, for which the geographical indication or the appellation of origin of goods is used, must comply with the requirements established by federal laws and other regulatory legal acts of the Russian Federation.

Since geographical indications have appeared in the Russian legislation relatively recently,[5] there has not yet been any significant practice. Appellations of origin, however, often affect business in the fields that are geographically specific.

For example, the registration of appellation of origin, *Essentuki*, was added to the state register on January 1, 1997, in relation to the mineral water goods according to the corresponding application. The exclusive right to use the *Essentuki* No. 4 appellation of origin was granted to *Zavod Mineralnyh Wod Oktyabr-A* LLC (in English, Mineral Waters' Plant Oktyabr-A). It indicated the place of origin (production) of the goods (boundaries of the geographical area) as the central section of the *Essentuki* mineral water deposit (wells No. 34-bis and No. 56), as evidenced by certificate No. 23/38, valid until May 16, 2022.

On April 25, 2018, *Kavminkurortresursy* JSC applied to Rospatent with a request to terminate certificate No. 23/38 because the goods produced by *Zavod Mineralnyh Wod Oktyabr-A* does not possess the special properties specified in the State Register of Appellations of Origin.

Kavminkurortresursy's request was satisfied by the decision of Rospatent of February 28, 2019; the validity of certificate No. 23/38 was terminated. Taking this decision, Rospatent proceeded from the following.

According to the information contained in the State Register of Appellations of Origin, the *Essentuki* mineral water belongs to the group of carbonic bicarbonate-chloride waters with a high degree of mineralization (8–14 g/l); it has specific composition and properties; the *Essentuki* mineral water refers to medicinal waters that have a complex effect on various functional systems of the body and used for various diseases of the digestive system and metabolism.

Certificate No. 23/38 was issued based on the application in which the wells noted above were indicated as the place of origin of the goods.

At the same time, Rospatent established that the contractual relationship for the supply of mineral water extracted from these wells between *Kavminkurortresursy*, which is a subsoil user of wells No. 34-bis and No. 56, and *Zavod Mineralnyh Wod Oktyabr-A* was terminated as it failed to be renewed. There were no intentions (expressions of will) to renew the agreement. As a result, *Zavod Mineralnyh Wod Oktyabr-A* was deprived of the opportunity to produce the *Essentuki* No. 4 mineral water, which corresponds with certificate No. 23/38.

There is no data about *Zavod Mineralnyh Wod Oktyabr-A* having access to other wells from which the *Essentuki* No. 4 mineral water is produced or having contractual or other relations with subsoil users that extract mineral water from the suitable wells.

Considering the above, Rospatent concluded that the loss of the possibility to produce the goods that meet the requirements set forth in certificate No. 23/38 indicates the loss of special properties of these goods pointed out in the state register. The court also supported Rospatent's position (Decision of the Intellectual Property Court of August 27, 2019, on case No. SIP-276/2019).

The next category of IP subject matter cannot be attributed to any of the above groups; therefore they are often called non-traditional IP subject matter. These include production secrets (know-how), selection achievements and topographies of integrated circuits.

By virtue of subclause 12, clause 1 of Article 1225 of the Civil Code, production secrets (know-how) are the result of intellectual activity. Nevertheless, civil legislation does not provide a procedure for mandatory state registration of this IP subject matter.

The essence of know-how is disclosed in Article 1465 of the Civil Code. The secret of production is information of any nature (production, technical, economic, organizational and others) about the results of intellectual activity in the scientific and technical sphere and the methods of carrying out professional activities that have real or potential commercial value due to being unknown to third parties if third parties do not have free access to this information on a legal basis and the copyright holder of the information takes reasonable measures to maintain its confidentiality, including via the trade secret regime. However, if information must be disclosed or it is unacceptable to restrict access to it in accordance with the law or other legal acts, it may not be defined as know-how (for more details about this IP subject matter, see section "Intellectual resources and human capital").

In accordance with Article 1412 of the Civil Code, the objects of intellectual rights to selective breeding achievements are plant varieties and animal breeds registered in the State Register of Protected Selection Achievements if these results of intellectual activity meet the requirements for these achievements.

A plant variety is a group of plants that, regardless of its protectability, is determined by the features that characterize the genotype or combination of genotypes and differs from other plant groups of the same botanical taxon by one or more features. A variety could be represented by one or more plants, part or several parts of the plant if such a part can be used to reproduce the whole plants of the variety. The protected categories of plant varieties are clones, lines, hybrids of the first generation and the population.

An animal breed is a group of animals that, regardless of their protectability, has genetically determined biological and morphological properties and characteristics, some of which are specific to this group and distinguish it from other groups of animals. The breed could be represented by a female or male individual or breeding material, that is, animals (breeding animals) intended to reproduce the breed, their gametes or zygotes (embryos). Protected categories of animal breeds are types and line crosses.

As said, selective breeding achievements refer to the registered results of intellectual activity. Data on them is entered in a special register, and a patent is issued (see section "Creation and registration of IP").

Selective breeding achievements are the result of creative activity. According to Eduard P. Gavrilov, they are "created, developed or discovered" (Article 1410 of the Civil Code) and therefore represent the results of intellectual activity (Gavrilov, 2011). Selection is described as the evolution of plants and animals directed by the will of the human, and such plants and animals undergo changes because of the humans' purposeful actions. This allows one to say, as noted by Alexander P. Sergeev, that the creative activity of the selection specialist is very similar to that of the inventor (Sergeev, 1995, p. 77). However, as pointed out by Pavel V. Krashenninikov (Krasheninnikov, 2010, p. 9), the Russian legislation considers selective breeding achievements as an object of special legal protection, which differs from patent protection of inventions. Selection achievements have a range of peculiarities due to their specific nature: being an intangible object with a material carrier. Material carrier is represented by plants and animals.

According to the current legislation, selective breeding achievements should meet the protection criteria and relate to botanical and zoological genera and species, the list of which is established in the Russian Federation by the federal executive authority that carries out legal regulation in the field of agriculture. This list has been approved in Russia. The list includes 435 botanical genera and species and 53 zoological genera and species (Order of the Ministry of Agriculture Russian Federation No. 369 of July 1, 2019, "On the Approval of the List of Botanical and Zoological Genera and Species Provided for by Article 1413 of the Civil Code of the Russian Federation").

Article 1413 of the Civil Code establishes the following criteria for the protection of selective breeding achievements:

- novelty,
- distinctness,
- uniformity,
- stability.

The plant variety and animal breed are considered new if, on the date of filing the application for the issuance of the patent, the seeds or breeding material of this selective breeding achievements were not sold or otherwise transferred by a selection specialist, his assignee or anybody else, with their consent, to other persons for the use of the selective breeding achievements:

1 in the territory of the Russian Federation more than a year prior to the specified date;
2 in the territory of another state more than 4 years or, if it concerns varieties of grapes, ornamental woody, fruit tree and woody forest species, more than 6 years prior to the specified date.

As emphasized in the Resolution of the Eighteenth State Commercial Court of Appeal of October 10, 2017, on case No. A47-9330/2015, only the fact of the sale or another type of transfer of the seeds or breeding material to third parties for the purposes of its use can refute the novelty of the selective breeding achievements.

This circumstance is analyzed in the Russian legal literature. A comparison was conducted of the novelty of a selective breeding achievement and the requirement for the novelty of technical and art and design solutions. In this connection, it was indicated that for selective breeding achievements, open-access information could not be used as one of the parameters for evaluating the novelty of the declared solution (Gorodov, 2011).

But distinctiveness as a criterion for the selective breeding achievement's protectability is very close to a sign of novelty in its traditional sense, in which it is usually used in patent law (Sergeev, 1995, p. 80). The Civil Code specifies that a selective breeding achievement should clearly differ from any other well-known selective breeding achievement existing at the time of filing the application for the patent. In this case, a well-known selective breeding achievement is a selective breeding achievement, the data on which is contained in official catalogues or reference databases, or a selective breeding achievement that has an accurate description in one of the listed publications.

Filing a patent application makes the selective breeding achievement well-known from the submission date if the patent has been issued for the selective breeding achievement.

The criterion of uniformity supposes that plants of the same variety and animals of the same breed should be sufficiently uniform in their characteristics, taking into account individual deviations that may occur due to some peculiarities of reproduction.

The selection achievement is considered stable if its main characteristics remain unchanged after repeated reproduction or, in the case of a special reproductive cycle, at the end of each reproductive cycle.

The last non-traditional IP subject matter is the topography of the integrated circuit.

According to Article 1448 of the Civil Code, the topography of an integrated circuit is a spatial-geometric arrangement of a set of elements of an integrated circuit and connections between them fixed in a material carrier. An integrated circuit is a microelectronic product, being final or intermediate, which is intended to perform the functions of an electronic circuit, the elements and connections of which are integrated into the interior space and (or) on the surface of the material serving as the basis for the item in question.

The legal protection that the Civil Code provides to the results of intellectual activity applies only to the original topography of an integrated circuit created as the result of the creative activity of the author and unknown to the author and (or) specialists in the field at the date of its creation. The topography of an integrated circuit is recognized as original until proven otherwise.

The topography of an integrated circuit, consisting of elements that are known to the integrated circuit topologies specialists at the date of its creation, shall be granted legal protection if the spatial-geometric arrangement of the set of the elements and the connections between them as a whole meet the originality requirement.

The legal protection does not cover ideas, methods, systems, technology or encoded information that may be embodied in the topography of an integrated circuit.

Thus, the Russian legislation regulates a wide range of IP subject matter that are provided with special legal protection. At the same time, the list of the results of intellectual activity and means of individualization protected in this order does not include domain names, names of non-profit organizations or names of the mass media. The rights to them are subject to protection based on the Civil Code's general provisions on civil rights protection.

Notes

1 The Civil Code of the Russian Federation includes four normative acts, they are: the Civil Code of the Russian Federation (Part I) No. 51-FZ of November 11, 1994; the

Civil Code of the Russian Federation (Part II) No. 14-FZ of January 26, 1996; the Civil Code of the Russian Federation (Part III) No. 146-FZ of November 26, 2001; the Civil Code of the Russian Federation (Part IV) No. 230-FZ of December 18, 2006. So, the Civil Code is divided into four parts each of which shall regulate a specific segment of social relations. Part I of the Civil Code includes general provisions on civil relations, right of ownership and other rights in rem (property rights) and general provisions on the law of obligations; part II of the Civil Code stipulates various types of obligations; part III of the Civil Code covers succession law and private international law; part IV of the Civil Code specifies the rights to the results of intellectual activities and means of individualization. All parts of the Civil Code were adopted and came into force separately, in different years.

2 The standard provides additional clarification and is not mandatory for compliance in the territory of the Russian Federation (Federal Law No. 184-FZ of December 27, 2002, "On Technical Regulation")

3 In Russia, the expression "joint stock company" is used as the English equivalent of "*aktsionernoe obshchestvo*". It should be noted that *aktsionernoe obshchestvo* is an organizational legal form of a legal entity under Russian law. This is a corporate form of a commercial legal entity.

4 In Russia, the expression "limited liability company" is used as the English equivalent of "*obshchestvo s ogranichennoy otvetsvennost'yu*". It should be noted that *obshchestvo s ogranichennoy otvetsvennost'yu* is an organizational legal form of a legal entity under Russian law. This is a corporate form of a commercial legal entity.

5 The corresponding changes were made to the Civil Code with the Federal Law No. 230-FZ of July 26, 2019.

2 Characteristics of intellectual property rights

As follows from Article 1226 of the Civil Code, the following rights exist in the intellectual property (IP) sphere:

- exclusive right,
- personal non-property (moral) rights,
- other rights.

The specific list of rights depends on the IP subject matter; however, the so-called exclusive right applies to all of them. In civil law, exclusive rights are rights that provide the right per se and the ability to prohibit other people from exercising it (Serebrovsky, 1956, p. 23).

An exclusive right is a property right. It has a validity period, which depends on the IP subject matter. It is this right that allows the involvement of IP in civil circulation. First, it implies the possibility of using the result of intellectual activity or the means of individualization in any way that does not contradict the law. Second, the exclusive right can be transferred. Third, the exclusive right contains the right to remuneration (clause 36 of Resolution of the Plenum of the Supreme Court No. 10).

Despite the fact that the specifics of the realization of the named right is determined by a specific IP subject matter, in the most general sense, it implies both using the IP subject matter independently and allowing/prohibiting its use by others (lack of prohibition does not count as consent).

Thus, Article 1270 of the Civil Code contains the non-exhaustive list of actions considered as the use of a work regardless of the purpose of making a profit or its absence:

- reproduction of a work, that is, making one or more copies of a work or part of it in any material form, including in the form of sound or video recording, making one or more copies of a two-dimensional work in three dimensions and one or more copies of a three-dimensional work in two dimensions;
- distribution of the work by sale or other alienation of its original or copies;
- public display of the work;

- import of an original or copies of a work for distribution purposes;
- rental of the original or a copy of the work;
- public performance of the work;
- broadcasting;
- cable broadcasting;
- retransmission;
- translation or other processing of the work;
- practical implementation of an architectural, design, urban planning or landscape gardening project;
- making the work available to the public in such a way that any person can access the work from any place and at any time of his own choice (bringing to the public).

Article 1358 of the Civil Code includes examples of the term "exploitation" regarding inventions, utility models and industrial designs. According to the article, exploitation means the import into the territory of the Russian Federation, manufacture, application, sale offer, sale, other introduction into civil circulation or the storage of a product for these purposes in which an invention, utility model or industrial design is used; and the mentioned operation in regards to a product being a direct result of the application of the patented methods; the devices, the exploitation of which, in accordance with their purpose, implies the realization of a patented method; the product intended for use in accordance with the purpose specified in the invention claims while protecting the invention in the form of limiting the product's use for a specific purpose; implementation of a method in which the use of the invention is required, including the application of this method.

As for the trademark, the exclusive right can be exercised for the individualization of goods, works or services in respect of which the trademark is registered, in particular, by placing the trademark on goods, including labels, packaging of goods that are produced, offered for sale, sold, demonstrated at exhibitions and fairs or otherwise introduced into civil circulation in the territory of the Russian Federation, or stored or transported for this purpose or imported into the territory of the Russian Federation; when performing work or rendering services; on documentation related to the introduction of goods into civil circulation; in offers for the sale of goods, the performance of work, the provision of services, as well as in announcements, on signs and in advertisements; on the internet, including in the domain name and with other methods of address (Article 1484 of the Civil Code).

However, there are situations where unauthorized persons will use IP with or without remuneration. For example, the public performance of a phonogram published for commercial purposes and its broadcasting on air or by cable is allowed without the permission of the exclusive right holder, but with the payment of remuneration to them (Article 1326 of the Civil Code). The right to remuneration also arises in the case of the reproduction of phonograms and audiovisual works exclusively for personal purposes. The remuneration is paid to the exclusive right holders with funds payable by manufacturers and importers of equipment and material carriers used for such reproduction.

But it should be borne in mind that such restrictions on the exclusive rights are possible only subject to meeting the following normatively defined conditions: the restrictions shall not contradict the norms of the normal use of works of science, literature and art, objects of related rights, industrial designs and inventions and unreasonably infringe upon the legitimate interests of the right holders; as regards trademarks, the restrictions shall take into account the legitimate interests of the right holders and third parties.

At the same time, the Civil Code defines cases of gratuitous use of IP subject matter in the absence of permission from the right holder. Thus, the law specifies the following cases of free use of works of science, literature and art and objects of related rights.

a) *Free reproduction of a work for personal purposes*

Personal purposes may be defined as subsequent non-commercial use of the corresponding copy to meet the needs of a person or the ordinary circle of the person's family (clause 97 of Resolution of the Plenum of the Supreme Court No. 10).

As noted in clause 93 of the named resolution, deciding whether persons belong to an ordinary family circle, the court must take into account family and personal ties, periods of communication, the nature of the relationship and other significant circumstances.

The person can reproduce a work without the consent of the author or right holder except for:

- reproduction of works of architecture in the form of buildings and similar constructions;
- reproduction of databases or their essential parts and computer programs, except for the cases provided for in Article 1280 of the Civil Code, which regulates the right of the computer program and database user;
- reproduction of books (in full) and musical texts, that is, their facsimile reproduction using any technical means, not carried out for the purpose of publication;
- video recording of an audiovisual work during its public performance in a place open to free attendance or in a place where there is a significant number of persons who do not belong to the usual family circle;
- reproduction of an audiovisual work using professional equipment not intended for use at home.

The person can reproduce the work if it was legally made public and the person had a need to do it. Clause 97 of Resolution of the Plenum of the Supreme Court No. 10 explains that the need to use a work means use in single copies (limited quantities), the number of which is justified and necessary to meet the named needs.

b) *Free use of the work for informational, scientific, educational or cultural purposes*

The work can be used without the consent of the author and remuneration on the condition of the indication of the author and the work to reach special goals, which are really important for public interests. For instance, citation in the original and in translation for scientific, polemical, critical, informational and educational purposes in order to reveal the creative intention of the author of lawfully published works in the amount justified by the purpose of citation, including the reproduction of excerpts from newspaper and magazine articles in the form of press reviews is allowed. It must be taken into account that the person can cite any work, including photographic work (clause 98 of Resolution of the Plenum of the Supreme Court No. 10). Furthermore, it is extremely essential to observe the citation conditions, as mentioned by the Intellectual Property Court in view of the failure to comply with the conditions for citing the works, the purpose of their use (informational, cultural or other socially significant purposes) does not matter (Resolution of the Intellectual Property Court of September 18, 2017, on case No. A46-13488/2016).

The described situation is not the only example of free use of a work for informational, scientific, educational or cultural purposes. The law also contains other grounds, such as the use of lawfully published works and excerpts as illustrations in publications, radio and television broadcasts, sound and video recordings of an educational nature to the extent justified by the goal, recording on an electronic medium, including recording in computer memory, and bringing the author's abstracts (summary) of these records to the general knowledge.

c) *Free use of the work by libraries, archives and educational organizations*

The specific activities of libraries, archives and educational organizations also implies the need for free use of works. Thus, according to Article 1 of Federal Law No. 78-FZ of December 29, 1994, "On Library Service", a library is an informational, cultural, educational organization or structural unit of an organization that has an organized fund of documents and provides them for temporary use to individuals and legal entities.

Public libraries, as well as archives, have access to archival documents that is not limited and in the absence of the purpose of making a profit, have the right, without the consent of the author or other right holder and without payment of remuneration, to provide for temporary free use (including through the mutual use of library resources) originals or copies of works lawfully introduced into civil circulation. With respect to electronic copies, access to them is granted only in the library's or archive's territory, provided that the possibility of making further copies of works in electronic form is excluded. Posting works on the internet, which, although it is called a library, allows copying and can be considered a violation (Appellate Ruling of the Moscow City Court of August 17, 2016, on case No. 33-22821/2016).

Educational organizations, provided that there is no purpose for making a profit, have the right, without the consent of the author and payment of remuneration but with the obligatory indication of the name of the author whose work is used and the source of borrowing, to create copies, including in electronic form, of individual articles and small-volume works lawfully published in collections, newspapers and other periodicals and short excerpts from other legally published written works (with or without illustrations) and provide these copies to students and teaching staff for examinations, classroom studies and self-study in the necessary quantities.

d) *Free use of the work that is permanently located in a place open to the public*

This rule applies to a work of fine art or photographic work that is permanently located in a place open to free access, except for cases where the work's image is the main object of use or the work's image is used to make a profit, and images of works of architecture, urban planning and of garden and park art located in a place open to the public, or visible from this place. The reproduction and distribution of copies, broadcast or cable broadcast making available to the public is allowed in this case.

As said in clause 100 of Resolution of the Plenum of the Supreme Court No. 10, when applying this norm, the courts should take into account that the internet and other information and telecommunication networks do not belong to places open to free visits.

e) *Free public performance of a lawfully released piece of music*

It is allowed, without the consent of the author or other right holder and without payment of remuneration, to publicly perform a lawfully published piece of music during an official or religious ceremony or funeral to the extent justified by the nature of such a ceremony.

In this case, it is extremely important to establish whether the event being held is an official ceremony. Otherwise, the use of music may be considered an infringement.

For example, the organizers of the City Day concert believed that the event was subject to the free use legal norm. However, the courts upheld the position of the All-Russian non-governmental organization, Russian Authors Society (RAO; see section"The state regulation of IP"), according to which they should have concluded an agreement on granting the right to public performance of works with the right holder or the collective management organization and pay the due remuneration. As the Intellectual Property Court explained, an official ceremony is conducted on behalf of the state and the constituent entities of the Russian Federation and local authorities (for example, the inauguration of the President, the reception of leaders of another state, the laying of wreaths at memorial complexes, a ceremony in honour of the opening or restoration of a socially significant object, etc.). At the same time, a concert, in fact, is musical entertainment, in this case, an entertainment event. At concerts, musical works are of primary importance. They do not serve as a "background" since the concert consists of consistently performed musical works (Decision of the Intellectual Property Court of February 2, 2018, on case No. A32-15565/2017).

f) *Free reproduction of a work for enforcement purposes*

The reproduction of a work to carry out proceedings in an administrative offence case, to conduct investigation or court proceedings is allowed without the consent of the author or other right holder and without payment of remuneration to the extent justified by this purpose.

As mentioned in the Decision of the State Commercial Court of Moscow City of February 29, 2016, on case No. A40-216504/14-15-1785, the procedure for securing evidence in the field of copyright is established by the described provision. In addition, within the framework of the consideration of this case, the Intellectual Property Court clarified the issue of the subject of who can apply this norm. As said by the RAO, as an accredited organization in the field of the collective management of copyright that acts in the interests and on behalf of right holders, all its actions in collecting evidence should be considered as actions of the right holders themselves, committed in the self-protection of civil rights (Article 14 of the Civil Code). Based on this, the reproduction of a work (subclause 1, clause 2 of Article 1270 of the Civil Code) by RAO used for the subsequent protection of the rights of the copyright holder cannot be recognized as the illegal use of this work. According to the court, this method of self-protection is proportionate to the violation and does not go beyond the limits of the actions necessary to suppress it.

g) *Free recording of the work by a broadcasting organization for short-term use*

A broadcasting organization has the right, without the consent of the author or other right holder and without payment of additional remuneration, to make a recording for the purposes of short-term use of the work in respect of which this organization has received the right to broadcast, provided that the broadcasting organization makes such a recording with the help of its own equipment and for its own transmissions. In this case, the organization is obliged to destroy such a record within six months from its production date unless a longer period is agreed with the right holder or is not established by law. Such a record can be saved without the consent of the right holder in state or municipal archives if it is exclusively documentary in nature.

The Intellectual Property Court explains that this legal norm does not provide for the right of broadcasting organizations to create their own content for its subsequent use without the consent of the right holders to the composite objects of the final product (Resolution of the Intellectual Property Court of September 20, 2019, on case No. A40-133665/2016).

It should also be noted that there is the so-called principle of exclusive rights exhaustion. The corresponding rule provides for the use of originals or copies of a creative work, including those protected by the exclusive right of the Publisher and a published phonogram. If the original or copies of a creative work or a published phonogram are lawfully introduced into civil circulation on the territory of the Russian Federation through their sale or other type of alienation, further distribution of its original or copies shall be allowed without the consent of the exclusive right holder and without payment of remuneration to them (except works, covered by resale right). Regarding the exclusive right to a trademark, its use by other people shall not be classified as a violation had the goods being introduced into civil circulation in the territory of the Russian Federation directly by the right holder or with their consent. As for the patent sphere, the following operations involving IP subject matter shall not be considered unlawful: import of a product into the territory of the Russian Federation, its use, offer for sale, sale, other methods of its introduction into civil circulation or storage for these purposes; if the product incorporates an invention, utility model or an industrial design and if this product or article been previously introduced into the civil circulation in the territory of the Russian Federation by the patent holder or another person with or without the patent holder's permission but provided that such introduction into civil circulation is carried out lawfully in the circumstances indicated in the Civil Code. Thus, IP rights are separated from the rights to the material objects in which the IP is contained. As stated in Article 1227 of the Civil Code, intellectual rights do not depend on property rights and other rights to a material carrier (thing), in which the corresponding result of intellectual activity or means of individualization is expressed.

The exclusive right is also limited by the duration, which depends, first of all, on the particular IP subject matter, but it can also be determined by other circumstances.

According to Article 1281 of the Civil Code, the exclusive right lasts during the lifetime of the author plus 70 years, counted from January 1 of the year following the author's year of death. Its duration shall be extended in the following situations:

- if the author was repressed and was posthumously rehabilitated, a 70-year period counting from January 1 of the year following that of the author's rehabilitation;
- if the author was working during the Great Patriotic War (June 22, 1941, to May 9, 1945) or was a participant, the term of the exclusive right is increased by 4 years.

Previously, there was a 50-year term of the exclusive right to a work. However, if this term expired after December 31, 1992 (but before the entry into force of Federal Law No.72-FZ of July 20, 2004, "On Amendments to the Law of the Russian Federation on Copyright and Related Rights", which established the 70-year copyright term) and the work passed into the public domain, since January 1, 2008, the exclusive right to this work is renewed and its validity period is calculated according to the rules provided for by Article 1281 of the Civil Code.

The actions of persons who used, prior to the entry into force of part IV of the Civil Code (January 1, 2008), works that were in the public domain before this date and complied with the provisions of Article 28 of Law of the Russian Federation No. 5351-1 of July 9, 1993, "On Copyright and Related Rights" (hereinafter Copyright Law), despite the renewal of the exclusive right to a work, cannot be considered a violation. At the same time, further use of the work can be carried out only in compliance with the provisions of part IV of the Civil Code. This explanation is given in clause 29 of the Resolution of the Plenum of the Supreme Court No. 10.

If several authors create the work, the exclusive right is valid for the entire life of the author who has outlived the others, plus 70 years, counting from January 1 of the year following that of his or her death.

Suppose the work was made public anonymously or under a pseudonym. In that case, the term of the exclusive right expires after 70 years, counting from January 1 of the year following that of its lawful publication. But in the case of revealing the identity of the author, the ordinary rules apply.

Suppose the work was made public after the author's death. In that case, the validity period of the exclusive right runs from January 1 of the year following that of its publication, provided that the work was made public within 70 years after the author's death.

The exclusive right to a performance is valid for the entire life of the performer, but not less than 50 years, counting from January 1 of the year following that in which the performer or conductor performed it, recorded it or it was broadcasted or brought to the public. The rules on the extension of the exclusive rights' term, described earlier, is also applied to the performer.

The exclusive right of the director to stage a production is valid for his entire life but not less than 50 years, counting from January 1 of the year following that in which the first public performance of the production took place (Article 1318 of the Civil Code).

The exclusive rights for phonograms last 50 years, counting from January 1 of the year following that in which the record was made. If it is made public, the exclusive right is valid for 50 years from January 1 of the year following that in which it was made public, provided that the phonogram was made public within 50 years after the recording.

The exclusive right to broadcasting and cable broadcasting is valid for 50 years, counting from January 1 of the year following that in which it took place.

The exclusive right of the manufacturer of the database arises at the time of completion of its creation and is valid for 15 years, counting from January 1 of the year following that of its creation. The exclusive right of the manufacturer of a database made public during the specified period is valid for 15 years, counting from January 1 of the year following that of its publication.

The publisher's exclusive right to a work arises at the time of the publication of this work and is valid for 25 years, counting from January 1 of the year following that of its publication.

The duration of exclusive rights for an invention is 20 years, for utility models 10 years and for industrial designs 5 years from the filing date of the initial application. It may be renewed several times for 5 years for industrial designs, but in general for no more than 25 years.

The exclusive right for selective breeding achievements lasts 30 years (for grapes, ornamental trees, fruit crops and forest species 35 years), counting from the date of their state registration in the relevant register.

The exclusive right to the topography of integrated circuits is valid for 10 years. Its start is determined by the day of its first use or day of its registration, depending on which occurred earlier.

The term of the trademark's exclusive right is 10 years from the filing date of the application for state registration. It may be prolonged an unlimited number of times on the right holder's application during the last year of the exclusive right duration. Although, in relation to a well-known trademark, legal protection is indefinite.

The exclusive right to a geographical indication or an appellation of origin of goods lasts 10 years from the date of filing an application to Rospatent and may be extended at the request of the right holder.

For some objects of intellectual rights, the duration of the exclusive right is determined depending on certain circumstances.

Thus, the exclusive right to a trade secret is valid as long as the confidentiality of the information constituting its content is preserved. The exclusive right to a company name terminated due to its exclusion from the Unified State Register for Legal Entities (USRLE). The exclusive right to a commercial name ends if the right holder does not use it continuously during the year.

The territorial aspect is of great importance for the exclusive right. This is directly enshrined in Article 1231 of the Civil Code, according to which the exclusive rights to the results of intellectual activity and the means of individualization established by international treaties of the Russian Federation and the Civil Code apply in the territory of the Russian Federation. This rule is concretized in the provisions of the Civil Code on the corresponding objects of IP rights. Thus, when deciding on the application of the exclusive right in the Russian Federation, the following will be taken into account: for works - the place of work's publication or expression in an objective form (if it is not made public), for inventions, utility models, industrial designs - a patent issued by Rospatent or a patent valid in the Russian Federation on the basis of the international agreements, for commercial names - the location of the enterprise for which it is used.

The exclusive right can belong either to one or several persons. This rule does not apply to the company name; this exclusive right belongs only to one commercial entity. However, as noted in clause 35 of Resolution of the

Plenum of the Supreme Court of the Russian Federation No. 10, this does not mean that these persons have the right to divide the exclusive right into shares.

This seems to indirectly indicate the indivisibility of the exclusive right. However, the doctrine provides distinct opinions on this issue. On the one hand, it points out the lack of a direct prohibition on the division of the exclusive right (Gutnikov & Sinitsyn, 2019), but, on the other hand, it is said that analysis of the current Russian legislation indicates the impossibility of alienating a part of the exclusive right from the whole (for example, under an agreement on the alienation of the exclusive right, the exclusive right shall be transferred in full – Article 1234 of the Civil Code), and in other articles of the Civil Code of the Russian Federation there is no mention of a possible separation of parts (Gavrilov, 2019).

It should be borne in mind that the permission to divide the exclusive right into shares will entail an inevitable revision of the mechanism for the exclusive rights accounting and, as a result, the introduction of their mandatory registration, regardless of the specific type of IP. It will also be necessary to document the transfer of the rights. The creation of special registers for all IP subject matter will be required too, although nowadays, the registration shall be carried out only in cases expressly stipulated by the Civil Code or at the request of the right holder (for more information, see section "Creation and registration of IP"). In addition, such issues as the procedure for determining the share and possible actions in case of its insignificance, e.g., compulsory acquisition, will inevitably arise. What is more, the procedure for obtaining permission by third parties wishing to use IP is not entirely clear. All this seems to testify to the inexpediency of the division of the exclusive right into shares.

Currently, as a general rule, the use of the exclusive right can be carried out by any right holder at their own discretion. The disposal of the exclusive right shall be carried out by them jointly, and the income arising in connection with it shall be distributed among all the right holders in equal shares. Changes to these provisions are possible upon the conclusion of a special agreement. Right holders may conclude an agreement and provide for a different procedure. In addition, each right holder has the right to independently take measures in order to protect their rights to the result of intellectual activity or to the means of individualization.

An analysis of these provisions clearly shows the desire to ensure a balance of the right holders' interests and at the same time, take into account the opinion of each. This approach is reflected in judicial practice. For example, one of the patent holders objected to the grant of the patent because the patent did not meet the novelty criterion. The patent was declared invalid, but the second patent owner's opinion regarding their willingness to amend the formula to partially preserve the technical solution was not requested. The court noted that if an objection to the grant of a patent is filed by one of the patent holders, then their will to revoke the patent is expressed. In such circumstances, another patent holder (other patent holders), by virtue of paragraph four of clause 3 of Article 1229 of the Civil Code, cannot be deprived of their right to protect the issued patent and preserve its legal protection, albeit to a lesser extent (Resolution of the Intellectual Property Court of October 28, 2019, on case No. SIP-540/2017).

As for co-authors, in the absence of the agreement, the work is used by them together. In cases of collaborative work, the result of which forms an undividable whole, none of the authors has the right to prohibit the use of such a work without sufficient grounds. A part of the work, the use of which is possible independent of the other parts, that is, a part that is of unique significance, can be used by its author at their own discretion unless otherwise provided by an agreement between the co-authors (Article 1258 of the Civil Code). Thus, divisible and indivisible works are distinguished.

The court recognized a song as a divisible work because as a result of intellectual activity, it does not represent an indissoluble whole. Each part (the music and the lyrics) is created by a particular author, and the possibility of their independent use does not raise doubt (Resolution of the Presidium of the Chukotka Autonomous District Court of April 18, 2018, on case No. 2-35/2017). In judicial practice, opera, as well as collective works in which the authors of individual parts (sections, chapters, etc.) of the collective work are recognized as such too (Resolution of the Federal State Commercial Court of the North Caucasus Circuit of March 28, 2011, on case No. A63-6048/2009; Ruling of the Kemerovo Regional Court of December 19, 2013, on case 33-11998/2013).

To a certain extent, works created in the framework of divisible authorship may resemble composite works, but the difference lies in single creative vision behind such divisible work.

The related rights to joint performance are, in their turn, exercised by the head of the group of performers, and in their absence, by the members of the group of performers jointly, unless otherwise provided by an agreement between them. Given that the number of co-executors can be significant, this provision is aimed at increasing regulation efficiency.

If an exclusive right arises in relation to all IP subject matter, then personal non-property rights can arise only in certain cases provided in the Civil Code. They are closely connected with the person who possesses them. In this regard, their alienation is impossible since they are inseparable from their holders. The amount of the author's personal non-property rights directly depends on the IP subject matter created by them. And this is about the results of intellectual activity, not about the means of individualization.

The following personal non-property rights belong to the author of a work of science, literature and art:

- the right of authorship,
- the author's right to a name,
- the right to the protection of the work,
- the right to publish the work,
- the right of withdrawal.

The author of an invention, utility model, industrial design, selection breeding achievement or topography of an integrated microcircuit acquires the right of authorship.

Personal non-property rights also arise in the sphere of related rights; for example, a performer has the right of authorship, the right to the name and the right of integrity of the performance.

Personal non-property rights help identify the creator of the IP subject matter and protect the very embodiment of the author's intention. Thus, the right of authorship is the right to be recognized as the author, the right to the name is the right to use or permit the use of a work under one's own name or a fictitious name (pseudonym) or anonymously. These rights are inalienable and non-transferable. Refusal of them is null and void.

The right of integrity of a work or performance is aimed at protecting the result of intellectual activity, since making changes, abbreviations and additions to their work, adding illustrations, foreword, afterword, comments or any explanations to the work without the consent of the author is not allowed.

The right of integrity should be distinguished from the adaptation right, which is one of the exclusive right elements. The adaptation of a work involves the creation of a new (derivative) work based on the existing one. The right of integrity (paragraph 1, clause 1 of Article 1266 of the Civil Code) concerns such changes in a work that are not related to the creation of a new work based on the existing one (clause 87 of Resolution of the Plenum of the Supreme Court No. 10).

For example, posting an author's article complemented by illustrations representing advertising messages and announcements, but not signed as such and not related to the work on the website, was found to be a violation of this right (Appeal Ruling of the Moscow City Court of March 10, 2020, on case No. 33-9211/2020). Adding comments to a photograph was also recognized as an infringement of this right (Appeal Ruling of the Sverdlovsk Regional Court of March 17, 2016, on case No. 33-3900/2016).

The author can agree that some changes may be introduced to the work in the future should the correction be required (correction of errors, clarification or addition of factual information, etc.) under the following conditions:

- the author's intention will not be distorted,
- the integrity of the work is not breached.

As explained in clause 87 of Resolution of the Plenum of the Supreme Court No. 10, such consent can be given by the author in the following cases:

- the author has made a public announcement (informed an indefinite number of people by posting a corresponding message on the official website of the federal executive body responsible for the placement of such statements) that provides any person with the opportunity to use a work belonging to them or an object of related rights on the conditions and within the period specified by the author free of charge (public (free) licence) (clause 5 of Article 1233 of the Civil Code);

- the author has granted the right to use the works for the creation of a new result of intellectual activity within the limits and under the terms of an open licence (clause 2 of Article 1286.1 of the Civil Code) (see section "The transfer of IP rights").

After the author's death, permission to make changes passes to the person who has the exclusive right to the work. In this case, it is necessary to take into account the author's will, definitely expressed in a testament, letters, diaries or another written form. Such actions should not contradict the author's wish.

The close connection between the author's personality and their work is also reflected in the position according to which changes to the work defaming the author's honour, dignity or business reputation, as well as attempts at such actions, give the author the right to demand protection of their honour, dignity or business reputation (after their death, this requirement can be declared by interested parties). However, in this case, the fact of the right infringement and the defamatory nature of these violations shall be proved (Ruling of the Eighth General Jurisdiction Court of Cassation of June 4, 2020, on case No. 88-5636/2020; Ruling of the Moscow City Court of November 3, 2015, on case No. 4g/8-11086/2015).

The right to publish a work and the right to withdraw it reflect the polar opposite approaches the author might opt for in relation to their work. In the first case, they make the work available to the public (publication, public display, public performance, broadcast or cablecast or in any other way); in the second case, they abandon the earlier decision to publish it. Meanwhile, an author who has transferred a work to another person under a contract for use is deemed to have agreed to the publication of this work. As for the right of withdrawal, it may be exercised before the actual publication of the work, subject to compensation for damages caused by such a decision to the person who got the exclusive right or the right to use the work. It should be pointed out that the right to withdraw does not apply to computer programs, work created under an employment contract and works included in a complex object.

There is also a category of so-called "other rights". The group of other rights includes those intellectual rights that cannot be attributed to the categories described above. The reason for their isolated status causes debate among scholars (Chernichkina, 2019). However, according to Alexandr L. Makovsky's justified opinion, this is due to, firstly, the very wording of the article of the Civil Code that describes intellectual rights. Thus, according to Article 1226 of the Civil Code intellectual rights are recognized to the results of intellectual activity and the means of individualization equated to them, which include an exclusive right that is a property right, and, in cases specified in the Civil Code, also personal non-property rights and other rights (the resale right, access right, etc.). Only the exclusive right was identified as a property right, but the property nature is inherent in some other rights too (for example, the right to remuneration for a work created under an employment contract, the resale right). The second reason is the lack of any clear criteria for dividing rights into property and personal non-property, taking into account the specificity of the modern IP sphere (Makovsky, 2008).

The Civil Code (Article 1225) provides an open list of other rights that explicitly mention the resale right and the right of access. The resale right is the author's right to collect a royalty on each resale of the original of a fine artwork and author's manuscripts (autographs) of musical and literary works. The participation of a legal entity or an individual businessman as an agent, buyer or seller (in particular, an auction house, an art gallery, an art salon, a shop) is an essential requirement for this right to arise. The right to access is the right of the author of an artistic work to require the owner of the original work to provide the right to reproduce their work. The author of a work of architecture has the right to demand from the owner of the original to take photographs and video of the work unless otherwise provided by the contract. The author does not have the right to demand delivery of the work from the owner of the original work.

Resolution of the Plenum of the Supreme Court No. 10 expands this list, although there it is not exclusive either. As follows from clause 32 of the Resolution, other rights include the resale right, the right of access, the right to remuneration for the result of intellectual activity created under an employment contract, the right to protect a phonogram from distortion during its use and the right to obtain a patent, etc. However, the Civil Code contains references to some other rights, for example, the rights of the author of a work of architecture, urban planning or gardening art to exercise the author's control over the preparation of the construction documentation and supervision over the construction site or other type of implementation of the corresponding project that the author of such a work comes across (Regulations on Authors Supervision over the Construction of Buildings and Structures, approved by Order of the Ministry of Construction of the Russian Federation No. 98/pr of February 19, 2016). The author of these copyright objects has the right to demand to participation in implementing their architectural, urban planning or landscape gardening project for the customer unless otherwise provided by the contract.

Talking about IP in business, the concept of "intangible assets" cannot be ignored. But these concepts are not identical. For example, in accounting, intangible assets are not limited to IP subject matter only. As follows from the Accounting Regulations "Accounting for Intangible Assets" (14/2007), the business's reputation arising in connection with the acquisition of an enterprise as a property complex (in whole or in part) is also taken into account as part of its intangible assets. Speaking about objects of IP rights, identification as intangible assets takes place only on the condition of compliance with the requirements.

Thus, in accordance with clause 3–4 of the Accounting Regulations 14/2007, in order to accept an object as an intangible asset for accounting, it should meet the following conditions simultaneously:

1 the object is capable of bringing economic benefits to the organization in the future; in particular, the object is intended for use in the production, the performance of work or in the provision of services for the managerial needs of the organization or use in activities aimed at achieving the goals of creating a non-profit organization (including its use in business activities carried out in accordance with the legislation of the Russian Federation);
2 the organization has the right to receive the economic benefits that this object is able to bring in the future (the organization shall have adequate documentation confirming the existence of the asset itself and the right of this organization to the result of intellectual activity or the means of individualization such as patents, certificates, other protection documents, an agreement on the alienation of the exclusive right to the result of intellectual activity or the means of individualization, documents confirming the transfer of exclusive rights without a contract, etc.); there are also restrictions on other person's access to such economic benefits (hereinafter control over the object);
3 selection or separation (identification) of an object from other assets are possible;
4 the object is intended to be used for a long time, i.e., useful life exceeding 12 months or normal operating cycle if it exceeds 12 months;
5 the organization does not intend to sell the object within 12 months or the normal operating cycle if it exceeds 12 months;
6 the actual (initial) cost of the object can be reliably determined;
7 the object has no material form.

If the above conditions are met, intangible assets include, for example, works of science, literature and art; computer programs; inventions; utility models; selective breeding achievements; production secrets (know-how); trademarks and service marks.

As stated in Article 257 of the Tax Code of the Russian Federation (hereinafter Tax Code),[1] intangible assets are the results of intellectual activity and other objects of IP (exclusive rights to them) acquired and (or) created by a taxpayer and used in the production (work performance, provision of services) or for the long-term management needs of an organization (duration over 12 months) (this is for the purposes of Chapter 25 of the Tax Code, "Corporate Profit Tax").

To be recognized as an intangible asset, the object must have the ability to bring economic benefits (income) to the taxpayer. Adequate documentation confirming the existence of the intangible asset itself and (or) the taxpayer's exclusive right to the results of intellectual activity (including patents, certificates, other protection-conferring documents, contract of assignment (acquisition) of a patent, trademark) is also necessary.

Intangible assets include, in particular:

1 the exclusive right of the patent holder to an invention, industrial design or utility model;

2 the exclusive right of the author and other copyright holders to use the computer program or database;
3 the exclusive right of the author or other copyright holder to use the topology of integrated circuits;
4 the exclusive right to a trademark, service mark, appellation of origin of goods and company name;
5 the exclusive right of the patent holder to selective breeding achievements;
6 possession of "know-how", secret formula or process, information regarding industrial, commercial or scientific experience;
7 the exclusive right to audiovisual works.

In accounting, including tax accounting, the intellectual and business qualities, qualifications and work skills of an organisation's employees are not considered intangible assets. In addition, in tax accounting, research, development and technological works that have not yielded a positive result are not recognized as intangible assets; in accounting, expenses associated with the formation of a legal entity (organizational costs) are not intangible assets.

Judicial practice indicates, citing Article 257 of the Tax Code of the Russian Federation and the provisions of the Accounting Regulations 14/2007, that an intangible asset is not the result of intellectual activity, but the exclusive right to use the result (Resolution of the Seventeenth State Commercial Court of Appeal of August 4, 2015, on case No. A60-6613/2009; Resolution of the Federal State Commercial Court of the Western Siberian Circuit of August 2, 2017, on case No. A27-7379/2014). According to GOST R 58591-2019, "National Standard of the Russian Federation. Intellectual Property. Accounting and Intangible Assets", approved and enacted by Order of Rosstandart No. 951-st of October 10, 2019, intangible assets include the IP exclusive rights as objects of non-financial assets.

As mentioned in the Resolution of the First State Commercial Court of Appeal of July 31, 2018, on case No. A11-5750/2016, intangible assets are a special type of an organization's assets since they do not have a tangible form. In accounting, and also tax accounting, intangible assets include exclusive rights to the results of intellectual activity and the means of individualization listed in Article 1225 of the Civil Code (clause 4 of the Accounting Regulations 14/2007, clause 3 of Article 257 of the Tax Code of the Russian Federation).

An IP subject matter can be recognized as an intangible asset only if a set of conditions are met (Ruling of the Supreme State Commercial Court of the Russian Federation of November 11, 2012, on case No. VAS-13774/12). In accounting, an asset is accepted as an intangible asset if all the conditions stipulated by the Accounting Regulations 14/2007 are fulfilled simultaneously, in tax accounting – if the requirements of Article 257 of the Tax Code of the Russian Federation are met (Resolution of the First State Commercial Court of Appeal of July 31, 2018, on case No. A11-5750/2016).

It should be noted that misinterpretation of the regulations on intangible assets leads to disputes that shall be resolved in court. For example, the value-added tax (VAT) on works and services performed and rendered by third-party organizations to create IP objects included in tax deductions prior to the IP subject matter's registration as an intangible asset may lead to additional VAT charges, as well as various fines and penalties. At the same time, the courts have pointed out that since an intangible asset cannot exist or be registered until the creation of the intangible assets has been completed, then the disputed tax amount can be claimed for deduction only after the completion of all stages of work on the creation of intangible assets and the transfer of the finished (existing) intangible asset (Resolution of the State Commercial Court of Moscow Circuit of March 7, 2019, on case No. A40-74076/2018; Ruling of the Supreme Court of the Russian Federation of May 19, 2017, on case No. A40-68072/2016).

An erroneous qualification of an IP subject matter as an intangible asset can also lead to litigation related to the accounting of its acquisition/creation costs as a lump sum or by depreciation (Resolution of the State Commercial Court of the Central Circuit of October 15, 2020, on case No. A35-3796/2019; Resolution of the State Commercial Court of Moscow Circuit of December 21, 2018, on case No. A40-56261/2017). It should be noted that according to Article 256 of the Tax Code, the results of intellectual activity and other subject matter of IP, that is owned by the taxpayer (unless otherwise provided by the Tax Code) and used by them to generate income are depreciable property. The results of intellectual activity and other objects of IP with a useful life of more than 12 months and an initial value of more than 100,000 rubles are depreciable property. According to the Accounting Regulations 14/2007, the cost of intangible assets is redeemed through depreciation over their useful life, unless otherwise provided by the relevant document. Intangible assets with indefinite useful lives are not depreciated.

Analyzing the nature of intellectual rights, the issue of their real meaning cannot be ignored. Subjective intellectual rights are aimed at providing an opportunity for the subject to give effect to their interests, including by establishing prohibitions for other persons and protection in case of violation. IP rights are no exception. At the same time, the differences between the groups of rights described above, of course, raises the question of whether one of them can be called prevailing or not. The maximum protection of the author and his creative intention will be achieved if the author has the entire set of rights. The lower their concentration in their hands, the less opportunities they have. For example, the author of a book sells the exclusive rights to it to a publisher. In this case, the author will no longer be able to determine issues related to the use of the work. Does this mean a complete separation of the person from the object created by them, as well as the loss of interest in it? No, because it would not be appropriate and rational. The figure of the author will always be primary for the results of intellectual activity since they carried out its creation. At the same time, under a favourable set of circumstances, the author will be able to further create objects of intellectual rights. The right holder is limited to the use of those objects that already exist.

Of course, considering IP as an intangible asset, attention will be paid to the exclusive right since its presence is one factor that makes it possible to recognize an IP subject matter as an intangible asset. In the process of IP valuation, the cost of exclusive (property) rights to the result of intellectual activity or means of individualization in monetary terms will be determined (GOST R 55386-2012).

However, for the author, the economic value of an intellectual result is not the only incentive for its creation. As Gabriel F. Shershenevich rightly noted, intellectual work is conditioned by internal stimuli that are born from spiritual needs (Shershenevich, 1890, p. 5). It seems that their absence greatly complicates the process of achieving the desired result and sometimes even makes it impossible. Therefore, the establishment of non-property rights for the author can be regarded as recognition of the significance of his activities and a kind of stimulation of the author for his further continuation.

In addition, when discussing intellectual rights, the question of the relationship between private and public interests inevitably arises. Thus, the Constitutional Court of the Russian Federation directly stated that law enforcers are obliged to apply the provisions of IP legislation not only on the basis of their systematic connection with the main provisions of civil legislation but also in the context of the general legal principles of equality and justice, and also taking into account the requirements of proportionality and compliance with the balance of competing rights and legitimate interests – private and public – arising from these principles (Ruling of the Constitutional Court of the Russian Federation of April 23, 2020, on case No. 994-O-P). Thus, the author's and the right holder's intellectual rights may be limited to a certain extent, but this does not diminish their importance. It is only a consequence of the need to consider the needs of society.

Note

1 The Tax Code of the Russian Federation includes two normative parts, they are: the Tax Code of the Russian Federation (Part I) No. 146-FZ of July 31, 1998, and the Tax Code of the Russian Federation (Part II) No. 117-FZ of August 5, 2000.

3 Legal regulation of intellectual property in the Russian Federation

In the Russian Federation, intellectual property (IP) is subject to regulation under national and international law.

The diversity of legal sources is due to the heterogeneity and complexity of IP discussed earlier.

The fundamental source of the national law is the Constitution of the Russian Federation. Freedom of literary, artistic, scientific, technical and other creative activities and the legal protection of IP are guaranteed by Article 44 of the Constitution.

However, it is Part IV of the Civil Code of the Russian Federation titled "The Rights to the Results of Intellectual Activity and Means of Individualization of Legal Entities, Goods, Works, Services and Enterprises" that must be considered as the main law regulating the abovementioned type of social relations. The act contains general provisions valid for all kinds of intellectual activities and means of individualization, while each of them is also regulated by specific norms stipulated therein.

Part IV of the Civil Code replaced the previous set of laws that used to regulate IP relations, e.g., Copyright Law, Law No. 3523-1 of September 23, 1992, "On Legal Protection of Programs for Computers and Databases"; Patent Law No. 3517-1 of September 23, 1992; Law No. 3520-1 of September 23, 1992, "On Trademarks, Service Marks and Appellations of Origin of Goods", etc.

According to Article 5 of Federal Law No. 231-FZ of December 18, 2006, "On the Introduction of Part IV of the Civil Code of the Russian Federation" (hereinafter Introductory Law), Part IV of the Civil Code is applied to all legal relations that take place after its implementation and, as for relations that had existed before that part of the Civil Code was introduced, Part IV of the Civil Code can only be applied to those rights and obligations arising from such relations that emerge after Part IV of the Civil Code came into force. However, in some cases, relations initiated before the implementation of Part IV of the Civil Code shall also fall under its legal power. For instance, authorship, author's name, works of art, literature and scientific research shall be protected even if they were not subject to legal protection at the time of their creation.

The codification of the IP laws was an important contribution in improving the field's legal regulation system and the development of the current legal system. The explanatory memorandum to the draft of Part IV of the Civil Code informs that one of the main reasons for the codification was the ever-increasing importance of IP in civil turnover.

The structure of Part IV of the Civil Code (Articles 1225–1551) includes:

- general provisions;
- copyright;
- rights related to copyright;
- patent law;
- right to selective breeding achievements;
- right to topologies of integrated circuits;
- trade secret rights (know-how);
- rights to the individualization of legal entities, goods, jobs, services and enterprises;
- right to a company name;
- trademark and service mark right;
- right to geographical indication and appellations of origin of goods;
- right to a commercial name;
- the right to integrate the results of intellectual activity into a complex technological solution.

However, the legal regulation of IP rights is not limited to one set of specialized laws. Norms regulating this domain can be generally divided into:

- norms that clarify the provisions of Part IV of the Civil Code,
- norms containing provisions on IP in various types of social relations,
- norms containing general provisions applicable to IP.

There are laws and bylaws that offer a more detailed specification of the norms of Part IV of the Civil Code. For example, Article 1247 of the Civil Code on Patent Attorney has a more specific explanation in Federal Law No. 316-FZ of December 30, 2008, "On Patent Attorney", while Government Order No. 745 of June 8, 2019, "On Establishing the Rules for Right Holders of Placing Statements on Providing Gratuitous Public Access to Works of Science, Literature, Art or Related Rights Objects on the Conditions and During the Period of Time Specified" provides a more detailed view on the content of clause 5 of Article 1233 of the Civil Code, which regulates so-called free licences. The peculiarities of the implementation procedure of certain Civil Code provisions can be found in the acts issued by corresponding federal executive bodies, e.g., the Ministry of Culture of the Russian Federation, the Ministry of Economic Development of the Russian Federation and Rospatent (Federal Service for Intellectual Property), etc. The abovementioned norms regulate IP relations directly and constitute the first and main group of norms.

The norms attributed to the second group are those used to regulate certain legal issues but specified in the normative acts that do not directly connect with the corresponding sphere of relations. For example, Article 14.4 of Federal Law No. 135-FZ of July 26, 2006, "On the Protection of Competition" (hereinafter Law on Protection of Competition) prohibits unfair competition related to the acquisition and use of the exclusive right to the means of individualization of a legal entity and of goods, works or services.

The third group contains norms of general character that can, however, regulate IP issues if not stipulated otherwise. It mostly has to do with the norms of Part I of the Civil Code that include provisions on good faith, entities and obligations that can also be applied to IP law being a subsection of the civil law. It must be mentioned one more time, though, that according to clause 3 of Article 1227, intellectual rights are not subject to regulation under section II, Part I of the Civil Code (the right of ownership and other property rights) if not specified otherwise in the special section of the Civil Code.

This division is, of course, rather conventional as the integral system of IP regulation is constituted by all sources together. What is certain is that the peculiarities of their interrelation and interaction must be taken into account.

Inferior normative acts may not contradict the acts that are superior to them, i.e., there is a certain hierarchy that reads as follows:

- The Constitution of the Russian Federation,
- Federal constitutional laws,
- Federal laws (including the Civil Code),
- Bylaws (presidential decrees, governmental orders, normative acts by federal executive bodies).

IP is subject to regulation under federal normative acts as in accordance with Article 71 of the Constitution of the Russian Federation, this type of relation is to be controlled by the Russian Federation. Thus, the constituent entities of the Russian Federation may not adopt laws or bylaws regarding IP.

Federal constitutional laws regulate the issues discussed in the Constitution of the Russian Federation (Article 108 of the Constitution). They do not regulate IP directly but are important for the implementation of rights and obligations within this field, e.g., Federal Constitutional Law No. 1-FKZ of December 31, 1996, "On the Judicial System of the Russian Federation" (hereinafter Law on the Judicial System) or Federal Constitutional Law No. 1-FKZ of April 28, 1995, "On State Commercial Courts of the Russian Federation".

Speaking about federal laws that also include the Civil Code, among them, the highest priority belongs to Part IV of the Civil Code. As Article 4 of the Introductory Law expressly states, until the laws and other normative acts existing in the Russian Federation fully comply with Part IV of the Civil Code, laws and other normative acts of the Russian Federation as well as the legislation acts of the Union of the Soviet Socialist Republics (USSR) that have legal power in the Russian Federation to the degree and effect determined by the

Russian Federation legislation, only apply to the extent to which they do not contradict Part IV of the Civil Code.

Bylaws include presidential decrees, governmental resolutions and directives and acts by ministries and other federal executive bodies. These are normative acts (they establish general rules of behaviour targeting the so-called indefinite group of persons and implying recurrent usage) adopted for the enforcement of laws. They may not be contrary to the existing laws.

Another possible regulator is a legal custom that represents a pattern of behaviour established and widely used within some business or different setting even though it is not officially stipulated in the legislation or any other document (Article 5 of the Civil Code). The litigants proving their position, as well as the court assessing the case, can refer to a legal custom which, nonetheless, may not contradict the fundamentals of the civil legislation, mandatory provisions in laws and other normative acts or the contract (clause 2 of Resolution of the Plenum of the Supreme Court of the Russian Federation No. 25 of June 23, 2015, "On Application by Courts of some Provisions of Part I of the Civil Code of the Russian Federation"; hereinafter Resolution of the Plenum of the Supreme Court No. 25).

The following examples of the application of legal customs in judicial practice can be cited:

- a defendant claims that based on the existing legal custom, authors who do not want their works to be used gratuitously tend to place into their books, albums and (or) internet publications an express prohibition on the use of their works without the author's written consent, i.e., without the licence agreement (Decision of the State Commercial Court of Moscow of January 26, 2016, on case No. A40-142345/15-15-1143);
- the court indicated that as per the legal custom on civil turnover, the plaintiff does not have to register specific violations of their exclusive authorship rights by the wrongdoer (Decision of the State Commercial Court of the Tatarstan Republic of May 12, 2015, on case No. A65-3735/2015).

Decisions on individual cases (both by the court and authorized executive bodies) cannot be considered sources of law but contribute to forming uniform approaches to interpreting normative stipulations. In this sense, studying legal practice proves quite relevant.

A special role in judicial practice is attributed to Resolution of the Plenum of the Supreme Court No. 10 adopted in order to ensure an adequate and uniform judicial resolution of disputes concerning IP rights protection. Despite the fact that such resolutions come from the court, they all help to make law implementation uniform by explaining and clarifying various legal practice issues. Such acts are not individually determined but rather universal and thus can serve as examples of interpreting the law.

Suppose no legal norm, contract or legal custom applies to the relations between parties. In that case, this blank space can be filled with a legal analogy using civil legislation regulating similar relations. In the absence of the latter, the legal relations are subject to the general provisions and meaning of the civil legislation (law analogy) and the requirements of good faith, sensibility and justice (Article 6 of the Civil Code).

International conventions are one of the important regulators of IP in the Russian Federation. Clause 1 of Article 7 of the Civil Code states that the generally recognized principles and norms of international law, as well as international agreements involving the Russian Federation, form part of the country's legal system according to the Constitution of the Russian Federation. Nowadays, the Russian Federation is a participant in a significant number of both bilateral and multilateral IP agreements such as

- the Berne Convention for the Protection of Literary and Artistic Works of September 9, 1886;
- the Paris Convention for the Protection of Industrial Property of March 20, 1883;
- the Nice Agreement Concerning the International Classification of Goods and Services for the Purposes of the Registration of Marks of June 15, 1957;
- the International Convention for the Protection of Performers, Producers of Phonograms and Broadcasting Organizations of October 26, 1961;
- the International Convention for the Protection of New Varieties of Plants of December 2, 1961;
- the Convention establishing the World Intellectual Property Organization of July 14, 1967;
- the Locarno Agreement Establishing an International Classification for Industrial Designs of October 8, 1968;
- the Patent Cooperation Treaty of June 19, 1970;
- the Strasbourg Agreement Concerning the International Patent Classification of March 24, 1976;
- the Budapest Treaty on the International Recognition of the Deposit of Microorganisms for the Purposes of Patent Procedure of April 28, 1977;
- the Madrid System for the International Registration of Marks of April 14, 1891;
- the Agreement on Trade-Related Aspects of Intellectual Property Rights (TRIPS) of April 15, 1994;
- the Eurasian Patent Convention of September 9, 1994;
- the World Intellectual Property Organization Copyright Treaty (WCT) of December 20, 1996;
- the Patent Law Treaty of June 1, 2000;
- the Singapore Treaty on the Law of Trademarks of March 27, 2006, etc.

The list of all multilateral and bilateral IP agreements (with texts) is available on the Rospatent official website.

In spite of the differences between IP legislation in various countries, international agreements allow some shared vectors of development and harmonize approaches to understanding the fundamentals of the regulation and interaction within this field. Throughout IP history, scientists kept pointing out (Boguslavsky, 1964; Yakovlev & Makovsky, 2007) that international agreements are aimed at protecting the rights of foreign authors and right holders. In 1894, Ilya D. Galperin-Kaminsky highlighted that the establishment of international authorship law proved important for authors and publishers as well as society in general (Galperin-Kaminsky, 1984, p. 66). Back then, the issue caused serious discussions (Lykoshin, 1899). Nowadays, however, IP rights regulation appears unimaginable without the international element. Moreover, the relevance of IP regulation is constantly growing, considering the fast development of information technologies and the ever-rising importance of online reality in our everyday lives.

Today's Russian Federation has a well-organized and consistent system of IP regulation composed of both international and national legal sources. The national part is characterized by 1) the hierarchy of the national acts with the superiority of the Constitution of the Russian Federation establishing the basic principles of IP regulation; 2) the legal code (Part IV of the Civil Code) being the main source of IP regulation in Russia; 3) other regulators that clarify and specify the Civil Code and do not contradict said normative act. International sources of law, including bilateral and multilateral agreements, form the basis for the stable development of the IP field and ensure the recognition and protection of the rights belonging to foreign authors and right holders.

4 Government authorities and other organizations operating in the field of management and protection of IP

In accordance with Article 10 of the Constitution of the Russian Federation, the governance of a state in Russia is based on the separation of powers: legislative, executive and judicial. All the authorities representing the above-listed branches of power are considered independent. All of them influence intellectual property (IP) regulation in one way or another.

In particular, the IP laws included in section "Legal regulation of IP" were adopted by the legislature and are binding upon all subjects within the Russian Federation, including government authorities.

The executive IP authorities ensure the exercise of IP rights while their protection is within the scope of the judicial authorities.

Since the structure of the Russian legislative authorities and the legislative process are not directly related to the topic, there is no need to focus on these issues here. However, it is worth recalling that since Russian IP legislative regulation can only be performed at the federal level, the issues under consideration may not be regulated by the acts of the constituent entities or the municipal units (see also section "Legal regulation of IP").

Describing the system of IP executive authorities, one should pay attention to the competence of the government of the Russian Federation.

According to Article 23 of Federal Constitutional Law No. 2-FKZ of December 17, 1997, "On the Government of the Russian Federation" (hereinafter Federal Constitutional Law on the Government of the Russian Federation), the government issues resolutions and directives on the basis and in pursuance of the Constitution, federal constitutional laws, federal laws, regulatory decrees of the president of the Russian Federation and ensures their implementation.

Acts of a normative nature are issued in the form of government resolutions. Acts regarding operational and other current issues that are not regulatory are issued in the form of directives.

Government resolutions and directives are legally binding in the Russian Federation.

These acts, as noted in section "Legal regulation of IP", are bylaws. They play a very important role as they facilitate the implementation of law provisions.

The first IP-related legal act that should be mentioned is Resolution of the Government No. 218 of March 21, 2012, which approved the Statute of the Federal Service for Intellectual Property (Rospatent) (Statute of Rospatent). This resolution was adopted in accordance with Presidential Decree No. 673 of May 24, 2011, "On the Federal Service for Intellectual Property".

Other important resolutions related to this field are as follows (the list of resolutions is not exhaustive):

- Government Resolution No. 524 of May 29, 1998, "On the Minimal Remuneration Rates for the Authors of Cinematic Works, the Production (Shooting) of which was Carried out Before August 3, 1992";
- Government Resolution No. 285 of April 19, 2008, "On Approval of the Rules for Payment of Remuneration to the Author in Case of the Resale of the Originals of Artistic Works or Manuscripts (Autographs) of Literary and Musical Works";
- Government Resolution No. 1416 of December 24, 2015, "On the State Registration of the Disposal of the Exclusive Right to an Invention, Utility Model, Industrial Design, Trademark, Service Mark, Registered Topography of an Integrated Microcircuit, a Computer Program, a Database Under a Contract and the Transfer of the Exclusive Right to them without a Contract".

The government also issues IP-related directives. In particular, the following directives should be mentioned:

- Government Directive No. 1791-r of December 1, 2008, "On the Reorganization of the Federal State Institution 'The Federal Institute of Industrial Property' of the Federal Service for Intellectual Property, Patents and Trademarks and the Federal State Institution 'The Chamber for Patent-related Disputes' of the Federal Service for Intellectual Property, Patents and Trademarks";
- Government Directive No. 1052-r of July 21, 2008, "On the Accession of the Russian Federation to the Treaty of the World Intellectual Property Organization on Copyright, adopted by the Diplomatic Conference on Certain Copyright and Related Rights Issues in Geneva on December 20, 1996".

In addition to the adoption of essential bylaws, the government directs the work of federal ministries and other federal executive authorities and controls their operation (Article 12 of the Federal Constitutional Law on the Government of the Russian Federation).

The state IP-related executive body with the biggest scope is the Federal Service for Intellectual Property (Rospatent). As indicated, its work is regulated by the Statute of Rospatent. The Federal Service for Intellectual Property is under the jurisdiction of the Ministry of Economic Development of the Russian Federation.

Rospatent's powers are defined in Section II of the Statute. This authority submits the drafts of federal laws, normative legal acts of the president and the government of the Russian Federation, and other documents on the issues within Rospatent's jurisdiction that require the government's decision to the Ministry of Economic Development. Rospatent also summarizes the practice of the Russian IP legislation's application and prepares proposals for its improvement.

The above Rospatent powers are essential for the development of IP legislation. Information on the most significant issues requiring additional elaboration can be found in Rospatent's regulatory and legal work schedule for 2019–2023 (https://rospatent.gov.ru/ru/activities/plan-normpravovoj-rosp). These include improving the regulation of the implementation of legally significant actions in the process of providing IP-related public services, developing the sphere of patent attorneys in Russia, etc.

Due to the powers granted to it, Rospatent is an active participant in a number of Russian target programs. Rospatent is implementing measures for IP digitalization within the framework of the Information Infrastructure federal project under the Digital Economy national program. The Action Plan of the Federal Service for Intellectual Property (Rospatent) for 2019–2024, approved by Rospatent on March 16, 2019, provides that special information systems and services have been created and are functioning within the framework of the specified federal project implementation. They are available at the following website: https://rospatent.gov.ru/ru/sourses.

In addition to the functions associated with the development of IP in Russia, Rospatent also performs some routine operations. For example, the Statute stipulates that Rospatent's competence also includes the following responsibilities:

- supervising the work of state customers and organizations executing state contracts that require the implementation of research, development and technological work funded from the federal budget;
- assessing and registering patent attorneys, issuing registration certificates to them and also monitoring the implementation of legal requirements by patent attorneys.

Rospatent carries out the assessment and registration in compliance with the "Administrative Regulations for the Provision by the Federal Service for Intellectual Property of the Public Service for the Assessment and Registration of Patent Attorneys of the Russian Federation, the Issuance of Certificates to Patent Attorneys", approved by Order of the Ministry of Economic Development of Russia No. 616 of September 29, 2016.

The regulations state that public services are provided by Rospatent either directly or with the assistance of the subordinate federal state budgetary institution, the Federal Institute of Industrial Property (FIIP), which is required for Rospatent to perform legally significant actions while providing public services.

The results of the provision of public services could be one of the following:

1. the assessment and registration of a patent attorney in the Register for Patent Attorneys of the Russian Federation, issuance of a certificate to the patent attorney and publication of the information on registration of the patent attorney in Rospatent's official bulletin;
2. issuance of a new certificate to a patent attorney;
3. making one of the following decisions and sending the corresponding notification to the applicant:
   a. refusal of admission to the qualification exam,
   b. refusal to certify as a patent attorney,
   c. refusal to register as a patent attorney,
   d. on the issuance of a new certificate,
   e. refusal to issue a new certificate.

As a general rule, the completion time for the provision of public services connected to the patent attorneys' certification and registration, as well as the issuance of certificates to patent attorneys amounts to nine months.

It should be noted that in addition to the indicated types of activity the authority resolves intellectual rights protection disputes related to:

- filing and considering applications for the issuance of documents on inventions, utility models, industrial designs, trademarks, service marks, geographical indications and appellations of origin of goods;
- the state registration of the results of intellectual activity and means of individualization;
- the issuance of the relevant title documents;
- challenging the legal protection of the mentioned results and means;
- termination of such legal protection.

As for patent attorneys, they are citizens who have received the special status in accordance with the lawfully established procedure and carry out activities related to the legal protection of the results of intellectual activity and means of individualization, the protection of intellectual rights, the acquisition of exclusive rights to the results of intellectual activity and means of individualization and the disposal of such rights (Article 2 of Federal Law No. 316-FZ of December 30, 2008, "On Patent Attorneys"; hereinafter Law on Patent Attorneys). The status of a patent attorney becomes valid from the date of registration of a citizen in the corresponding register maintained by Rospatent. This register will be described later.

Rospatent created a qualification commission to assess candidates for patent attorneys. A Rospatent official heads the commission. It should be noted that the qualification commission includes patent attorneys whose candidacy is listed by the patent attorneys' public associations and self-regulatory organizations. Patent attorneys constitute one-third of the members of the qualification commission. Patent attorneys included in the qualification commission are subject to rotation once every 3 years (clauses 1–2 of Article 6 of the Law on Patent Attorneys).

The assessment of candidates for patent attorneys is conducted at least twice a year.

The assessment procedure includes several stages.

The first stage is to check if they meet the requirements for patent attorneys. The following requirements are established by Article 2 of the Law on Patent Attorneys:

1 the citizen shall not be under 18 years old,
2 the citizen shall reside permanently in the territory of the Russian Federation,
3 the citizen shall have a university degree,
4 the citizen shall have at least 4 years of experience as a patent attorney in accordance with the specialization in relation to which the citizen expresses a desire to be certified and registered as a patent attorney.

Such experience can be confirmed, for example, by providing a copy of one's employment record book, a copy of an employment contract, a certificate containing information about the time, type, scope and (or) nature of the work that the candidate performed as an employee in some organization or under the guidance of a patent attorney or the job description from the previous place of employment (clause 23 of the "Procedure for the Operation of the Qualification Commission", approved by Order of the Ministry of Economic Development of the Russian Federation No. 617 of September 29, 2016).

It should be noted that the requirements regarding education and work experience are interrelated. The registration of patent attorneys is carried out more than 4 years after they obtained a university degree. As indicated in the Recommendations for the "Preparation of the Documents Confirming Four Years of Experience as a Patent Attorney", approved by the Qualification Commission of June 21, 2019, accumulating 4 years of work experience as a patent attorney seems difficult without higher education.

In other words, for a person employed in an IP company without having undertaken a higher education course but having a different level of education instead, this period of work does not count as the work experience specified in the requirements. Both the Intellectual Property Court and the courts of general jurisdiction stick to this position.

Thus, it was mentioned that the assessment procedure for a patent attorney is not allowed immediately after having obtained a higher education certificate. The applicant's lack of higher education during the period of their work raises doubts about whether the applicant actually possesses an appropriate level of professional training as a patent attorney in accordance with their specialization, as required by law (Appellate Ruling of the Moscow City Court of February 26, 2015, on case No. 33-6192).

Based on the results of the documentation verification, the qualification commission decides on the applicant's admission to the qualifying exam or its refusal.

The second stage of the assessment includes a qualification exam that checks whether the candidate possesses the knowledge necessary to carry out the work of a patent attorney and is capable of the practical application of that knowledge.

Based on the exam results, the qualification commission makes a decision on the positive assessment of the candidate or refusal to certify them as a patent attorney. Such a decision is made within a month and comes into force from the date of its adoption. This is the last stage of certification in accordance with the law (clause 4 of Article 6 of the Law on Patent Attorneys).

The qualification commission does not have the right to refuse a citizen who has successfully passed the qualifying exam certification as a patent attorney, unless after the qualifying exam have been passed, the following circumstances are revealed:

- a person does not meet the above requirements regarding age, education, experience, place of residence;
- a citizen is recognized as incapable or partially capable in the manner prescribed by the legislation of the Russian Federation;
- the citizen's activity as a patent attorney was suspended by a court decision for a certain period and the period has not expired yet, or the citizen has been excluded from the Register of Patent Attorneys for a certain period (this period has not expired either).

In accordance with clause 1 of Article 9 of the Law on Patent Attorneys, in order to control the assessment of candidates for patent attorneys and the work of patent attorneys, Rospatent also created an appeal commission.

The appeal commission considers complaints regarding the qualification commission's decisions and complaints from people regarding the actions of patent attorneys representing their rights and legal interests that were performed in violation of the legislation of the Russian Federation.

In case of the violation of the legislation by a patent attorney, as a result of which the rights and (or) legitimate interests of the persons represented by said attorney are infringed, taking into account the consequences that have occurred, the appeal commission may take one of the following decisions:

1. issue a warning to a patent attorney,
2. apply to Rospatent with a recommendation to send a claim to the court on the application of penalties provided in clause 1 of Article 10 of the Law on Patent Attorneys to the patent attorney.

This clause states that the court can impose the following types of penalties on a patent attorney: suspension of one's activities for up to 1 year or exclusion from the Register of Patent Attorneys for up to 3 years with the possibility of the subsequent recovery of status, subject to re-assessment or without it.

For example, when considering a case based on a complaint from a person whose interests were infringed, the appeal commission recommended that the head of Rospatent file a lawsuit against a patent attorney in the form of excluding him from the Register of Patent Attorneys for a period of up to 3 years with the possibility of the subsequent recovery of status subject to a re-assessment. An appropriate penalty measure was applied to the patent attorney by the court. This decision was based on the following. Said patent attorney and PermEnergoMash Limited Liability Company (LLC) developed long-term cooperation, including legal protection of utility models under certain patents. On August 8, 2017, Promrubezh LLC filed objections with Rospatent against the issuance of the mentioned patents. And that same patent attorney participated in the consideration of those objections on behalf of Promrubezh. The patent attorney provided explanations substantiating the non-compliance of the utility models with the conditions of patentability. Despite representing PermEnergoMash in the issues regarding certain patents and, thus, carrying out actions to obtain and maintain those patents in force, the patent attorney agreed to represent the interests of Promrubezh in a legal process that involved challenging the validity of said patents (Cassation Ruling of the First General Jurisdiction Court of Cassation of March 2, 2020, on case No. 2a-1365/2018). Such behaviour is unacceptable for a patent attorney.

Everything that was described testifies to the significant role of Rospatent in the formation, development and strengthening of the institution of patent attorneys in Russia. Moreover, the routine functions associated with the institution of patent attorneys are no less important than the previously considered functions of improving legislation. By influencing patent attorneys in the ways described above, Rospatent contributes to the implementation, enforcement and protection of the rights of interested persons in the IP field.

Among the significant routine administrative tasks of Rospatent are registration actions, which can be found in more detail in sections "Creation and registration of IP" and "The transfer of IP rights" of the book.

Particularly, Rospatent is responsible for the state registration of inventions, utility models, industrial designs, trademarks, service marks, geographical indications, appellations of origin of goods, computer programs, databases and topographies of integrated circuits, including the issuance of the originals and copies of the patents on the above IP items and certificates for them in accordance with the established procedure.

The scope of Rospatent also includes the registration of operations with intellectual rights. This state authority registers:

- transferring of exclusive rights to an invention, utility model, industrial design, trademark, service mark, registered topography of an integrated microcircuit, computer program or database;

- pledging of the exclusive right to an invention, utility model, industrial design, trademark, service mark or registered topography of an integrated circuit;
- granting the right to use the objects under the contract that were specified in the previous point;
- granting and termination of the right to use an invention, utility model or industrial design under a compulsory simple (non-exclusive) licence following the court's decision;
- transferring the exclusive rights to an invention, utility model, industrial design, trademark, service mark, appellation of origin of goods, registered topography of an integrated microcircuit, computer program or database that does not include the conclusion of a contract.

In addition, Rospatent's competence extends to the registration of transactions involving the use of an integrated technology outside the Russian Federation.

Other important Rospatent tasks include the maintenance of various registries in the field of IP. According to clause 5.9 of the Rospatent Statute, the body shall maintain the following registers:

- State Register for Inventions,
- State Register for Utility Models,
- State Register for Industrial Designs,
- State Register for Trademarks and Service Marks,
- List of Well-Known Trademarks,
- State Register for Geographical Indications and Appellations of Origin of Goods,
- Register for Computer Programs,
- Register for Databases,
- Register for Topographies of Integrated Circuits,
- Unified Register of the results of research, development and technological work used for military, special and dual-use purposes, the rights to which belong to the Russian Federation.

Regarding each of the registers, there is an established procedure of how each shall be filled. For example, the registration of an invention in the state register consists of assigning a state registration number to the invention and entering this number and other information into the state register.

The following data shall be included:

- the state registration number of the invention (patent number);
- the registration number of the application;
- the date of submitting the application;
- the date from which the validity period of the exclusive right to the invention and the patent certifying this right is calculated;
- information concerning the priority (priorities) of the invention;

- information about the author(s) of the invention. If the author wishes to abstain from having their name included in the data regarding the patent, then the note "not to be published" shall be put in the state register;
- information about the patent holder(s);
- the contact details of the patent holder;
- the title of the invention;
- additional information, if such seems relevant (in particular, mentioning that there is an application that expresses the obligation to conclude an agreement on the transfer of the patent; providing details on a representative of the patent holder if this is the case; providing information about the state customer if the patent was issued in the name of the executor of a state or municipal contract);
- the date of the state registration of the invention;
- the date of the patent grant publication and the number of the official bulletin.

This information is reflected in the "Administrative Procedures and Actions Guide Implementation within the Framework of the Provision of State Services for State Registration of an Invention and the Issuance of a Patent for an Invention, its Duplicate", approved by Order of Rospatent No. 236 of December 27, 2018.

As indicated earlier in the text, Rospatent also maintains the Register of Patent Attorneys. This is specified directly in the Law on Patent Attorneys. Article 7 of this law states that should there be no legal grounds for refusing the applicant a state registration, the federal executive authority shall enter the citizen certified as a patent attorney in the register for IP following the decision of the qualification commission to give the patent attorney a positive assessment and the patent attorney's application filled in the prescribed manner.

The following people may not be registered as patent attorneys in Russia (clause 4 of Article 2 of the Law on Patent Attorneys):

- civil servants, people holding offices in the federal government of the Russian Federation, public offices in the government of the subjects of the Russian Federation, municipal offices; municipal employees;
- employees of the organizations subordinate to Rospatent;
- persons recognized as incapacitated or partially incapacitated in the manner prescribed by the legislation of the Russian Federation.

The Register of Patent Attorneys contains the following information:

- the registration number of the patent attorney, which is also the number of the registration certificate of the patent attorney, and the date of registration of the patent attorney;
- the surname, name, and patronymic of the patent attorney;
- the number and date of the decision of the qualification commission on the positive assessment;

- the specialization of the patent attorney;
- the name of the employer of the patent attorney or an indication of their independent professional activities;
- the address in the territory of the Russian Federation for correspondence, as well as their e-mail, telephone number, fax number, if any, and the languages in which correspondence can be carried out;
- the penalties imposed on the patent attorney;
- the names of the public associations and self-regulatory organizations to which the patent attorney belongs as a member.

The register also contains information on the exclusion of patent attorneys and the recovery of their registration.

In accordance with Article 8 of the Law on Patent Attorneys, the grounds for excluding a patent attorney from the register are:

- patent attorney request;
- loss of Russian citizenship;
- departure from the territory of the Russian Federation for permanent residence;
- circumstances being revealed which prevent a person from being a patent attorney in the Russian Federation (indicated above);
- death or being declared as deceased or missing by the court;
- court's decision on the exclusion from the register.

Rospatent's responsibilities include the accreditation of a Russian scientific or educational organization as an organization that can perform preliminary information searches in relation to the claimed inventions or utility models and a preliminary assessment of their patentability. The government of the Russian Federation establishes the procedure for accrediting a scientific or educational organization, the requirements for it and the grounds and procedure for terminating one's accreditation.

Of course, Rospatent's functions are not limited to those described. The work carried out by Rospatent in the field of IP is a complex one, so a separate book can be devoted to the description of its functions and the procedure for their fulfilment. However, the key functions of this Russian authority seem sufficient within the framework of the given topic.

IP issues concerning selective breeding achievements are within the remit of the Ministry of Agriculture of the Russian Federation. In accordance with clause 5 of the Resolution of the Government of the Russian Federation No. 450 of June 12, 2008, "On the Ministry of Agriculture of the Russian Federation", the Ministry of Agriculture, on the basis of and pursuant to the Constitution, federal constitutional laws, federal laws and acts of the president and the government of the Russian Federation, adopts normative legal acts for the purpose of regulating IP relations connected with selective breeding achievements. Thus, the Ministry of Agriculture of Russia participates in the development of the normative IP regulation system.

It is noteworthy that two special divisions deal with IP issues in the Ministry of Agriculture. These are the Livestock and Breeding Department and the Department of Plant Growing, Mechanization, Chemicalization and Plant Protection.

The former department implements such functions assigned to the Ministry as state policy development and legal regulation and the provision of state services including those related to selective breeding achievements in animal husbandry. In order to regulate IP in this area, advisory drafts of normative legal acts are prepared (Regulations "On the Livestock and Breeding Department" approved by Order of the Ministry of Agriculture of Russia No. 89 of March 1, 2018).

The latter department implements similar functions in the field of crop production and prepares the corresponding draft regulatory acts (Regulation "On the Department of Plant Growing, Mechanization, Chemicalization and Plant Protection", approved by Order of the Ministry of Agriculture of Russia No. 67 of February 14, 2018).

The Ministry of Agriculture of the Russian Federation carries out registration actions related to the exclusive rights to selective breeding achievements.[1] In particular, Article 1414 of the Civil Code established the requirement for state registration of a selective breeding achievement in the State Register of Protected Selective Breeding Achievements, which entails the issuance of a patent on a selective breeding achievement in favour of the applicant by the Ministry of Agriculture.

In addition, the Ministry of Agriculture issues copyright certificates for selective breeding achievements (Article 1416 of the Civil Code).

Agreements on the disposal of the exclusive right to a selective breeding achievement are subject to registration in Russia. The types of agreements are as follows:

- an agreement on the transfer of the exclusive right to a selective breeding achievement (an agreement on the transfer of a patent),
- an agreement on the pledge of the exclusive right to a selective breeding achievement,
- an agreement on the grant of the right to use a selective breeding achievement.

The Ministry of Agriculture registers such agreements as well as the changes introduced therein and the agreement's termination.

Moreover, the state authority also registers the transfer of the exclusive right to a selective breeding achievement without an agreement (Resolution of the Government of the Russian Federation No. 384 of April 30, 2009, "On Approval of the Rules for State Registration of Agreements on the Disposal of the Exclusive Right to a Selective Breeding Achievement and the Transfer of Such Right without an Agreement").

In addition to the above, the Ministry of Agriculture resolves administrative disputes (see section "Protection of IP rights").

Since the company name of a commercial legal entity is considered an IP subject matter, another authority shall be mentioned, the Federal Tax Service of the Russian Federation. It operates in accordance with the "Regulations on the Federal Tax Service", approved by Resolution of the Government of the Russian Federation No. 506 of September 30, 2004. Registering commercial legal entities in the Russian Federation falls under the jurisdiction of the Federal Tax Service. This body maintains the United State Register for Legal Entities (USRLE), which has the power to refuse registration of a legal entity, including due to an improper company name.

For example, Russian legislation prohibits the inclusion of certain terms in the company name of a legal entity: full or abbreviated official names of foreign states as well as words derived from such names, full or abbreviated official names of the federal government authorities, the government authorities of constituent entities of the Russian Federation and the local governments, full or abbreviated names of public associations and designations that contradict public interests and the principles of humanity and morality (clause 4 of Article 1473 of the Civil Code).

Suppose the company name does not meet the necessary requirements. In that case, its registration may be refused (clause 1 of Article 23 of Federal Law No. 129-FZ of August 8, 2001, "On State Registration of Legal Entities and Individual Entrepreneurs"; hereinafter Law on State Registration of Legal Entities and Individual Entrepreneurs). Thus, the emergence, implementation and termination of the exclusive right to a company name are within the Federal Tax Service's remit. The corporate name itself will be discussed in more detail in section "IP in corporate relations".

The Federal Antimonopoly Service of Russia (FAS) occupies a special place in the system of executive authorities in the IP field.

The Federal Antimonopoly Service is a federal executive body that controls and supervises the observance of the legislation on competition in the product and financial services markets, natural monopolies, advertising, etc. (Resolution of the Government of the Russian Federation No. 189 of April 7, 2004, "Issues of the Federal Antimonopoly Service").

The functions of the FAS aimed at maintaining competition and thus protecting IP are significant both for the Russian economy in general and for separate business entities.

For example, there is a ban on unfair competition associated with the creation of confusion (Article 14.6 of the Law on Protection of Competition). Thus, a business entity may not perform actions (inaction) that can be confused with a competing business entity's activities or with goods or services introduced by a competing business entity into civil circulation in the Russian Federation.

Significant importance is attached to the illegal use of a sign identical to a trademark, company name, commercial name, appellation of origin of goods of a competing business entity or one that is confusingly similar, by placing it on goods, labels, packaging or otherwise used in relation to the goods, which are sold or otherwise introduced into civil circulation within the territory of the Russian Federation, as well as through its use on the internet, e.g., as part of a domain name or in other addressing modes.

Confusion can also occur when copying or imitating the appearance of a product introduced into civil circulation by a competing business entity, including its packaging, label, name, colour scheme, corporate design in general (the combination of the clothing, the design of the sales area, showcases) or other elements that individualize a competing business entity and (or) its product.

For instance, the antimonopoly authority qualified as a violation of law the actions of a business company that used a colour scheme that imitates the general style of another gas station network, as well as pictorial elements, symbols, letters, signs that are similar to the point of confusion to the trademarks owned and used by other business subjects, in the external design of its gas stations. As explained by FAS, even the owner of a product that is not actually in the market, but has the potential to enter the market, can be recognized as violating the corresponding provision of the Law on Protection of Competition ("Review of the Practice of Applying Antimonopoly Legislation by the Collegial Bodies of FAS Russia (for the period from January 5, 2016, to July 1, 2018)", approved by protocol of the Presidium of FAS Russia No. 10 of October 3, 2018).

One of the important functions of FAS is to prosecute the actions of business entities that aim to mislead consumers. For example, the monitoring of the food products sold in the *PYATEROCHKA* chain supermarkets in the city of Yoshkar-Ola revealed that the Nelly Kids Chocolate products have packaging similar to that of Kinder Chocolate.

After the violation had been established, an order was sent to the business entity that imported Nelly Kids Chocolate into Russia instructing them to transfer the illegally obtained income to the state budget and stop the violation of the antimonopoly legislation (Resolution of the Intellectual Property Court of July 29, 2020, on case No. A38-4009/2019).

Thus, both the interests of consumers and those of the right holders were protected by FAS.

At the same time, unfair competition associated with the obtaining and subsequent use of the exclusive right to the means of individualization of a legal entity, goods, works or services shall be prohibited (part 1 of Article 14.4 of the Law on Protection of Competition).

For example, within the framework of one FAS case, it was noted that the actions of a business entity were aimed at gaining advantages in business over a competitor by using its business reputation, which has developed since the competitor's registration as a legal entity, through the registration and subsequent use of the company name *Sotsial'naya Apteka* (in English, social pharmacy) (Decision of the Intellectual Property Court of February 1, 2018, on case No. SIP-587/2017).

The exclusive rights to the results of intellectual activity could be taken into account by FAS when determining the dominant position of a business. For example, determining the dominant position of Google Inc. in the market of the application store for Android-based devices, the antimonopoly authority found that the dominant position of the defendant was strengthened due to its rights to the Android operating system (clause 10 of Clarification of FAS No. 17 "On Certain Issues of the Analysis of the State of Competition", approved by protocol of the Presidium of the FAS Russia No. 3 of April 10, 2019).

All of the above is just a small part of the measures taken by FAS in order to maintain competition and protect IP.

FAS also fulfils a rulemaking function in Russia, including in the IP field. In particular, there is the "Agreement on Cooperation between the Federal Antimonopoly Service and the Federal Service for Intellectual Property, Patents and Trademarks," approved by FAS and Rospatent on April 9, 2010. According to clause 2.1. of this document, these authorities provide mutual assistance in developing proposals aimed at improving the legislation of the Russian Federation on IP and the antimonopoly legislation of Russia in order to enhance the efficiency of the protection of IP rights and counteraction to antimonopoly legislation violations. Indeed, as practice shows, many competition violations are associated with the violation of intellectual rights. Therefore, the indicated interaction of the state authorities seems to be especially important.

FAS also has the authority to consider administrative disputes (Order of FAS Russia No. 339 of May 25, 2012, "On Approval of the Administrative Regulations of the Federal Antimonopoly Service for the Execution of the State Function to Initiate and Consider Cases of Violations of the Antimonopoly Legislation of the Russian Federation").

In the framework of the discussion of the peculiarities of the legal and illegal use of IP in the modern world, the functions of the Federal Service for Supervision of Communications, Information Technology and Mass Media (Roskomnadzor) should be taken into account. The operation of Roskomnadzor is regulated by Government Resolution No. 228 of March 16, 2009, "On the Federal Service for Supervision of Communications, Information Technology and Mass Media".

According to clause 5.1.7 (1) of this act, Roskomnadzor has the authority to restrict access to certain information resources in the information and telecommunication networks, including the internet, as established by Federal Law No. 149-FZ of July 27, 2006, "On Information, Information Technologies and Information Protection" (hereinafter Law on Information). Article 15.6 of the law defines the procedure for restricting access to websites that have repeatedly and unlawfully posted information containing copyright and (or) related rights objects or explaining ways to obtain such objects using information and telecommunication networks. The normative procedure and the peculiarities of the implementation of corresponding regulations will be described in section "IP in digital economy".

"The Agreement on the Cooperation between the Federal Service for Intellectual Property and the Federal Service for Supervision of Communications, Information Technology and Mass Media" was concluded in Moscow on October 28, 2015. It aims to organize cooperation between these two authorities, which includes the exchanging of information in their possession. In accordance with clause 3.1 of the agreement, Roskomnadzor is given internet access to Rospatent's databases containing information from the State Register for Trademarks and Service Marks, the List of Well-Known Trademarks and the State Register for Geographical Indications and Appellations of Origin of Goods (independent information search allowed). Roskomnadzor, in turn, grants access to the information from the Unified All-Russian List of the mass media resources to Rospatent (clause 4.1). In addition, Roskomnadzor informs Rospatent of the mass media resources applying for registration if the name of a mass media resource to be registered is identical or confusingly similar to trademarks and service marks or appellations of origin of goods protected in the Russian Federation.

The Ministry of Culture of the Russian Federation is a federal executive authority responsible for the development and implementation of state policies, legal regulation in the field of copyright and related rights, as well as for their protection, control and supervision in the abovementioned area (clause 1 of "Regulations on the Ministry of Culture of the Russian Federation", approved by Resolution of the Government of the Russian Federation No. 590 of July 20, 2011; hereinafter Regulations on the Ministry of Culture). This authority approved the "Administrative Regulations for the Fulfilment by the Ministry of Culture of the Russian Federation of the State Function of Exercising State Controlling (Supervising) over the Observance of the Legislation of the Russian Federation on Copyright and Related Rights" (Order No. 2778 of December 16, 2016). According to clause 4 of this regulatory document, the state control (supervision) aims to ensure that legal entities (their branches, representative offices, separate structural divisions) or individuals registered as individual entrepreneurs using objects of copyright and related rights or complying with the mandatory requirements established by the legislation of the Russian Federation in this field, should follow the requirements of the Russian legislation on copyright and related rights.

The state function of supervision and control translates into:

- issuance of inspection certificates;
- issuance of orders instructing to eliminate violations of the copyright and related rights legislation that were revealed during the inspection;
- drawing up a report on an administrative offence and taking measures to make the person who committed the violation assume legal liability;
- sending information as per the prescribed procedure to other authorities: information on violations of regulatory legal acts of the Russian Federation that are not monitored by the Ministry of Culture of the Russian Federation

> shall be sent to the state control authorities with corresponding responsibility. Information on violations containing signs of crimes shall be sent to law enforcement agencies and prosecutorial authorities of the Russian Federation.

Thus, the Ministry of Culture monitors the observance of copyright and related rights legislation and works in cooperation with other authorities contributing to the maintenance of law, including in the field of IP.

The following example of the monitoring carried out by the Ministry of Culture of the Russian Federation can be given. Article 1245 of the Civil Code establishes that authors, performers, producers of phonograms and audiovisual works shall be assigned a reward for the free reproduction of the phonograms and audiovisual works exclusively for personal purposes. The reward is compensatory in nature and shall be paid to the copyright holders from the funds that are payable by manufacturers and importers of equipment and tangible media used for such reproduction. The list of equipment and tangible media, the amount of payment as well as the procedure for the collection thereof were approved by Government Resolution No. 829 of October 14, 2010, "On the Remuneration for the Free Reproduction of Phonograms and Audiovisual Works for Personal Purposes." The collection of the remuneration for the free reproduction of phonograms and audiovisual works for personal purposes shall be carried out by an accredited organization (discussed in more detail below). Failure to comply with the obligation to pay the corresponding fees may show up during a routine inspection of the Ministry of Culture.

This was the case with Panasonic Rus LLC. An inspection revealed that the import of equipment and tangible media used for the free reproduction of phonograms and audiovisual works into the territory of the Russian Federation was carried out without payments specified in Article 1245 of the Civil Code. After an inspection report had been made, an order was issued to the company to eliminate the detected violations. Panasonic Rus went to court. The court supported the position of the Ministry of Culture. At the same time, attention was drawn to the fact that the Supreme Court of the Russian Federation, in its judicial acts, repeatedly noted that it is the Civil Code that obliges manufacturers and importers to pay the remuneration fee and not the agreement that an accredited organization concludes with the payers; it is a duty, not a right. Therefore, it does not really matter whether such an agreement between the importer and the accredited organization exists (Resolution of the Ninth State Commercial Court of Appeal of December 29, 2014, on case No. A40-95170/14).

In addition to the above, the Ministry of Culture monitors the work of the accredited organizations responsible for the collective management of copyright and related rights (collective management organizations) (clause 5.4.10.8 of the Regulation on the Ministry of Culture; clause 6 of Article 1244 of the Civil Code).

Article 1244 of the Civil Code contains general regulations on the state accreditation of collective management organizations. Clause 1 of this article establishes a list of areas of collective management in which accreditation can be obtained. They are as follows:

- managing the exclusive rights to published musical works (with or without text) and excerpts from musical and drama works in regard to their public performance, broadcasting by air or by cable, including retransmission;
- exercising the rights of the authors of the musical works (with or without text), that were used in an audiovisual work, to remuneration for the public performance or broadcasting by air or cable of such audiovisual work, including retransmission;
- managing the resale right for a work of fine art, as well as an author's manuscripts (autographs) of literary and musical works;
- exercising the rights of authors, performers and producers of phonograms and audiovisual works to the remuneration for reproduction of phonograms and audiovisual works for personal purposes;
- exercising the rights of performers to the remuneration for public performance, as well as for air or cable broadcasting of phonograms published for commercial purposes;
- exercising the rights of producers of phonograms to the remuneration for public performance, as well as for air or cable broadcasting of phonograms published for commercial purposes.

The state shall accredit only one collective management organization to carry out activities in each of these areas of collective management. At the same time, a collective management organization can receive state accreditation to carry out activities in one, two or more areas of collective management. State accreditation is granted for 5 years to organizations accredited for the first time and 5–10 years for organizations that were previously accredited and did not have any reproofs from the regulatory authorities on their record (clause 20 of the "Regulations on the State Accreditation of Organizations Exercising Collective Management of Copyright and Related Rights, as well as on Establishing the Maximum Amount Retained by an Accredited Organization to Cover the Necessary Costs of the Collection, Distribution and Payment of the Remuneration, as well as that Amount that is Sent to Special Funds", approved by Government Resolution No. 992 of December 29, 2007; hereinafter Regulations on the Organizations State Accreditation).

In accordance with clause 21 of the Regulations on the Organizations State Accreditation, information about the organizations is posted by the authorized body on its official website: https://opendata.mkrf.ru/opendata/7705851331-copyright_accredited_organizations.

Currently, the following organizations in Russia have state accreditation in one of the previously mentioned six fields of activity:

- *Non-profit partnership, Partnership for the Protection and Management of Rights in the Field of Art (UPRAVIS).* It manages the resale rights for a work of fine art, as well as the author's manuscripts (autographs) of literary and musical works;
- *All-Russian non-governmental organization, Russian Union of Right Holders (RSP).* It exercises the rights of authors, performers and producers of phonograms and audiovisual works to remuneration for the reproduction of phonograms and audiovisual works for personal purposes.

Two accredited organizations operate in more than one of the areas of activity mentioned earlier.

The *All-Russian non-governmental organization, Collective Management Society of Neighbouring Rights "Russian Organization for Intellectual Property" (VOIS)* exercises:

- the rights of performers to remuneration for the public performance, as well as for the air or cable broadcasting of phonograms published for commercial purposes;
- the rights of producers of phonograms to remuneration for the public performance, as well as for the air or cable broadcasting of phonograms published for commercial purposes.

The second organization is the Russian Author's Society (RAO) which:

- exercises the rights of the authors of musical works (with or without text), which were used in an audiovisual work, to remuneration for the public performance or broadcasting by air or cable of such audiovisual work, including retransmission;
- manages exclusive rights to published musical works (with or without text) and excerpts from musical and dramatic works regarding their public performance, broadcasting by air or cable, including retransmission.

These accredited organizations are entitled to manage the rights of those right holders with whom they have entered into contracts and manage the rights and collect remuneration for those right holders with whom they have not concluded such agreements.

It should be noted that the existence of the accredited organization does not preclude the creation of other collective management organizations, including in the areas of collective management indicated above (see also section "IP use in business"). Such organizations have the right to enter into agreements with users only if this lies within the interests of the right holders who have given them the authority to manage their rights.

Russian courts play a special role in the system of IP authorities. The decisions of the courts in the Russian Federation, which have been entered into legal force, as well as legal orders, requirements, instructions, summons and other appeals issued by the courts, are mandatory for all state authorities, local governments, public associations, officials, other individuals and legal entities without exception and shall be followed throughout the country. Failure to comply with a court decision, as well as any other contempt of court entails legal responsibility (Article 6 of the Law on the Judicial System).

It should be noted that the foundations of the judicial system of the Russian Federation are established in the Constitution. According to Article 118, justice in Russia can only be delivered by a court. In this case, judicial power is exercised through constitutional, civil, state commercial administrative and criminal proceedings. All types of legal proceedings can take place when it comes to IP. This is due to the peculiarities of the normative regulation of legal relations in Russia, including in the field of IP.

For instance, constitutional proceedings refer to the work of the Constitutional Court of the Russian Federation. In order to protect the foundations of the constitutional system, fundamental human and civil rights and freedoms and ensure the supremacy and direct action of the Constitution throughout the country, the Constitutional Court has the following powers among others:

- to hear and pass judgement on cases questioning whether the following legal documents and acts comply with the Constitution of the Russian Federation: federal laws, normative acts of the president, federation council, state duma, government; regulatory acts of the constituent entities of the Russian Federation, agreements between the authorities of the Russian Federation and the authorities of its constituent entities, contracts between the authorities of the constituent entities of the Russian Federation; international treaties of the Russian Federation that have not yet entered into force;
- to hear and pass judgement on cases on the distribution of responsibility between authorities in Russia;
- to check the constitutionality of the law applied in a particular case if there is a complaint on the violation of the citizens' constitutional rights and freedoms;
- to interpret the Constitution of the Russian Federation.

Should constitutional proceedings be the case, the Constitutional Court refrains from establishing and investigating the factual circumstances when this function falls within the competence of other courts or other authorities (Articles 1 and 3 of Federal Constitutional Law No. 1-FKZ of July 21, 1994, "On the Constitutional Court of the Russian Federation").

An interesting example of how the Constitutional Court can participate in determining the constitutionality of IP normative provisions and their interpretation is Resolution of the Constitutional Court of the Russian Federation No. 28-P of July 3, 2018, "On the Case of Checking the Constitutionality of Clause 6 Article 1232 of the Civil Code of the Russian Federation in Connection with the Request of the Intellectual Property Court".

According to the provision contested by the Intellectual Property Court, in case of non-compliance with the requirement for the state registration of the transfer of the exclusive right to the result of intellectual activity or to means of individualization under the exclusive right alienation agreement or without a contract, the pledge of an exclusive right or the grant of the right to use such a result or such a means to another person under a contract, the transfer of the exclusive right, its pledge or the grant of the right to use an IP subject matter shall be considered to have not taken place.

Working on one of the cases, the Intellectual Property Court decided that the constitutionality of this clause could not be declared with certainty and, having suspended the proceedings, applied to the Constitutional Court. In the opinion of the Intellectual Property Court, there was uncertainty regarding the moment of transfer of the exclusive right to a trademark in the event of the reorganization of a legal entity by merging with another legal entity (the right holder of this trademark), as well as regarding the option for the reorganized legal entity (the legal successor of the trademark right holder) to apply to Rospatent for the renewal of the exclusive right to a given trademark if the transfer of the right to the trademark in question had not been previously registered with Rospatent. This, as decided by the Intellectual Property Court, leads to the arbitrary implementation of law and, thus, to the violation of the guarantees of the state protection, including the judicial one, of the constitutional rights and freedoms of citizens.

The Constitutional Court did not recognize this normative provision as unconstitutional. However, it explained the specifics of its implementation, taking into account both IP norms and the norms on the reorganization of legal entities. The court clarified that the established administrative procedure presupposes that during the reorganization, a legal entity (the one which the right holder joins) must first register that the exclusive right to a trademark has been transferred to it and only after that apply to Rospatent for an extension of this right. The time of administrative procedures significantly increases, and in some cases there is a risk of losing the right to the trademark. However, the rational organization of the activities of Russian authorities may not be the basis for restricting human and civil rights and freedoms. This is the position of the Constitutional Court, which has been repeatedly pointed out.

Therefore, in such a situation, despite the administrative procedure, Rospatent should consider the issue of the state registration of the transfer of the exclusive right to a trademark and the issue of extending the validity of this right at the request of the holder of the exclusive right to a trademark simultaneously.

At the same time, the constitutional and legal meaning of clause 6 of Article 1232 of the Civil Code, identified by the Constitutional Court in the described resolution, is generally binding, and excludes any other interpretation of it in the legal practice.

No matter how significant the acts of the Constitutional Court are, the main judicial burden, IP cases included, is borne by other Russian courts. The

Russian judicial system is unified (Article 4 of the Law on the Judicial System). At the same time, IP cases are not subject to the jurisdiction of all the courts of the Russian Federation.

The federal courts, whose activities are important for the protection of IP rights, are as follows:

- the Constitutional Court, which has already been mentioned;
- the Supreme Court of the Russian Federation;
- federal courts of general jurisdiction: cassation courts of general jurisdiction, courts of appeal, supreme courts of the regions, courts of federal cities, district courts;
- federal state commercial courts: state commercial courts of circuits, state commercial courts of appeal, state commercial courts of the constituent entities of the Russian Federation and specialized state commercial court (Intellectual Property Court).

In accordance with Article 26.1 of the Law on the Judicial System in the Russian Federation, there is a specialized state commercial court that resolves, within its competence, disputes related to the protection of IP rights, as a court of first and cassation instance. It is called the Intellectual Property Court. At the same time, the fact that such a court exists in the Russian judicial system does not mean that all IP disputes are resolved by this particular court.

In the Russian Federation, competence of the courts is determined by special acts. In addition to those mentioned earlier, there is also Federal Constitutional Law No. 1-FKZ of February 7, 2011, "On Courts of General Jurisdiction in the Russian Federation"; Civil Procedure Code of the Russian Federation No. 138-FZ of November 14, 2002, (hereinafter Civil Procedure Code); State Commercial Procedure Code of the Russian Federation No. 95-FZ of July 24, 2002, (hereinafter State Commercial Procedure Code); Code of the Russian Federation on Administrative Offences No. 195-FZ of December 30, 2001, (hereinafter Code on Administrative Offences); Administrative Procedure Code of the Russian Federation No. 21-FZ of March 8, 2015, (hereinafter Administrative Procedure Code).

In order to ensure the correct and uniform resolution of IP disputes by the courts, the Supreme Court gave special clarifications, including those on procedural issues. They are contained in Resolution of the Plenum of the Supreme Court No. 10.

To explain the competence of courts in the field of IP, some key points will be given.

In clause 3 of Resolution of the Plenum of the Supreme Court No. 10, it is noted that, based on the Civil Procedure Code, the courts of general jurisdiction hear cases related to the application of part IV of the Civil Code, with exception of the cases that are under the competence of the state commercial courts, in accordance with the laws. State commercial courts hear cases on economic disputes and other cases related to business and other economic activities (clause 1 of Article 27 of the State Commercial Procedure Code).

In particular, IP cases, as a general rule, are subject to hearing in a court of general jurisdiction if one of the parties to the dispute is a citizen who does not have the status of an individual entrepreneur or if one of the parties to the dispute is an individual entrepreneur, but the case was not initiated in connection with their business activity (clause 1 of part 1 of Article 22 of the Code of Civil Procedure).

Disputes concerning the authorship of the result of intellectual activity are heard by the courts of general jurisdiction as they are not related to business and other economic activities, with the exception of disputes on the authorship of inventions, utility models, industrial designs, selective breeding achievements and production secrets (know-how) which, according to the State Commercial Procedure Code, shall be decided by the Intellectual Property Court as a court of first instance. Thus, according to clause 4 of Article 34 of State Commercial Procedure Code, the Intellectual Property Court, as a court of first instance, considers the following cases:

- on challenging the regulatory legal acts of the federal executive authorities in the field of patent rights and rights to selective breeding achievements, rights to the topographies of integrated circuits, know-how rights, rights to means of individualization of legal entities, goods, works, services and enterprises and right to use results of intellectual activity as part of an integrated technology;
- on granting or termination of legal protection of results of intellectual activity and equated means of individualization of legal entities, goods, works, services and enterprises (with the exception of objects of copyright and related rights, topographies of integrated circuits), including:
  - challenging the decisions by FAS on recognizing the unfair competition of actions related to the obtaining of the exclusive right to the means of individualization of a legal entity, goods, works, services and enterprises;
  - on determining the patent holder;
  - on early termination of the legal protection of a trademark due to its non-use etc.

At the same time, cases on the amount of royalties are within the competence of the courts of general jurisdiction.

Clause 4 of Resolution of the Plenum of the Supreme Court No. 10 explains that the court hearing disputes on the protection of intellectual rights, including cases on violations of intellectual rights to the results of intellectual activity and to appellations of origin of goods, on violation of the right of prior use and the right of post-use and disputes on the disposal of the exclusive right, is determined based on the parties to the dispute and the nature of the disputed legal relationship, unless otherwise provided by law.

"Otherwise" means, for example, IP disputes that involve collective management organizations, which, by virtue of subclause 6, clause 6 of Article 27 of the State Commercial Procedure Code, are subject to hearing by state commercial courts, regardless of whether such organizations appear in court on behalf of the right holders (legal entities, individual entrepreneurs or citizens who are not individual entrepreneurs) or on their own behalf.

Regardless of the persons participating in the case, disputes concerning the means of individualization (except for disputes on appellations of origin of goods) are subject to hearing in state commercial courts. Such cases do not include disputes related to the application of consumer protection legislation, inheritance disputes and disputes over the division of spouses' property.

The fact that determining competent courts is not an easy matter should not be a reason for refusing to go to court to protect one's IP rights. The complexity is levelled by the detailed normative regulation as well as the existing explanations on IP provided by the highest courts, the Supreme and Constitutional Courts of the Russian Federation.

Thus, IP relations in Russia a subject to regulation by various state authorities, the competence of which depends on the functions they perform and is normatively defined at all levels. Such an extensive system of authorities provides an opportunity to properly regulate, enforce and protect the rights of IP right holders.

Note

1 Registration functions are performed directly by the State Commission of the Russian Federation for Selective Breeding Achievements Test and Protection (FSBI *Gossortcommission*), created in accordance with Order of the Ministry of Agriculture of Russia No. 368 of April 9, 2002.

References

Bogdanova, O.V. *Protection of Intellectual Copyright by Civil Law Methods. Monograph [Zashchita intellektual'nykh avtorskikh prav grazhdansko-pravovymi sposobami: monografiya].* Moscow, Yustitsinform, 2017.

Boguslavsky, M.M. *International Agreements in the Field of Inventions and Trademarks (Paris Convention): Course book [Mezhdunarodnye soglasheniya v oblasti izobreteniy i tovarnykh znakov. Parizhskaya konventsiya: Uchebnoe posobie].* Edited by Bakastov, V.N. Moscow, Central Research Institute of Patent Information and Economic Research, 1964.

Chernichkina, G.N. Other Intellectual Rights of the Fourth Part of the Civil Code of the Russian Federation [Inye intellektual'nye prava chasti chetvertoy Grazhdanskogo kodeksa Rossiyskoy Federatsii]. *Modern Law [Sovremennoe pravo].* 2019. No. 3. P. 61–73.

Civil Law: Textbook: in 2 Volumes [Grazhdanskoe pravo: Uchebnik. V 2 t.]. Edited by Gongalo, B.M. 3rd ed. Vol. 1. Moscow, Statut, 2018.

Commentary on Part Four of the Civil Code of the Russian Federation (on Chapters) [Kommentariy k chasti chetvertoy Grazhdanskogo kodeksa Rossiyskoy Federatsii (poglavnyy)]. Edited by Makovsky, A.L. Moscow, Statut, 2008.

Commentary on the Civil Code of the Russian Federation (Educational and Practical). Parts One, Second, Third, Fourth Itemized [Kommentariy k Grazhdanskomu kodeksu Rossiyskoy Federatsii (uchebno-prakticheskiy). Chasti 1–4]. Edited by Stepanov, S.A. 2nd ed. Moscow, Prospect; Yekaterinburg, Institute of Private Law, 2009.

Dozortsev, V.A. *Intellectual Rights. Concept. System. Codification Tasks: Collection of Articles [Intellektual'nye prava. Ponyatie. Sistema. Zadachi kodifikatsii: Sbornik statey].* Moscow, Statut, 2003. P. 238–276.

Eremenko, V.I. On the Legal Protection of Related Rights in the Russian Federation [O pravovoy okhrane smezhnykh prav v Rossiyskoy Federatsii]. *Legislation and Economics [Zakonodatel'stvo i ekonomika].* 2012. No. 2. P. 30–55.

Galperin-Kaminsky, I.D. *General Benefits of Copyright Law: Featuring Émile Zola's Letter Addressing Russian Publishers and the Text of Laws on Literary and Creative Property of the American, Belgian and Spanish, the 1886 Berne Convention and the 1852 French Decree [Obshchaya pol'za avtorskogo prava: S prilozheniem pis'ma k russkoy pechati Emilya Zolya i teksta zakonov o literaturnoy i khudozhestvennoy sobstvennosti amerikanskogo, bel'giyskogo i ispanskogo, Bernskoy konventsii 1886 g. i frantsuzskogo dekreta 1852 g.].* Saint-Petersburg, Izdanie knizhnogo magazina A.F. Tsinzerlinga, 1984.

Gavrilov, E.P. About the Legal Protection of Selective Breeding Achievements [O pravovoy okhrane selektsionnykh dostizheniy]. *Business and law [Khozyaystvo i pravo].* 2011. No. 1. P. 3–11.

Gavrilov, E.P. When the Exclusive Right to Identical Objects Belongs Simultaneously to Several Persons [Kogda isklyuchitel'noe pravo na tozhdestvennye ob"ekty prinadlezhit odnovremenno neskol'kim litsam]. *Patents and Licenses [Patenty i litsenzii]*. 2019. No. 9. P. 8–16.

Gorodov, O.A. *Industrial Property Law: Textbook [Pravo promyshlennoy sobstvennosti. Uchebnik]*. Moscow, Statut, 2011.

Gutnikov, O.V. and Sinitsyn, S.A. Plurality of Holders of Exclusive Rights: Problems of Theory and Practice [Mnozhestvennost' obladateley isklyuchitel'nogo prava: problemy teorii i praktiki]. *Laws of Russia: Experience, Analysis, Practice [Zakony Rossii: opyt, analiz, praktika]*. 2019. No. 12. P. 67 – 73.

Ioffe, O.S. *Soviet Civil Law (Course of lectures). [Part III]: Legal Relations Associated with the Products of Creative Activity; Family law; Inheritance law [Sovetskoe grazhdanskoe pravo: Kurs lektsiy.Ch. 3. Pravootnosheniya, svyazannye s produktami tvorcheskoy deyatel'nosti. Semeynoe pravo. Nasledstvennoe parvo]*. Leningrad, Izdatel'stvo Leningradskogo universiteta, 1965.

Ionas, V. Ya. *Works of Creativity in Civil Law [Proizvedeniya tvorchestva v grazhdanskom prave]*. Moscow, Yuridicheskaya literatura, 1972.

Korneev, V.A. and Kolsdorf, M.A. Disputable Issues of Database Regulation [Spornye voprosy regulirovaniya baz dannykh]. *Statute [Zakon]*. 2019. No. 5. P. 157–167.

Lykoshin, A.I. On Literary Conventions [O literaturnykh konventsiyakh]. *The Bulletin of Law [Vestnik prava]*. 1899. No. 3 (March). P. 1–56.

Novoselova, L.A. and Rozhkova, M.A. *Intellectual Property: Some Aspects of Legal Regulation. Monograph [Intellektual'naya sobstvennost': nekotorye aspekty pravovogo regulirovaniya: monografiya]*. Moscow, Norma: INFRA-M, 2014.

Ownership: Topical Issues [Pravo sobstvennosti: aktual'nye problemy]. Edited by Litovkin, V.N., Sukhanov, E.A., Chubarov, V.V. Moscow, Statut, 2008.

Rozhkova, M.A. Databases and Services of Online Classifieds: Use of the Database and Use of Information [Bazy dannykh i servisy onlayn-klassifaydov: pol'zovanie bazoy i ispol'zovanie informatsii]. *Journal of the Intellectual Property Court [Zhurnal Suda po intellektual'nym pravam]*. 2019. No. 26. P. 25–32.

Sagdeeva, L.V. The Vindication of Intellectual Property [Vindikatsiya intellektual'noy sobstvennosti]. *Journal of Russian Law [Zhurnal rossiyskogo prava]*. 2019. No. 3. P. 74–83.

Semenova, A.A. Memes: Issues of Legal and Incorrect Use [Memy: voprosy pravomernogo ispol'zovaniya], in M.A. Rozkova (ed.). *Law on the Internet: Collection of [Articles Pravo v sfere interneta: sbornik statey]*. Moscow, Statut, 2018.

Serebrovsky, V.I. *Questions of Soviet Copyright [Voprosy sovetskogo avtorskogo prava]*. Moscow, Izdatel'stvo Akademii nauk SSSR, 1956.

Sergeev, A.P. *Legal Protection of Non-traditional Objects of Intellectual Property in the Russian Federation [Pravovaya okhrana netraditsionnykh ob"ektov intellektual'noy sobstvennosti v Rossiyskoy Federatsii]*. Saint-Petersburg, Izdatel'stvo Sankt-Peterburgskogo universiteta, 1995.

Sergeev, A.P. Section II "Ownership" and other Property Rights Applied to Intellectual Property Relations [Primenenie pravil razdela II «Pravo sobstvennosti i drugie veshchnye prava» Grazhdanskogo kodeksa RF k otnosheniyam intellektual'noy sobstvennosti]. *Statute [Zakon]*. 2018. No. 12. P. 87–95.

Shershenevich, G.F. *Economic Justification of Copyright. Composition [Ekonomicheskoe obosnovanie avtorskogo prava]*. Kazan, Tipografiya Imperskogo universiteta, 1890.

Shershenevich, G.F. *Favorites [Izbrannoe]*. T. 3. [Introductory speech, compiled by: P.V. Krasheninnikov]. Moscow, Statut, 2017.

The Fifth Session of the Supreme Soviet of the USSR: Verbatim report. Part XV: June 10 - 21, 1991 [Pjataja sessija Verhovnogo Soveta SSSR: Stenograficheskij otchet. Chast' XV: 10 – 21 ijunja 1991]. Moscow, Izdanie Verhovnogo Soveta SSSR, 1991.

The Right to a Selection Achievement: Commentaries Chapter 73 of the Civil Code of the Russian Federation [Pravo na selekcionnoe dostizhenie: Postatejnyj kommentarij glavy 73 Grazhdanskogo kodeksa Rossijskoj Federacii]. Edited by Krasheninnikov, P.V. Moscow, Statut, 2010.

Vitko, V.S. Legal Nature of 'Work Title' Notion [Pravovaja priroda ponjatija "nazvanie proizvedenija"]. *IP. Copyright and Related Rights [IS. Avtorskoe pravo i smezhnye prava].* 2020. No. 7. P. 23–36.

Yakovlev, V.F. and Makovsky, A.L. On Part IV of the Russian Civil Code [O chetvertoj chasti grazhdanskogo kodeksa Rossii]. *Journal of Russian Law* [*Zhurnal rossijskogo prava*]. 2007. No. 2. P. 3–13.

Yurchenko, A.K. *Problems of Soviet Inventive Law [Problemy sovetskogo izobretatel'skogo prava].* Leningrad, Izdatel'stvo Leningradskogo universiteta, 1963.

Part Two

Intellectual property as an organization's internal resource

5 General provisions on the creation and registration of intellectual property

Intellectual property (IP) can be created by a person independently, or a group of persons. As for legal entities, IP can be created by a employees or with the help of an outside expert. The former is discussed in section "Intellectual resources and human capital".

If external specialists are involved in the creation of IP, a legal agreement must be concluded. The form of said agreement shall be determined, firstly, by the object to be created and, secondly, by the type of participating counterparties. However, the creation of IP can result from an agreement that does not expressly stipulate the creation of that product. Part IV of the Civil Code specifies the following types of agreement:

- an author's commissioning agreement;
- a commissioning agreement;
- a contract for the performance of work (refit contract);
- a contract for the performance of research, development and technological work;
- state or municipal contracts.

The diversity of contracts used in this field testifies to IP's ever-growing importance and its active turnover in the market. There is a clear tendency to try to ensure normative coverage of all kinds of situations. That is why, apart from the traditional author's commissioning agreement which implies the creation of a work, other types of contracts, which can involve other kinds of counterparties, are also used. Besides, there are legal norms that regulate incidentally created IP in the framework of an agreement that does not expressly stipulate its creation as the desired result. The choice of a contract can also be due to the specific type of intellectual activity or means of individualization. Each of the contractual forms has its peculiarities. That is why it seems reasonable to consider the mentioned contracts in detail.

According to the author's commissioning agreement, one party (the author) shall create for the other party (the client) a work of art, science or literature specified in the agreement and provide it fixed in a tangible or otherwise agreed type of medium (Article 1288 of the Civil Code). Such an agreement regarding works of art, science or literature can only be signed by the author. Nowadays, the author of the result of intellectual activity is the citizen who created that result through their creative skill and labour (Article 1288 of the Civil Code). It is worth noting that the Civil Code uses the term "citizen", which, in this case, should be interpreted as a natural person and not as a person being a citizen of some state. Previously, the country's legislation contained provisions on organizations' authorship rights to periodic or other editions, companies' authorship rights to films and television films (Articles 485 and 486 of the Civil Code of the Russian Soviet Federative Socialist Republic; RSFSR). Based on clause 2 of Article 6 of the Introductory Law, Resolution of the Plenum of the Supreme Court No. 10 decided that a legal entities' copyright that came into force before August 3, 1993 (before the introduction of the Copyright Law) shall expire upon 70 years from the publication of the work or, had it never been revealed to the public, from the day of its creation. Corresponding norms from Part IV of the Civil Code are applied to such legal relations, with legal entities being considered the creation's authors in this case.

As for the means of individualization of goods, works, services and enterprises, the question of authorship is not raised in relation to them, as they are designed to distinguish a product and not to convey the author's intention or show their creative potential. However, some visual art can be protected as an object of copyright and be a registered trademark.

What kind of terms and conditions an author's commissioning agreement should contain is widely discussed by the representatives of scientific research and practising lawyers.

However, to avoid controversies and disputes, one should determine the conditions that will minimize the risk of controversy between the parties:

a) *the subject matter of the agreement*

An author's commissioning agreement implies that the author shall create a work of art, science or literature fixed in a tangible or otherwise agreed type of carrier, i.e., a description of the desired result of creative activity must be included in the agreement. As at the moment of concluding the agreement, the creative work does not yet exist, a detailed list of its characteristics should be provided. However, it is hard to say to what degree it will meet the requirements until the work has been created (Resolution of the State Commercial Court of Moscow Circuit of March 19, 2018, on case No. A40-163366/15). That is why disagreements may occur during the acceptance of the work.

A provision on the exclusive rights to the work is also most advisable. Article 1228 of the Civil Code indicated that an author's commissioning agreement could include a disposition in favour of the client of the exclusive rights to the work that will be created by the author or entitle the client to use the creative work within the limits specified in the contract. Whether such a term is obligatory is still subject to discussion (Novoselova, 2017b).

On the one hand, the analysis of normative provisions does not allow one to conclude with certainty if such an imperative prescription exists. At the same time, judicial practice contains a direct reference to the disposition principle that is applied to the transfer of exclusive rights to a work created under a legal agreement (Resolution of the Intellectual Property Court of June 06, 2019, on case No. A55-20118/2017).

As noted in sections "Intellectual property: concept and types" and "Characteristics of IP rights" of this book, Article 1227 of the Civil Code clearly indicates that IP rights do not depend on the right of ownership or other property rights to a physical carrier (thing) in which the results of intellectual activity or means of individualization are fixed. Article 1291 of the Civil Code stipulates that the rights to the original of a creative work can be transferred while the exclusive rights will remain in favour of the author. However, it should be borne in mind that this provision is not just about all the originals of the works, but about the manuscript, the original work of a painting, sculpture and similar items. It may indicate the special nature of this legal norm and its extension only to those objects that have intrinsic value due to special external expression.

On the other hand, why anyone would commission a work without actually possessing the rights to it in the future is not quite clear. Their absence may pose a risk of the impossibility of further use and liability for infringing the author's rights. At the same time, judicial practice shows that the absence of the disposition rights provision in the agreement does not imply that the person who commissioned the work will not be able to use it in accordance with the goals by which said agreement was concluded. This is because the client's interest cannot possibly lie in the mere act of having a work created and obtaining a material carrier to fix it in without claiming the rights to the work as they are what represent the material value of the protectable result (Resolution of the Intellectual Property Court of December 12, 2019, on case No. A83-14576/2018).

The above approach seems justified as creating a work just for the sake of creating and fixing it in a material carrier does not look rational in the framework of running a business.

Such contracts tend to be concluded to achieve some commercial objective that often presupposes that the entrepreneur sees the result of the intellectual activity as a means of gaining profit and not as a creative object. For instance, Evgenyi A. Nefediev called deals between the author and the publisher a means for commercial turnover (Nefediev, 1900, p. 91).

To avoid the uncertainty that may well lead to financial losses, including litigation fees, it seems only logical to establish an exclusive rights arrangement within the agreement.

b) *the completion time*

The completion time is one of the essential conditions of an author's commissioning agreement. Considering the specific character of such agreements,

Article 1289 of the Civil Code provides the possibility of prolonging the agreement (if need be and if there are valid reasons) to finish the creation. The list of valid reasons is not in the Civil Code but, as a rule, valid reasons are an illness, hospital stay, etc. This extra time is called a grace period and it generally constitutes one-quarter of the term set for the fulfilment of the contract (the parties can agree on a longer period). The client also has the right to terminate the agreement upon the expiration of the term if the agreement fails to be fulfilled on time, and it is clear from the provisions of the agreement that the client is not interested in the results of the agreement, provided the agreement has expired. Say, the creation of a work implies several stages, and at the first stage, the author fails to fulfil their obligations that are of vital importance for the work as a whole or the work, which has not been created on time, was intended as part of an event. In such situations, the creative work loses its consumer value for the buyer, which determines the possibility of annulling the contract without providing extra time to finish the work.

c) *remuneration paid to the author or indication of its absence*

According to Article 1288 of the Civil Code, an author's commissioning agreement may specify a remuneration to be paid to the author or stipulate its absence expressly. The agreement is by default not gratuitous if not stated otherwise.

Remuneration paid to the author can assume various forms: a firm sum of money or a royalty payment based on the wholesale cost of the products or the cost of the products sold. In the case of literary works, the fixed amount of consideration can be calculated depending on the volume of the text. The measurement unit in this situation is most often the so-called author's sheet, which is equivalent to 40,000 characters, including spaces. Arkadyi I. Vaksberg pointed out the inevitable controversy that could arise when a talented and hard-working author, who put serious effort into making their work laconic and meaningful, was going to get less than the person who artificially boosted the volume of the book, not caring about the quality of the text (Vaksberg, 1958, p. 122).

The agreement may contain an advance payment provision. Royalty-based consideration depending on the sale(s) of the work can lead to legal disputes due to the insufficient, in the author's opinion, usage of the product or the overall refusal to use the product that then results in a low financial income and makes the author want to terminate the agreement in court.

Suppose an author's commissioning agreement contains terms and conditions on the exclusive rights disposition or its limited use. In that case, it becomes subject to the Civil Code provisions on the exclusive rights disposition or licence agreement (see section "The transfer of IP rights"). That is why the provision regarding the payment conditions is important as its absence in the above-mentioned agreements is the reason to consider them not concluded.

Suppose an author's commissioning agreement does not contain provisions on exclusive rights, the gratuitous or non-gratuitous character of the agreement and (or) the amount of consideration. In that case, the doctrine fails to provide a uniform interpretation of the situation. Some researchers suggest that one should apply the principle according to which payment is taken for similar goods, services and labour (Article 424 of the Civil Code); the presumption of non-gratuitousness also comes into effect here (Novoselova, 2017a). Other researchers say that such an approach is virtually impossible due to the unique character of the work being created and the impossibility of finding any equivalent goods or services (Berezin, 2018).

d) *the acceptance procedure*

Another important provision of an author's commissioning agreement is the acceptance procedure which includes the requirements for transferring the work created and the conformance check.

Article 508 of the Civil Code of the Russian Soviet Federative Socialist Republic (RSFSR) indicated the acceptance and approval procedure. Nowadays, however, the parties to the agreement are free to determine their own acceptance procedure.

Considering that creative works are the result of creative activity, there is a risk that the goal of the agreement will not be achieved. And this is not due to the party's refusal or lack of desire to fulfil their contractual obligations but rather because the creation of such work proves virtually impossible.

The above situation can be explained as follows: firstly, creative activity reflects how an author perceives reality. Secondly, creation is directly connected to inspiration, which can be considered its integral part. Without a doubt, creative activity cannot be reduced to these two aspects as there is a rational element in creative processes. The mere act of closing an agreement to create a work has rational bases to it but not emotional ones. However, an author's commissioning agreement requires, to a certain degree, that the rational and the emotional should co-exist, which is not always possible. The discord between them can have a negative impact on the overall result. The specific character of creative activity does not allow a definite assertion of whether the desired result can be achieved. The author, putting all possible effort into the work, may run into what is called a creative failure, which means that it was not due to their fault or bad faith that the client's idea could not be realized. The risks associated with creative failures can be considered as the client's risk, i.e., the client does not necessarily receive the result at which the agreement was aimed. Can the author be responsible for not being able to create what was expected?

On the one hand, having signed an agreement, the author takes on the responsibility that they cannot reject unilaterally. On the other hand, the legislators took into consideration the specific character of the creative activity. They limited the author's responsibility to the compensation of real damage (i.e., the financial losses that the party suffered or would suffer if their rights were infringed because of the need to recover the infringed rights, the loss of or damage to their property, see also Part 3 of the book). As per clause 2 of Article 1290 of the Civil Code, in case of the non-fulfilment or improper fulfilment of an author's commissioning agreement for which the author is responsible, the author shall return the advance to the client and pay the penalty fee should it be specified in the agreement. The total fee shall not exceed the amount of the real damage incurred.

Another possible outcome is that the author fulfils their obligations properly, but the result does not meet the client's expectations. This may be the case of the author's creative failure or the client's subjective perception of the work. Suppose the work conforms to the criteria stipulated in the agreement (objective conformation – special verification tests can be conducted). The refusal to accept it stems from the differences in creative views or personal preferences. In that case, there are no grounds not to accept the work as well as to refuse to pay the full remuneration to the author or demand the return of the advance (Resolution of the Intellectual Property Court of December 23, 2016, on case No. A40-222033/2015; Appeal Ruling of the Saint Petersburg City Court of October 6, 2016, on case No. 2-4296/2016).

If the work does not fully conform with the objective requirements, then the risk of creative failure can be considered the reason for it. This, however, cannot be the ultimate criterion for assessing the fulfilment of the agreement. The objective non-conformity with the requirements means that the contractual obligations were not fulfilled properly.

The provisions listed above represent the most significant terms and conditions of an author's commissioning agreement. However, this list is not complete as an author's commissioning agreement (as well as any other agreements) requires that the parties include the necessary provisions for their field to minimize the risks of controversies and disputes.

It should be noted that the parties of the agreement makes it rather specific. A number of special conditions (e.g., grace period, limited responsibility) can be interpreted as providing extra protection to the weaker party of the agreement (the author) and helps to balance the stronger party (the client). However, this kind of agreement presupposes high risks for the client: first, because of the special concessions just mentioned and, secondly, due to the indefinite character of the result. Any contract aimed at creating an object, even a material one, can lead to a result that will not meet the client's expectations. However, in an author's commissioning agreement, the decisive factor is the author's subjective interpretation of the work to be created. Should there not be any objective discord between the work and the conditions of the agreement, the client does not possess any means to resolve the situation in their favour even if the result is not satisfactory.

The Civil Code of the Russian Federation also mentions a commissioning agreement that involves an entity that is not the author of the work to be created. This fact distinguishes it from an author's commissioning agreement (clause 107 of Resolution of the Plenum of the Supreme Court No. 10).

Even though there is no legal definition of a commissioning agreement, its goal is obviously to create IP. While an author's commissioning agreement implies the creation of a work of art, literature or science, a commissioning agreement is not limited to this category of work. Also, it encompasses industrial designs, selective breeding results and topographies of integrated circuits. Here a question arises if a commissioning agreement can be used for inventions and utility models, etc., considering there is no such indication in the Civil Code. On the one hand, the "everything that is not forbidden by law is allowed" principle sees it as possible. On the other hand, a more logical approach seems to consider the type of object to be created.

For instance, inventions and utility models do not normally appear as the subject matter of such a contract (Novoselova, 2014). It is due to their specific nature, which can be described as finding a solution to a practical task (Ioffe, 1965, p. 86). The agreement may contain the description of the desired result but what the client wants to get in the end is an innovative approach to the solution and not just a summary of existing approaches. Moreover, there are no guarantees that the desired solution will be found. As was rightly stated by V.A. Dozortsev, the uncertainty typical of spiritual production, although it decreases from fundamental research to implementation stage, however, does not completely disappear which leads to negative result and creative failures (Dozortsev, 1978, p. 97). The above casts doubt upon the possibility of fulfilling the agreement and questions the object's patentability.

As a rule, the exclusive rights distribution in the case of a commissioning agreement are as follows:

- the exclusive rights and the right to obtain a patent belong to the client;
- the performer has the right to use the created IP subject matter for their own purposes (it means the contractor's need to use the IP object in their work) under a gratuitous, simple (non-exclusive) licence until the exclusive rights period expires if the exclusive rights and the right to obtain a patent belong to the client;
- the client has the right to use the created IP subject matter for which the corresponding agreement was created under a gratuitous, simple (non-exclusive) licence until the exclusive rights period/patent expires if the exclusive rights and the right to obtain a patent belong to the performer.

These provisions agree with the dispositive principle, i.e., they come into effect if the agreement does not indicate otherwise.

As soon as the exclusive rights distribution is an integral condition of this type of agreement, it may be assumed that the provisions on the exclusive rights disposition agreement (Article 1234 of the Civil Code) and licence agreement (Article 1235 of the Civil Code) shall apply to the relations between the parties. Failure to indicate the amount of remuneration and the absence of the procedure of its calculation are reasons to declare the agreement as not concluded. Moreover, as a general rule, the gratuitous alienation of exclusive rights is prohibited when it comes to the relations between two commercial legal entities.

Considering the lack of author means of protection and a clear distribution of the exclusive rights, this type of agreement proves less risky than an author's commissioning agreement, although the uncertainty of the result is still an issue.

IP is also relevant in the framework of a state or municipal contract. The regulation of this type of agreement is not limited to the Civil Code of the Russian Federation. However, it can be based on the provisions of Federal Law No. 44-FZ of April 3, 2013, "On the Contract System in the Procurement of Goods, Works, Services for the State and Municipal Purposes" (hereinafter Law on Contract System) that explains the organization of contractual relations between parties (e.g., peculiarities of the contracts' conclusion aimed at the creation of a work).

According to Article 3 of the Law on Contract System, a state contract and municipal contract are civil law contracts for the supply of goods, works and services (including the purchase or rent of real estate) and concluded on behalf of the Russian Federation, a constituent entity of the Russian Federation (state contract), or a municipality (municipal contract) by a state or municipal authority in order to satisfy the state or municipal needs. The peculiarity of this type of contract lies in the specific character of the client party.

Part IV of the Civil Code includes provisions about the rights of the state and municipal clients and the contractor (Review of Intellectual Property Judicial Practice, 2015):

Article 1298 – works of science, literature and art;
Article 1373 – inventions, utility models, industrial designs;
Article 1432 – selective breeding achievements;
Article 1464 – integrated circuit layouts;
Article 1471 – production secrets (know-how);
Chapter 77 – integrated technologies.

If the contract does not stipulate otherwise, the exclusive right and the right to obtain a patent on the created object belong to the performer. In this case, a client requires granting a gratuitous, simple (non-exclusive) licence to a specified person for the state or municipal needs. Suppose the client and the performer have shared rights. In that case, the client has the right, with prior notification of the performer, to grant a gratuitous, simple (non-exclusive) licence for the use of the IP subject matter should it be required to satisfy the state or municipal needs. A state or municipal contract can stipulate that this right belongs to the Russian Federation, a constituent entity of the Russian Federation, a municipality on behalf of which the state or municipal client act. Thus, the performer must transfer all the rights to the Russian Federation, the constituent entity of the Russian Federation and the municipality and may request for reimbursement of acquiring the rights.

IP can also be created within the contractual relations between parties that have no direct purpose to achieve such a result. It mostly has to do with a contract for the performance of work (refit contract) or a contract for the performance of research, development and technological work. Legal provisions on these types of contracts can be found in Part II of the Civil Code as they do not represent IP contracts as such. The exclusive rights distribution related to them is explained in Part IV of the Civil Code.

As for the performance of the work (refit contract), one party (the performer) is obliged to fulfil a task defined by the other party (the client) while the client is obliged to accept the result of the work and pay for it (Article 702 of the Civil Code). The direct result of such a contract is the creation of a thing (a material object). Its indirect result or a by-product can include the creation of IP, e.g., in the design and installation of equipment, a technical solution related to the equipment is found. The essential terms of this contract will be the subject matter of the contract and the completion time.

A contract for the performance of research means that the researcher is obliged to conduct research according to the client's technical task. In contrast, in a contract for the development and technological work, the contractor has to design a new product and prepare all the technical documentation for it or elaborate on new technology. The client is obliged to accept and pay for the work done (Article 769 of the Civil Code).

The Civil Code contains a direct instruction that the terms of a contract for the performance of research, development and technological work shall conform to the laws and other normative acts on exclusive rights. The above indication shows the high probability of IP creation when executing such contracts. The essential terms of this type of agreement include the subject matter and the completion time.

Article 769 of the Civil Code stipulates that, unless otherwise specified by law or the contract, the risks of the unexpected impossibility of fulfilling a contract for the performance of research, development and technological work are those of the client.

Suppose in the course of the research contract's execution, it is discovered that the achievement of the desired results is impossible due to circumstances beyond the control of the researcher. In that case, the client is legally obliged to pay for the work done before it was discovered that the results specified in the contract for research and development are not achievable. The payment shall not exceed the cost of the corresponding part of the works stipulated in the agreement (Article 775 of the Civil Code).

An interesting doctrinal position on the need to distinguish between the risks of negative results and the risks of occasional creative failures was expressed by Mihail P. Ring (Ring, 1967, p. 178). When a negative result means that the achievement of the goal is impossible, the risk of occasional creative failures can be determined by certain aspects of the work being done, e.g., the wrong choice of approach, which does not necessarily suppose that the obligations undertaken by the performer cannot be fulfilled. But they probably can be, provided the performer corrects the mistakes that were made.

Despite the differences in the described contracts' subject matter, the legislation provides uniform rules for exclusive rights distribution. In this case, it is the incidental creation of IP that has a decisive role. If the contract does not state otherwise, the exclusive right and the right to obtain a patent belongs to the performer. If not otherwise agreed, the client has the right to use the IP subject matter for which the contract was created under the terms of a simple (non-exclusive) licence until the exclusive rights/patent expires, without having to make additional financial contributions. This right is also preserved when the performer wants to transfer the exclusive right to a third party. Suppose the IP subject matter's exclusive rights were given to the client or a third party associated with the client. In that case, the performer has the right to use the IP subject matter created for their own purposes under the terms of a simple (non-exclusive) licence until the expiry of the exclusive rights/patent, unless otherwise agreed in the contract.

Although there is no direct involvement of the author in some contracts, the author as a participant of the creative process does not lose their legal power as they are not just considered a party to the contract. The author's non-property right, being inalienable and non-transferable, is preserved. If the author is no longer in possession of the exclusive right, they are entitled to a financial consideration.

However, in some cases, the full use of IP is only possible upon state registration. State registration shall be conducted for inventions, utility models, industrial designs, trademarks, collective marks, service marks, appellations of origin of goods, geographical indications, selective breeding achievements, company names, topographies of integrated circuits, computer programs and databases.

Such tasks are generally attributed to the scope of Rospatent; however, the state registration of selective breeding achievements falls within the responsibility of the State Commission of the Russian Federation for Selective Breeding Achievements Test and Protection (hereinafter State Sort Commission), while the registration of company names is the responsibility of the Federal Tax Service (also, see section "The state regulation of IP").

Upon the successful completion of the registration, the protected results of intellectual activities and means of individualization are included in one of the registers listed below:

- State Register for Inventions,
- State Register for Utility Models,
- State Register for Industrial Designs,
- State Register for Trademarks and Service Marks,
- List of Well-Known Trademarks,
- State Register for Geographical Indications and Appellations of Origin of Goods,

- Register for Computer Programs,
- Register for Databases,
- Register for Topographies of Integrated Circuits,
- Unified State Register for Legal Entities (USRLE),
- State Register for Selective Breeding Achievements.

The procedures for registering different types of IP and means of individualization have their own peculiarities, and their goals can vary. This, actually, depends on the objects to be registered.

The need for registering inventions, utility models and industrial designs is due to the legal provision according to which the exclusive rights to inventions, utility models and industrial designs certified by patents are recognized in the Russian Federation (Article 1346 of the Civil Code).

This does not mean that the absence of a patent entails the inability to use the invention, utility model or industrial design. However, it may restrict it if the patent is obtained by somebody else. In this case, one can try to exercise the right of prior use, explained in Article 1361 of the Civil Code.

According to Article 1361, if a person been exploiting (see section "Characteristics of IP rights"), in good faith, a solution identical to the invention or a solution that differs from it only in some comparable features, created regardless of the author, within the territory of the Russian Federation and before the priority date of the invention, utility model or industrial design, or had they made necessary preparations for it, such a person retains the right to further non-compensated use of said identical solution without the extension of the scope of use. This is called the right of prior use.

It should be noted that based on judicial practice, the right of prior use can be exercised by the person who creates/manufactures the products and not by the dealer or buyer, for instance (Decision of the State Commercial Court of the Samara Region of December 26, 2019, on case No. A55-24376/2019). This is not confirmed by specific judicial acts only, but also by the provisions of Resolution of the Plenum of the Supreme Court No 10. According to clause 128 of the act, necessary preparations for exploitation presuppose the intention (confirmed by the case circumstances) to use, in a certain company, a solution identical to the patented object in some technological process, provided that said solution determines the procedure of the above technological process, the implementation of which should be objectively possible. Scientific and other research unconnected to the direct implementation of a manufacturing technology or a method are not considered preparation for exploiting an identical solution. Therefore, exploitation implies production and excludes other forms of use.

Despite the fact that court decisions do not determine the prior user right, the question of its existence arises in legal disputes quite frequently: as a response to suits regarding breaches of a patent holder's exclusive right or as an independent lawsuit aimed at preventing claims from the patent holder (clause 126 of Resolution of the Plenum of the Supreme Court No. 10).

However, it should be borne in mind that the ability to exercise the right of prior use implies the establishment of the following facts (Decision of the State Commercial Court of Moscow City of January 24, 2020, on case No. A40-202611/2019):

- solution development regardless of the author,
- the identical character of the solution or its difference from the invention only in comparable aspects,
- use in good faith or necessary preparations for it,
- scope of use and the territory of use.

In such cases, the participation of an expert is rather widespread, for instance, to determine the number of manufactured products or to identify the similarities between the invention claim and the technical documentation of the corresponding product.

Although such a procedure is not obligatory, sometimes the refusal to engage experts may lead to new case revision (Resolution of the Intellectual Property Court of January 29, 2018, on case No. A53-5891/2017; Resolution of the Intellectual Property Court of January 25, 2018, on case No. A56-26863/2015).

The burden of proof of the prior user right is usually on the potential prior user. Russian legislation does not contain the presumption of the existence of the right of prior use by the person invoking such a right (Resolution of the Intellectual Property Court of August 28, 2015, on case No. A48-3161/2014).

The right of prior use can be viewed as a means of protection, as a means of creating competitive advantage (Raygorodskiy, 1949, p. 239), as a guarantee of ensuring technical creativity freedom, allowing one to continue using the independently created object (Yaichkov, 1961, p. 172) and as a way of achieving a balance of interests between bona fide parties (Lazareva, 2015, p. 3).

It is noteworthy that in some circumstances, the open use of an identical solution before the priority date by the prior user can serve as a basis for the invalidation of the patent due to non-conformity with the novelty standard ("Information on the Issues Related to Disputes on the Right of Prior Use", approved by Resolution of the Presidium of the Intellectual Property Court of November 14, 2014, on case No. SP-21/14).

It is also necessary to mention the right of subsequent use. It means that a person who began to use an invention, utility model or industrial design or made the necessary preparations between the date of termination of a patent for an invention, utility model or industrial design and the date of publication in the official bulletin of the federal executive body for IP of information on the restoration of the patent, retains the right to further use free of charge without expanding the scope of such use (Article 1400 of the Civil Code).

As clause 133 of Resolution of the Plenum of the Supreme Court No. 10 clarifies, this right is retained if the person proves that the production (preparation for production) of the goods in which the invention, utility model or industrial design was carried out in the period before the restoration of the patent.

It is worth noting that the patent may be terminated due to nonpayment of the fee for maintaining the patent in force. However, it may be restored at the request of the patent holder or the assignee of that person, which is filed within 3 years from the date of expiry of the term for payment of the patent fee, but before the expiration of the patent validity period. This information is published in the official bulletin.

The right of subsequent use may be transferred to another person only together with the enterprise where the invention or solution, which differs from the invention only in equivalent features, utility model or industrial design, was used or the necessary preparations were made.

However, it is the patent that confirms the exclusive right to an invention, utility model or industrial design (clause 122 of Resolution of the Plenum of the Supreme Court No. 10). The patent owner has the exclusive right to use the patented objects in any way that does not contradict the law, to dispose of the exclusive right and protect it.

Despite the obvious advantages that obtaining a patent means for the patent holder (strengthening their position in the market, determining the purposes of use, protection against unauthorized use, possibility of commercialization, attracting investment, etc.), one should carefully evaluate the expediency of obtaining a patent, considering all the money and time expenditures, as well as various provisions on a compulsory licence due to the insufficient use or non-use of a patent and the disclosure of information about the subject matter of the patent.

The processing of a patent application contains several steps that may be summarized as follows:

- filling a patent application,
- formal examination of the application,
- substantive examination of the application,
- grant of a patent or refusal to grant it.

Rospatent grants patents with the assistance of the Federal Institute of Industrial Property (FIIP), which is its subordinate. The application can be submitted:

- in electronic form (the official website of Rospatent) (FIIP) or through the federal state information system, the Public Services Portal of the Russian Federation (PSP) on the internet,[1]
- in person by the applicant (their representative),
- by post,
- by fax.

The procedure is regulated by the Civil Code of the Russian Federation (Part IV), as well as by orders of the Ministry of Economic Development of the Russian Federation:

- Administrative Regulations for the Familiarization with the Application Documents for the Patent on an Invention, Utility Model or Industrial Design; providing copies of the said documents (Order No. 615 of August 28, 2015)
- Administrative Regulations for the State Registration of an Invention and the Grant of a Patent (Order No. 315 of May 25, 2016)
- Administrative Regulations for the State Registration of a Utility Model and the Grant of a Patent (Order No. 702 of September 30, 2015)
- Administrative Regulations for the State Registration of an Industrial Design and the Grant of a Patent (Order No. 696 of September 30, 2015)
- Procedure for the Familiarization with the Application Documents for the Grant of a Patent on an Invention, Utility Model, Industrial Design and the Issuance of Copies of Such Documents, the Request Procedure for the Familiarization with the Application Documents for the Grant of a Patent on an Invention, Utility Model, Industrial Design and the Issuance of Copies of Such Documents (Order No. 614 of August 28, 2015)
- Rules for the Preparation, Submission and Consideration of the Documents that are Obligatory to Initiate the Legally Significant Actions Required for the State Registration of Inventions; Types of Documents (Order No. 316 of May 25, 2016)
- Rules for the Preparation, Submission and Consideration of the Documents that are Obligatory to Initiate Legally Significant Actions for the State Registration of Utility Models; Types of Documents (Order No. 701 of September 30, 2015)
- Rules for the State Registration of Industrial Designs (see section "Intellectual property: concept and types").

The guidelines for implementing the administrative procedures and actions for the inventions, utility models and industrial designs registration adopted by Rospatent are also of great importance for the patenting procedure. They are non-obligatory in nature but reflect the established practice in this area. They can be found on the official website.

The right to apply for a patent belongs to:

- the author of an invention, utility model, industrial design/co-authors;
- the assignee of the author (co-authors) of an invention, utility model, industrial design (another natural or legal person) to whom the right to obtain a patent is transferred in cases and on the grounds established by the legislation of the Russian Federation, including the rule of universal succession[2] or a contract, in particular, an employment contract;

- the assignee of the persons who have the right to obtain a patent in cases and on the grounds established by the legislation of the Russian Federation, by a contract or by a state or municipal contract, including the Russian Federation, a constituent entity of the Russian Federation or a municipality on behalf of which a state or municipal customer acts.

An application can be submitted either in person by the above-mentioned people or by their representatives. The representative's powers are certified by a power of attorney, except the legal representatives of a child up to the age of 14 (parents, adopted parents, guardians), and legally incapable persons (guardian). Minors aged 14–18 can apply independently, without the consent of legal representatives.

Credentials are confirmed by the corresponding documents, for example, a birth certificate, a certificate of adoption, a certificate on the appointment of a guardian or a contract of guardianship. The power of attorney must be notarized. However, the law specifies cases where powers of attorney are considered notarized by default, namely (Article 185.1 of the Civil Code):

1 powers of attorney of military personnel and other persons undergoing treatment in hospitals, sanatoriums and other military medical institutions, which are certified by the head of such an institution, their medical department deputy, and, in their absence, by the senior or on-call doctor;
2 powers of attorney of military personnel and also powers of attorney of employees, members of their families and family members of military personnel in the places of deployment of military units, formations, institutions and military educational institutions where no notary offices and other bodies performing notarial acts can be found, which are certified by the commander (chief) of these military units, formations, institutions or establishments;
3 powers of attorney of people in prison, certified by the head of the corresponding place of deprivation of liberty;
4 powers of attorney of adult capable citizens living in stationary social service organizations, certified by the administration of this organization or the head (their deputy) of the corresponding body for social protection of the population.

As for the legal entities, a power of attorney on behalf of a legal entity shall be certified by its head or another person authorized to do so per the law and the constituent documents. The head of a legal entity represents its interests without power of attorney.

According to the Russian law, the head of a legal entity represents its interests but is not its representative in the generally accepted sense. A director is a body of a legal entity, an integral part of it, but not an independent entity; therefore, a relationship of representation does not arise. According to Article 53 of the Civil Code, the constituent document may provide that the authority to act on behalf of a legal entity is granted to several persons acting jointly or independently of each other. Information about this must be included in the USRLE.

It should be noted that a patent attorney can act as a representative. Moreover, according to Article 1247 of the Civil Code, citizens permanently residing outside the Russian Federation and foreign legal entities communicate with Rospatent through patent attorneys registered with the indicated federal body, unless otherwise provided by an international treaty of the Russian Federation. The Intellectual Property Court has repeatedly stated that conducting business through patent attorneys does not deprive one of the right to get acquainted with and know the status of the corresponding application from open sources, including information posted on the official Rospatent and FIIP websites (Resolution of the Presidium of the Intellectual Property Court of April 5, 2018, on case No. SIP-444/2017).

As stated in the message of Rospatent of December 28, 2, posted on the official website (https://rospatent.gov.ru/ru/documents/informatsionnoe-pismo-28022019), business cooperation with IP agencies can be carried out without resorting to patent attorneys in the framework of the intergovernmental agreements that apply to the following states:

- Azerbaijan Republic (Agency for Intellectual Property of the Azerbaijan Republic)
- Republic of Armenia (Intellectual Property Agency of the Ministry of Economic Development and Investments of the Republic of Armenia)
- Republic of Belarus (National Centre for Intellectual Property)
- Republic of Kazakhstan (National Institute of Intellectual Property of the Ministry of Justice of the Republic of Kazakhstan)
- Kyrgyz Republic (State Service for Intellectual Property and Innovation under the Government of the Kyrgyz Republic)
- Republic of Moldova (State Agency for Intellectual Property of the Republic of Moldova)
- Republic of Tajikistan (National Patent Information Centre of the Ministry of Economic Development and Trade of the Republic of Tajikistan)
- Turkmenistan (State Service for Intellectual Property of the Ministry of Finance and Economy of Turkmenistan)
- Republic of Uzbekistan (Agency for Intellectual Property under the Ministry of Justice of the Republic of Uzbekistan)
- Ukraine (Ministry of Economic Development and Trade of Ukraine)

Meanwhile, a person working with Rospatent on their own or through a representative who is not a patent attorney registered with said federal body shall provide their address in the territory of the Russian Federation for correspondence at the request of Rospatent (Article 1247 of the Civil Code).

The powers of a patent attorney are confirmed by a power of attorney, which does not require notarization if the patent attorney has corresponding specialization (the necessary information, including information about the foreign language(s) in which a patent attorney can carry out correspondence, is contained in the Register of Patent Attorneys of the Russian Federation). A power of attorney issued in the territory of another state following its national legislation can be used to confirm the authority of a Russian patent attorney or a foreign patent attorney to work with Rospatent on behalf of a foreign applicant in the cases stipulated by the international agreements of the Russian Federation.

Rospatent requires that all the documentation should be provided in Russian. If the power of attorney is presented in a language other than Russian, it shall also be translated into Russian. The translation does not require notarization.

The composition of the filed application depends on the subject of patenting. At the same time, any application will include a request for a patent (the above-mentioned orders establish forms of patent request) with the name of the author and the applicant, the person who has the right to obtain a patent as well as the place of residence or location of each of them.

An application for an invention and a utility model also contains:

- a description of the invention/utility model that shall reveal its essence;
- claims of invention/utility model;
- drawings and other materials, if they are necessary for understanding the essence of the invention/utility model (other materials are various types of graphic materials explaining the essence of the invention, for example, diagrams, drawings, graphs, photographs and tables, etc.);
- abstract.

An application for an industrial design includes a set of product images that provide a complete understanding of the industrial design and its essential features constituting the aesthetic of the product appearance, a drawing of the general view of the product, a list of materials, if they are necessary to reveal the essence of the industrial design, and description of the industrial design.

As a general rule, the date of applying is the date of its receipt by Rospatent. The priority of an invention, utility model or industrial design is established according to date of receipt.

The application will not be accepted in the following cases:

- an application submitted on paper does not contain a request;
- the request is illegible or is not presented in Russian;
- the request does not indicate the applicant, their location or place of residence or address for correspondence;
- submission of a paper application, the processing of which is impossible due to technical reasons related to the condition of the paper;
- non-compliance of the documents submitted in an electronic form with the requirements;

- a "commercial secret" stamp on the application documents (commercial secret regime is incompatible with the openness of the patent data).

The applicant has the right to make additions, clarifications and corrections to the application documents by submitting additional materials at the request of Rospatent if these do not change the application in substance, convert the application into an application of a different type or withdraw the application.

According to Article 1378 of the Civil Code, the applicant has the right to make additions, clarifications and corrections to the invention, utility model or industrial design application documents by submitting additional materials at the request of Rospatent before the decision to grant or refuse a patent or recognize the application as withdrawn is made if these additions, clarifications and corrections do not change the substance of the invention, utility model or industrial design application.

The applicant can make changes on their own initiative if said changes do not relate to the substance of the subject matter being patented, for example, the information about the author, the applicant, as well as the correction of obvious and technical errors. For this purpose, a corresponding request must be submitted.

Then, having received the report on the information search, the applicant has the right to submit the amended invention claim on their own initiative once only, should it not change the substance of the invention application, and introduce appropriate changes to the description.

From August 1, 2021, the applicant will have the right to submit the amended claim on their own initiative, provided that it does not change the substance of the invention application, and make appropriate changes in the description when filing a request for the substantive examination of the application and (or) after receiving the preliminary information search or information search report, as well as the right to submit the amended claim of a utility model, if it does not change the substance of the utility model application, and to amend the description after receiving the preliminary information search report.

It should be noted that the changes that come into force on August 1, 2021, will also affect issues related to information search. A preliminary information search in relation to inventions or utility models and the preliminary assessment of their patentability will be carried out by Russian scientific or educational organizations that are accredited for such a job.

The Civil Code defines the cases in which additional materials change the substance of the application. Concerning inventions and utility models, this happens if the additional materials contain:

- another invention that does not meet the unity of invention requirement concerning an invention or a group of inventions accepted for consideration, or another utility model;

- features that are subject to inclusion in the claim of an invention or utility model and have not been mentioned in the application documents;
- an indication of the technical result provided by an invention or a utility model that is not related to the technical result contained in the same documents.

Additional materials change the substance of the industrial design application if :

- they contain images of the product on which another industrial design that does not meet the unity of the industrial design requirement in relation to the industrial design or the group of industrial designs shown in the images accepted for consideration is represented;
- they contain essential features of the industrial design that are absent in the images presented on the application filing date;
- they contain images of the product on which the essential features of the industrial design presented on the application filing date are absent.

An invention application can be converted into a utility model or industrial design application, a utility model application can be converted into an invention or industrial design application and an industrial design application can be converted into an invention or utility model application. An invention application can be converted before the information about the invention application has been published but no later than the day the decision to grant a patent on the invention is made. Suppose the decision is made to refuse a patent on the invention or recognize the application as withdrawn. In that case, the conversion shall be performed before the period to object to the decision has expired.

The decision by Rospatent to grant a patent on an invention, to refuse a patent on an invention or to declare an application withdrawn can be challenged by filing an objection to Rospatent within seven months from the date of receiving the notification about the relevant decision or obtaining copies of the materials requested from Rospatent that are indicated in the decision on the refusal to grant a patent, provided that the applicant requests copies of these materials within three months from the date of receipt of the notification (clause 3 of Article 1387 of the Civil Code).

The conversion of a utility model application into an invention or an industrial design application or an industrial design application into an invention or a utility model application shall be allowed upon the request filed by the applicant to Rospatent until the day the decision to grant a patent is made and, in the case of the decision to refuse a patent or to recognize the application as withdrawn, before the period to object the decision has expired (clause 3 of Article 1387 of the Civil Code applies by analogy).

The applicant has the right to withdraw their invention, utility model or industrial design application prior to the state registration of the invention, utility model or industrial design in the corresponding register (Article 1380 of the Civil Code).

In the course of the formal examination, the organization responsible checks whether all the necessary documents are included in the application and whether they comply with the established requirements; however, the essence of the subject matter is not analyzed. Suppose the documents are missing or inconsistent with the requirements. In that case, a corresponding request within a period not exceeding two months from the start of the formal examination will be sent to the applicant.

Provided that the documents meet all the requirements, a decision to conclude the formal examination with a positive result is made. The applicant is notified of the decision taken, and the application is forwarded to the department carrying out the substantive examination.

The substantive examination of the invention or utility model application includes:

- an information search concerning the claimed subject matter for the determination of the prior art, which shall be later considered during the patentability check;
- verification for compliance with the conditions of patentability and requirements for the subject matter of patent rights;
- verification for the sufficiency of the invention/utility model substance description in the application documents for implementing the invention by a specialist skilled in the corresponding technical field.

Substantive examination of an industrial design means:

- an information search regarding the declared industrial design for the detection of publicly available information that later shall be considered during the patentability check (information contained in the source of information, which may be accessed by any person, is considered to be publicly available);
- verification for the compliance of the industrial design with the requirements concerning objects that feature official symbols, names and distinctive signs, as well as the conditions of patentability.

It should be noted that, unlike the examinations of an industrial design and utility model, which begin after the positive conclusion of the previous stage, the examination of an invention needs a special request that can be either filed by the applicant (within 3 years from the date of filing the application) or included in the invention application.

If the patentability of the object is confirmed, then a decision to grant a patent is made. Otherwise, a decision to refuse the grant of a patent is made.

To obtaining a patent, patent fees shall be paid. Their Regulations on Patent and Other Fees, approved by Decree No. 941 of the Government of the Russian Federation of December 10, 2008, established the amount of the patent fees. Subsequently, keeping the patent in force also implies paying fees.

It is important to note that the patent obtainment procedure implies informing an indefinite number of people about the subject matter of the patent. Information about the granting of a patent is disclosed in a special bulletin and a corresponding register, which gives the right to any person to get access to the application documents and the information search report. For this, it is necessary to submit a request and pay a fee. However, in the case of inventions and industrial designs, information about the application is also published in the official bulletin (Article 1385 of the Civil Code). For inventions, such publication is made after 18 months from filing the invention application that has undergone formal examination with a positive result. Information may be published earlier should there be an applicant's request filed before the expiration of 12 months from the date of filing the invention application. Publication shall not be made if, before the expiration of 15 months from the date of filing, the application was withdrawn, recognized as withdrawn or the registration was performed on its basis. In all cases, the author has the right to refuse to have their name mentioned in such a publication.

When making a decision on patenting, it should be considered that there is the risk that an interested person can obtain a so-called compulsory licence. This can happen in the case of the non-use or insufficient use of the object of patent rights (for an invention or an industrial design it is within 4 years from the date of granting the patent, for a utility model, it is within 3 years), which leads to shortages of the corresponding goods, works or services in the market.

In this case, it is a question of maintaining a balance of private and public interests because, on the one hand, the patent is obviously aimed at protecting the rights of the author and the patent owner who put in the effort to create and register it, but, on the other hand, as follows from the provisions of the law, a certain market demand arises, and it is this demand that determines the possibility of obtaining a compulsory licence. Scientific literature even points out the similarity of this legal structure with an easement (Sagdeeva, 2018; Mikryukov, 2007). It is noteworthy that the earlier legal acts referred to the "significant importance for the state" (Raigorodsky, 1949; Regulations on Inventions and Technical Improvements, approved by the Council of People's Commissars of March 3, 1941; Regulations on Industrial Designs, approved by the Resolution of the Council of Ministers of the USSR No. 539 of August 6, 1981), but it is not identical to the current rule.

A person interested in obtaining a patent initially applies to the patent holder. In the event of their refusal to conclude a licence agreement on terms consistent with the established practice person concerned can go to the court with a claim to provide a compulsory simple (non-exclusive) licence allowing the use of the invention, utility model or industrial design in the territory of the Russian Federation.

If the patent holder proves that the non-use or insufficient use of the subject matter is due to valid reasons, the court will not satisfy the claim. Otherwise, the licence will be granted, and the total amount of payments for such a licence set in a court decision may not be lower than the price of the licenses determined under comparable circumstances.

However, even the issuance of a licence does not mean that the patent holder no longer has any leverage to influence the situation, since the law establishes one's right to go to court with a claim to terminate such a permit if the circumstances that led to its granting cease to exist and their re-occurrence is unlikely. In this case, the court establishes the term and procedure for terminating the compulsory simple (non-exclusive) licence and the rights arising in connection with the receipt of this licence.

Obtaining a compulsory licence on this basis has a number of difficulties connected with proving the shortage of offers for goods, works and services, as well as the validity of the reasons for non-use. However, the risk of such a situation cannot be excluded.

Thus, when deciding on obtaining a patent, one should weigh the pros and the cons, since patenting for the sake of patenting may not bring the desired result, and the spent resources will not be reimbursed. In addition, it is also important to consider the limited period of patent protection: 20 years for inventions; 10 years for utility models; 5 years for industrial designs (may be renewed several times for 5 years, but in general for no more than 25 years). However, the pros of having a patent, expressed in the possibility of its widespread use, are control over other persons' actions regarding the patented object, including the prosecution of illegal and dishonest actions, protection of IP, its commercialization, etc. In the case of competent IP management, a patent can give an IP owner some undeniable market advantages, which nowadays seem to be an extremely significant aspect of an effective business.

The registration of a trademark is necessary for a certain sign to be recognized as a trademark since the sign that is submitted for state registration and examined by Rospatent cannot be considered a trademark until the date of its registration in the State Register of Trademarks.

As explained by the Federal Antimonopoly Service (FAS) in Letter No. IA/74666/15 December 24, 2015 "On the Application of the Fourth Antimonopoly Package", the violation of the exclusive rights to a trademark can only take place when a certificate for a trademark (Article 1504 of the Civil Code) is available, not a registered application (Article 1492 of the Civil Code).

The procedure for trademark registration is regulated by the Civil Code (Part IV), and orders of the Ministry of Economic Development of the Russian Federation:

- Administrative Procedure for the State Registration of a Trademark, Service Mark, Collective Mark and the Grant of a Patent and the Grant of a Certificate for a Trademark, Service Mark, Collective Mark, its Duplicate (Order No. 483 of July 20, 2015; hereinafter Administrative Procedure for the State Registration of a Trademark)

- Rules for the Preparation, Submission and Consideration of the Documents that are Obligatory to Initiate Legally Significant Actions for the State Registration of Trademarks, Service Marks, Collective Marks. Requirements for the Documents Enclosed with the Application for the State Registration of a Trademark, Service Mark, Collective Mark, Types of the Documents to be Attached. The Procedure for Converting an Application for the State Registration of a Collective Mark into an Application for the State Registration of a Trademark, Service Mark and Vice Versa. Data Indicated in a Trademark (Service Mark) Certificate Form, in a Collective Mark Certificate Form; Trademark (Service Mark) Certificate Forms, Collective Mark Certificate Forms (Order No. 482 of July 20, 2015)
- Administrative Procedure for the Recognition of a Trademark or a Sign Used as a Trademark as a Well-known Trademark in the Russian Federation (Order No. 602 of August 27, 2015; hereinafter Administrative Procedure for the Recognition of a Trademark or a Sign Used as a Trademark as a Well-Known Trademark)

The explanations offered by Rospatent and FIIP should be considered, for instance, the "Guidelines for the Implementation of the Administrative Procedures and Actions for the State Registration of a Trademark, Service Mark, Collective Mark, the Grant of the Certificates for Trademark, Service Mark, Collective Mark, their Duplicates", adopted by Order of FIIP No. 12 of January 20, 2020 (hereinafter Guidelines on the State Registration of a Trademark, Service Mark, Collective Mark); "Methodological Recommendations on Certain Issues of Examination of the Trademark Registration Applications", adopted Order of Rospatent No. 26 of March 27, 1997; Information Letter of Rospatent No. 1 of February 19, 2010 "On Some Issues of the Examination of Trademarks used in Technical Regulations and National (State) Standards" and others. These acts contain explanations of the practical aspects of the registration procedures.

An application for a trademark registration can be filed by a legal entity or an individual entrepreneur. According to Article 1478 of the Civil Code, the owner of the exclusive right to a trademark can be a legal entity or an individual entrepreneur. This rule also imposes other restrictions. For example, the exclusive right to a trademark and service mark that belonged to an individual entrepreneur (clause 1 of Article 1484 of the Civil Code) and inherited by a citizen who is not registered as an individual entrepreneur must be alienated within a year from the date that the inheritance came into force (except for cases where the heir registers as an individual entrepreneur within this period). An association of persons can submit an application for a collective mark.

In accordance with clause 13 of the Administrative Procedure for the State Registration of a Trademark, the time for the provision of public services of receiving, registering, examining an application and issuing a certificate for a trademark amounts to 18 months and two weeks. However, in practice, the average duration of the application's consideration under the national procedure requires 5.59 months, and its duration under the international procedure is 6.33 months (see the Rospatent Annual Report, 2019).

The registration procedure includes the following steps:

- filing an application,
- examining the application (formal examination and examination of the sign),
- making a decision on the state registration of a trademark and granting a certificate.

Application documents are submitted to Rospatent:

- online (the official website of Rospatent) (FIIPS) or through the PSP,
- in person,
- by post,
- by fax.

A trademark application includes:

1 a request for state registration of the sign as a trademark indicating the name of the applicant and their place of residence or location;
2 the sign to be registered (from January 17, 2021, if the applicant so wishes, a three-dimensional model in an electronic form can be submitted);
3 the list of goods for which the state registration of a trademark is requested and which are grouped by classes defined by the International Classification of Goods and Services for the Purposes of the Registration of Marks under the Nice Agreement (hereinafter ICGS);
4 a description of the sign.

If a collective mark is registered, then the charter of the collective mark must also be submitted. The charter contains the name of the association authorized to register the collective mark in its name (right holder), a list of persons entitled to use this collective mark, the purpose of the registration of the collective mark, a list of the uniform characteristics of quality or other general characteristics of the goods that will be indicated by the collective mark, conditions for the use of the collective mark, provisions on the procedure for monitoring the use of a collective mark and provisions on the liability for violation of the charter of a collective mark.

The documents of the application are submitted in Russian or another language. If these documents are submitted in another language, their translation into Russian shall be attached to the application.

The priority of a trademark is established by the date of filing an application for a trademark to Rospatent. The priority of a trademark can be established by the date of filing of the first application for a trademark in a country that is a party to the Paris Convention for the Protection of Industrial Property (convention priority). It can also be established by the date when the open display of the exhibit on which the trademark is placed starts in official or officially recognized international exhibitions organized on the territory of one of the member states of the Paris Convention for the Protection of Industrial Property (exhibition priority) if the application for a trademark is filed with the federal executive body for IP within 6 months from the relevant date. The priority of a trademark may be established by the date of the international registration of the trademark in accordance with international treaties of the Russian Federation.

The grounds for the refusal to accept the application are:

- an application submitted on paper does not contain a request. The request is illegible or is not presented in Russian. The request does not indicate the name of the applicant, their location or place of residence, or address for correspondence;
- an application submitted on paper cannot be processed for technical reasons related to the condition of the paper;
- non-compliance of the documents submitted in electronic form with the requirements.

After registration of the application, in accordance with clause 1 of Article 1493 of the Civil Code, all the necessary information is published by Rospatent in the Rospatent official bulletin in order to ensure that any person can have access to it. The bulletin is published and posted on Rospatent's and the FIIP's websites at least twice a month in the "Official Publications" section. Access to it is free of charge.

The following information is subject to publication:

- registration number of the application;
- date of receipt of the application;
- date of the publication of the application in the official bulletin;
- reproduction of the trademark;
- the full name of the legal entity and the address of the location of the legal entity (according to the constituent document) indicating the name of the country or the last name, first name, patronymic (the latter, if any) of the individual entrepreneur and their place of residence, indicating the name of the country;
- the address for correspondence indicated in the application;
- the list of goods specified in the application.

Access to the documents of the application for the state registration of a trademark, service mark or collective mark and the issuance of copies of such documents are carried out at the request of any person. The form of the request is stipulated in the "Procedure for Accessing the Documents of the Application for the State Registration of a Trademark, Service Mark, Collective Mark and the Issuance of Copies of Such Documents, Application Forms for Accessing the Documents of the Application for the State Registration of a Trademark, Service Mark, Collective Mark and the Issuance of Copies of such Documents", adopted by Order of the Ministry of Economic Development of the Russian Federation No. 607 of August 27, 2015.

It is important to note that after the publication of information about the application and before a decision is made on the state registration of a trademark, any person has the right to submit an objection to Rospatent in writing.

In this case, the person filing objections should consider the grounds for refusing the state registration of a trademark, provided in Article 1483 of the Civil Code.

First, state registration of trademarks is not allowed for signs that are not distinctive or consist only of elements:

1. *that are commonly used to indicate goods of a certain type.* Examples of signs that have come into general use as designations for goods of a certain type are cellophane, thermos, lanolin, petroleum jelly, saccharin, celluloid, escalator, primus, gramophone, tape recorder, linoleum, nylon, etc. (Guidelines on the Classification of the Declared Signs, Trademarks and Service Marks as Generally used Designations of Goods and Services of a Certain Type, approved by Order of Rospatent No. 26 of March 27, 1997);
2. *that are generally accepted symbols and terms.* For example, the term "claims", written in English, was recognized as a generally accepted term in the field of law (Decision of the Intellectual Property Court of March 25, 2020, on case No. SIP-750/2019);
3. *providing the characterization of the goods, including indicating their type, quality, quantity, features, purpose, value, as well as the time, place and method of their production or sale.* For example, the claimed sign "Cakepops" characterizes a product, indicating its type, features (a cake on a stick) and is perceived by consumers as an indication of a flour-based confectionery product (Ruling of the Judicial Collegium for Economic Disputes of the Supreme Court of the Russian Federation of October 31, 2019, on case No. SIP-691/2018);
4. *representing the form of the goods, which is determined exclusively or mainly by the property or purpose of the goods* (realistic shape of the product).

These kinds of elements can be included in a trademark as unprotected elements if they do not occupy a dominant position in it. It is also worth noting that the described rule does not apply to cases in which signs have acquired distinctiveness as a result of their use, consist only of the specified elements and form a combination that has a distinctive ability.

Second, state registration of signs as trademarks shall not be permitted for signs that fully or partially consist of elements that are false or capable of misleading the consumer in respect of the product or its manufacturer or are contrary to the public interests and principles of humanity and morality.

Third, it is prohibited to register signs that cause persistent associations with certain well-known objects as trademarks. For example:

- objects that include official symbols, names and distinctive emblems;
- the official names and images of some especially valuable objects of cultural heritage of the peoples of the Russian Federation or objects of the world's cultural or natural heritage, as well as images of cultural values stored in collections and funds, if registration is requested in the name of the persons who are not their owners, without the consent of the owners or the persons authorized by the owners to register such signs as trademarks. If the object is privately owned, consent is given by the owner or a person authorized by them. If the object is in state ownership, consent is given by legal entities authorized by the legislation: organizations which, by decree of the President of the Russian Federation, are classified as especially valuable objects of cultural heritage of the peoples of the Russian Federation (the Bolshoi Theatre, the State Hermitage, the Russian Academy of Arts) (Presidential Decree No. 294 of December 12, 1991), including those contained in the World Heritage List; state nature reserves and national parks, including those contained in the World Heritage List; state institutions (directorates) empowered by regulatory acts of the constituent entities of the Russian Federation to manage the natural parks, Lenskie Stolby of the Republic of Sakha (Yakutia) and the Volcanoes of Kamchatka included in the World Heritage List; cultural organizations, including museums (or their directorates);
- the name of a famous work of science, literature or art, known in the Russian Federation on the date of filing an application for the state registration of a trademark (Article 1492 of the Civil Code), a character or a quote from such a work, a work of art or a fragment thereof, without the consent of the right holder, if the rights to the corresponding work were obtained earlier than the priority date of the registered trademark;
- the name (Article 19 of the Civil Code), pseudonym (clause 1 of Article 1265 and subclause 3, clause 1 of Article 1315 of the Civil Code) or a sign derived from them, a portrait or facsimile of a person known in the Russian Federation on the date of filing the application, without the consent of that person or their heir;
- signs that represent or contain elements that are protected in one of the signatory countries of an international treaty as signs that identify wines or alcoholic beverages as originating from its territory (produced within the boundaries of that state) and having a special quality, reputation or other characteristics, which are mainly determined by their origin, if the trademark is intended to indicate wines or spirits not originating from the territory of a given geographical location.

Fourth, as a general rule, state registration of signs is not allowed for signs that are identical or confusingly similar to other subject matters of intellectual rights, such as:

- geographical indications or appellations of origin of goods and the signs submitted for registration before the priority date of a trademark. Except in cases where such geographical indication or such name or a confusingly similar sign is included as an unprotected element in a trademark registered in the name of a person entitled to use such a geographical indication or such name, provided that the registration of the trademark is carried out in respect of the same goods for the individualization of which such geographical indication or such appellation of origin of goods was registered;
- a company name or commercial name (their individual elements) or the name of a selective breeding achievement registered in the State Register of Protected Breeding Achievements, the rights to which, in the Russian Federation, were obtained earlier than the priority date of the registered trademark and belong to other people (for homogeneous goods);
- an industrial design or a mark of conformity, the rights to which were obtained earlier than the priority date of the registered trademark and signs, the elements of which are another persons' means of individualization protected in accordance with the Civil Code of the Russian Federation (except for objects for which permission can be obtained).

Fifth, signs identical or confusingly similar to existing trademarks or signs submitted for registration, which have an earlier priority concerning similar goods, cannot be registered as trademarks. Registration as a trademark in relation to homogeneous goods of a sign similar to the point of confusion to any trademark is allowed with the consent of the right holder if such registration does not mislead consumers. The right holder cannot revoke consent. This exclusion does not apply to well-known trademarks and collective marks.

For the reasons described above, legal protection is also not granted to trademarks registered in accordance with the international treaties of the Russian Federation.

During formal examination, the application is checked to see if it includes:

- the request for state registration of the sign indicating the applicant's name and their place of residence or location;
- the sign being registered;
- the list of goods in respect of which the state registration of a trademark is requested and that are grouped according to the classes of the ICGS;
- descriptions of the sign, as well as the name and location of the applicant's representative, if any.

Furthermore, it is checked to see if the following documents are included and comply with the established requirements:

- documentary confirmation of the consent to the processing of personal data of the applicant's representative if the application is submitted by a representative who is not a patent attorney;
- the charter of the collective mark if the application is filed for the state registration of the collective mark;
- a power of attorney certifying the authority of the patent attorney and other representatives to deal with Rospatent or a certified copy of a document of the established form confirming the powers of the legal representative if the applicant deals with Rospatent through a legal representative;
- translation of documents attached to the application if not filed in Russian.

The term of the formal examination is one month.

Suppose the application is missing documents, without which it is impossible to conduct a formal examination. In that case, a request is sent to the applicant indicating the grounds for the need to submit additional materials and a proposal to submit the missing and (or) corrected information and (or) documents within three months from the date of the request.

Based on results of the formal examination, the application is accepted for consideration or a decision is made to refuse to accept it for consideration, and the applicant is notified of this.

The examination of the sign implies establishing the trademark priority and conducting an information search to check if the sign used by the applicant is identifiable with the goods it should indicate and see its correlation with a specific product of the particular class of ICGS, the correctness of the grouping of goods according to the classes of ICGS carried out by the applicant as well as the sign's compliance with the requirements of the Russian legislation.

Guidelines on the State Registration of a Trademark, Service Mark or Collective Mark contain a special section, "Checking the Compliance of the Designation to be Registered with the Requirements of the Russian Legislation" (No. 4), which explains its features in sufficient detail and provides examples.

Suppose during the application consideration process (before making a decision based on the results of the examination of the sign) there is an appeal from any interested person indicating the number of the application under consideration and containing documented information on the non-compliance of the sign with the requirements of the Russian legislation. In that case, the information provided is considered when making a decision based on the results of the examination of the sign.

Based on the results of the examination of the claimed sign, Rospatent decides to grant or refuse state registration of a trademark. The relevant information is posted on Rospatent and FIIP websites and in the Rospatent official bulletin, "Trademarks, service marks and appellations of origin of goods". Within a month from the state registration of a trademark in the State Register of Trademarks, a trademark certificate is issued. From January 17, 2021, it is issued in electronic form and, at the applicant's request, on paper.

During the period of the examination of the application for a trademark, the applicant has the right to supplement, clarify or correct the materials of the application, including by submitting additional materials, before the decision is made. An applicant can file a divisional application for the same sign. It can be done during the examination of a trademark application or consideration of an objection for a decision on the state registration of a trademark or on the refusal to register a trademark made based on the fact that the claimed sign is identical or confusingly similar to other trademarks submitted for registration or protected in the Russian Federation as well as other trademarks officially recognized as well known. A divisional application must contain a list of goods taken from among those indicated in the initial application, as of the date of its filing, and different from those goods on the list contained in the initial application for which the original application remains in force. The applicant also has the right to withdraw the application at any stage of its consideration but no later than the date of the state registration of the trademark.

It is noteworthy that non-use of a trademark continuously for 3 years could become the basis for early termination of legal protection regarding all goods or a part of the goods for the individualization of which the trademark is registered. It implies the termination of the exclusive right to this trademark.

In this case, the interested person sends the right holder a proposal to apply to Rospatent with an application for the waiver of the right to a trademark or to conclude an agreement with the interested person on the alienation of the exclusive right to a trademark in respect of all the goods or a part of the goods for the individualization of which the trademark is registered. If within two months from the date of sending the proposal the right holder does not take appropriate actions, the interested person, within 30 days after the specified two months, has the right to apply to the court with a claim for the early termination of the legal protection of the trademark due to its non-use. The court shall make the decision on early termination of the legal protection. Legal protection of a trademark is terminated from the date the court decision is entered into force. The interest is manifested in the plaintiff's wish to use a sign to designate homogeneous goods identical or confusingly similar to controversial sign with or without its legal protection as a means of individualization (clause 165 of Resolution of the Plenum of the Supreme Court No. 10).

To maintain the legal protection of a trademark, the right holder must prove the actual (not pretended) use of the trademark in respect to each product for which the trademark is registered and for which the plaintiff has provided proof of non-use due to which the early termination of legal protection is required. In such cases, the evidence of non-use of the trademark for reasons beyond the control of the right owner can be taken into account (clauses 166–67 of Resolution of the Plenum of the Supreme Court No. 10).

The interested person can send a new proposal to the trademark right holder not earlier than three months from the date of sending the previous proposal.

As for the right of prior use, it is not normatively provided for trademarks; however, in practice, there have been attempts to apply the provisions on the right of prior use of the objects of patent rights to trademarks. However, the courts proceed from the fact that there is no right of prior use concerning trademarks (the principle of actual use, the principle of first use) (Resolution of the Presidium of the Intellectual Property Court of May 31, 2019, on case No. SIP-242/2019; Resolution of the Intellectual Property Court of April 8, 2019, on case No. A32-11407/2018; Resolution of the State Commercial Court of the Republic of Tatarstan of October 17, 2016, on case No. A65-9183/2016).

Recognition of a trademark as well known is of considerable interest for businesspeople. This is due to a number of advantages described earlier. At the same time, the number of trademarks recognized as well known in Russia is low and, according to data as of the beginning of September 2020, amounts to 213. Despite the apparent simplicity of the registration procedure, the main difficulty lies in proving that the trademark is well known.

As a rule, the period for consideration of an application is 10 months. The procedure includes:

1) acceptance and registration of the application;
2) verification of the payment of the fee and submission of necessary documents;
3) consideration of the application;
4) the inclusion of a well-known trademark in the list of well-known trademarks and issuance of a certificate (from January 17, 2021, well-known trademark recognition certificates are issued in electronic form and, at the applicant's request, on paper).

As per the Administrative Procedure for the Recognition of a Trademark or a Sign Used as a Trademark as a Well-known Trademark, the fact that a trademark or a sign is well known can be confirmed by documents containing the following information:

- the active use of the trademark or the sign within the territory of the Russian Federation, in particular. On the applicant's initiative, the date of the trademark's first use, the list of towns and cities where the sale of goods marked with the trademark or the sign is carried out, the sales of these goods, ways of using the trademark or the sign, the average annual number of consumers of the product, the position of the manufacturer on the market, etc., are also stated;
- the countries in which the trademark or the sign have become well known;
- the expenses for the advertising of the trademark or the sign (for instance, the annual financial report);
- the cost (value) of the trademark according to the annual financial reports;
- the results of a consumer survey about the well-known trademark or the sign carried out by a specialized independent organization.

In addition to the documents confirming that a trademark or a sign are well known, the following papers shall also be submitted:

- request form for recognition of a trademark or a sign as a well-known trademark;
- power of attorney certifying the authority of the applicant's representative, should the applicant be submitting the application through a representative;
- translation of a power of attorney and (or) materials into Russian, signed by the translator, should they be submitted in another language;
- sample of a sign used as a trademark, drawn up in accordance with the requirements (if the submitted application is for a sign used as a trademark).

The acceptance of the documents can be refused due to the following reasons:

- the request is unreadable,
- the request was submitted in a language other than Russian,
- the request does not indicate the applicant or their location or place of residence,
- the data storage device that contains the request is out of service.

This list is exhaustive.

If no problems related to the documents arise and the state fee has been paid, the application shall be considered at Rospatent's board meeting. The board considers all the materials submitted by the applicant and hears the arguments of the applicant or the applicant's representative. At the end of the meeting, the board announces the results of the application consideration.

Rospatent refuses to recognize a trademark or a sign as well known if at least one of the conditions listed below occurs:

- the materials submitted by the applicant do not confirm that a trademark (sign) has been well known from the date specified in the application (for example, a trademark is known only to specialists and not consumers);
- the trademark and the sign have become widely known after the priority date of an identical or confusingly similar trademark of another person, intended for use in relation to similar goods.

In addition, the specialists of Rospatent point out that a connection between the applicant and the goods in respect of which the trademark/sign is used shall be required. If such a connection is not established, recognition of the trademark as well known can be refused. However, such a refusal can be challenged in court.

It should be noted that when considering refusals to recognize a trademark as well known in a judicial proceeding, the courts refer to the "Joint Recommendation on the Provisions Regarding the Protection of Well-Known Marks", adopted September 20–29, 1999, by the Assembly of the Paris

Union for the Protection of Industrial Property and the General Assembly of the World Intellectual Property Organization (WIPO) at the 34th Series of Meetings of the WIPO Member States Assembly.

In addition to the risk that a trademark will be refused recognition as well known, there is also a risk of the termination of its legal protection based on the loss of the features of a well-known trademark. However, the recognition of a trademark as well known, of course, can become a significant asset for an organization, strengthening its position on the market.

Appellations of the origin of goods and geographical indication also require state registration since it leads to their recognition and protection.

Applications shall be submitted to Rospatent. There are currently four application forms:

1) an application for the state registration of a geographical indication and the granting of an exclusive right to such a geographical indication (hereinafter application for a geographical indication);
2) an application for the granting of an exclusive right to a previously registered geographical indication (hereinafter an application for a previously registered geographical indication);
3) an application for the state registration of an appellation of origin and for the granting of an exclusive right to such an appellation (hereinafter an application for an appellation of origin);
4) an application for granting an exclusive right to a previously registered appellation of origin (hereinafter an application for a previously registered appellation of origin).

The applicants can be one or more citizens or one or more legal entities as well as an association of persons whose creation and activities do not contradict the legislation of the country of origin of the goods.

The application includes:

- a request, the form of which was approved by Order of the Ministry of Economic Development No. 398 of July 3, 2020 (depending on the selected type of application);
- the sign being registered;
- an indication of the goods in respect of which the state registration of the geographical indication or appellation of origin of goods or the granting of the exclusive right are requested;
- an indication of the place of origin (production) of goods (boundaries of a geographical object);
- an explanation of the relation between the goods' characteristics and its place of origin (production) (for geographical indication)/between the specific properties of the goods and the geographical object (for the appellation of origin of goods);
- a description of the product characteristics (for a geographical indication)/ specific properties of the goods (for an appellation of origin of goods),

including the source material used to manufacture the product, the physical, chemical, microbiological, organoleptic or artistic features of the product;

- a description of the production method, as well as the conditions of the goods' storage and transportation if this has a significant impact on the formation and preservation of the characteristics of the goods (for a geographical indication)/specific properties of the goods (for an appellation of origin of goods);
- a description of the procedure for the monitoring of the product's compliance with the conditions of production and the preservation of the product's characteristics (for a geographical indication)/specific properties of the goods (for an appellation of origin of goods) in respect of which the legal protection is sought;
- a list of persons entitled to use the sign (for a geographical indication/an appellation of origin of goods) (if an application is filed by an association of persons, then the conditions for the use of the geographical indication/appellation of origin of goods are presented too);
- information confirming the right to carry out the production of goods if it is required by federal laws.

According to Article 1522 of the Civil Code, the application shall include the documents confirming that the products produced by the applicant comply with the requirements related to the geographical origin as well as other data mentioned above.

As follows from Article 1522.1 of the Civil Code, an application for an appellation of origin of goods shall be accompanied by the conclusion confirming that the applicant produces goods, the special properties of which are determined by the natural conditions and (or) human factors typical of the given geographical object, as well as the documents confirming that such an appellation is known in relation to this type of goods. An application for exclusive right includes the conclusion of the authorized authority that the applicant produces goods with special properties specified in the State Register of Geographical Indications and Appellations of Origins of Goods within the boundaries of a given geographical object.

In accordance with Decree of the Government of the Russian Federation No. 1195 of August 8, 2020, "On Federal Executive Authorities Authorized to Issue Conclusions Necessary for the State Registration of an Appellation of Origin and the Implementation of Legally Significant Actions in Relation to a Registered Appellation of Origin of Goods, and the Invalidation of Some Acts of the Government of the Russian Federation", the Ministry of Health (concerning medical mud and mineral water), the Ministry of Industry and Trade (concerning arts and crafts and musical instruments), the Ministry of Agriculture (concerning agricultural products and food products, except for mineral water, alcohol and alcohol-containing products) and the Federal

Service for the Regulation of the Alcohol Market (concerning alcohol and alcohol-containing products) have the authority to do it.

The registration procedure includes the following steps:

- filing an application,
- formal examination,
- examination of the sign claimed as a geographical indication or an appellation of origin of goods,
- making a decision on the application.

The application is submitted to Rospatent. Payment of a state fee is required. Application documents are submitted:

- online (the official website of Rospatent or through the PSP),
- in person,
- by post,
- by fax.

The formal examination involves checking the availability of the necessary documents and their compliance with the requirements. If additional materials are needed, then a proposal is sent to the applicant to provide the necessary information within three months from the date of the request. If the formal examination ended positively, then a decision is made to accept the application for substantive consideration. In this case, Rospatent publishes information about it in the official bulletin to provide an opportunity for any person to get acquainted with it. After the publication of the information, any person, within three months, has the right to submit an objection to the grant of legal protection and (or) to the granting of the exclusive right.

In addition, Rospatent shall notify the supervisory authorities,[3] the highest official of the corresponding constituent entity of the Russian Federation (the head of the supreme executive body of the relevant constituent entity), as well as the professional associations of manufacturers, information about which is posted on Rospatent's official website of such applications.

The examination of a sign claimed as a geographical indication includes checking its compliance with the characteristics of a geographical indication and the possibility of its registration as such, and the availability of the necessary information and documents. The same applies to the appellation of origin of goods.

It should be noted that according to Article 1516 of the Civil Code, state registration as a geographical indication or an appellation of origin of goods shall not be allowed for a sign:

1. that, although it refers to the name of a geographical object, is commonly used as a sign of a certain type of product, no matter its place of production;

2 registered as a geographical indication or appellation of origin of goods in relation to goods of the same type;
3 identical or similar to a trademark that has an earlier priority, if the use of such a geographical indication or such an appellation of origin can mislead the consumer about the goods or their manufacturer;
4 representing the name of a plant variety or an animal breed, if the use of such a geographical indication or such an appellation of origin of goods can mislead the consumer about the goods or their manufacturer;
5 capable of misleading the consumer about the product or its manufacturer;
6 filed for the state registration as a geographical indication or appellation of origin of goods for products that do not meet the legal requirements for geographical indications and appellations of origin of goods.

In the case of a positive decision by Rospatent on the state registration of a geographical indication/appellation of origin and the granting of an exclusive right to it and (or) the decision granting an exclusive right (if the registration of a geographical indication or an appellation of origin took place earlier), the corresponding data is entered into the State Register of Geographical Indications and Appellations of Origins of Goods, and a certificate is issued. The information is also published in the official bulletin.

The exclusive right to a geographical indication or an appellation of origin of goods is valid for 10 years from the date of filing an application. It can be extended at the request of the right holder.

The registration provides an opportunity to use geographical indication or appellation of origin of goods. However, the legal protection of the corresponding objects can be terminated. The provisions, indicated below, applies to the appellations of origin of goods as well.

This occurs in the case of:

1 the disappearance of the characteristics typical of the given geographical object and the impossibility of producing goods with the characteristics indicated in the State Register of Geographical Indications and Appellations of Origins of Goods concerning this geographical indication;
2 termination of the legal protection of a geographical indication in the country of origin.

The termination of the legal protection of a geographical indication in the country of origin can occur in the following situations:

- the goods produced by the right holder is inconsistent with the characteristics of the goods indicated in the State Register of Geographical Indications and Appellations of Origins of Goods concerning this geographical indication;
- the right holder loses the right to the production of goods with the characteristics specified in the State Register of Geographical Indications and Appellations of Origins of Goods concerning this geographical indication;

- the goods do not comply with the requirements based on the geographical indication or the appellation of origin established by federal laws and other regulatory legal acts of the Russian Federation;
- systematic violation of the production method and the storage and transportation conditions indicated in the State Register of Geographical Indications and Appellations of Origins of Goods;
- termination of the legal protection of the object;
- termination of the legal entity, cessation of the individual entrepreneur's status, or death of the owner (for right holders);
- expiration of the exclusive right;
- the owner of the exclusive right submits a corresponding application to Rospatent;
- a foreign legal entity, a foreign citizen or a stateless person loses the right to the given geographical indication in the country of origin of the goods.

Selection breeding achievements (plant varieties and animal breeds) are also subject to state registration, but it is not carried out by Rospatent but by the State Sort Commission. State registration, as a result of which a patent is issued, mediates the recognition and protection of an exclusive right. The period of validity of the exclusive right to a breeding achievement is 30 years. It is calculated from the date of the state registration of the breeding achievement in the State Register of Protected Breeding Achievements.

It is important to note that, in accordance with Article 1436 of the Civil Code, a selective breeding achievement for which an application is filed obtains temporary legal protection from the application date and until the date of the issuance of a patent for a breeding achievement. A patent for the selective breeding achievement certifies the priority of the selective breeding achievement, its authorship and the exclusive right to the breeding achievement.

As it was pointed out in section "The state regulation of IP" the author of a breeding achievement has the right to obtain an author's certificate.

The priority of a selective breeding achievement is established by the date of receipt of a patent application.

Issues regarding obtaining a patent for a breeding achievement are regulated by the Civil Code, as well as by the "Rules for the Preparation and Filing of an Application for the Grant of a Patent for a Breeding Achievement", approved by the Ministry of Agriculture and Food of the Russian Federation No. 2-01/3 of October 14, 1994.

The right to file an application and obtain a patent belongs to the author of the selection breeding achievement. However, it can be transferred to another person.

The application contains the following documents:

- a request form,
- a profile of a plant variety or a breed,

- a document confirming the right to submit an application (for legal successors and intermediaries).

An application for granting a patent for a selective breeding achievement and all corresponding documents are submitted in Russian or another language. If the documents are submitted in another language, their translation into Russian shall be attached to the application. The name of the foreign breeding achievement is recorded in the applicant's language and Russian.

A patent can be obtained if the selection breeding achievement meets the following criteria: novelty, distinctness, uniformity, stability (also, see section "Intellectual property: concept and types"). The above is confirmed through special verification activities.

After filing an application, a preliminary examination is carried out, during which the availability of the necessary documents and their compliance with the established requirements are checked; this takes one month. After its completion, the accepted status of the application is published in the official bulletin. This makes the information available to an unlimited number of people so that any interested person can request the claimed selective breeding achievement be examined for novelty (within six months from the date of publication of the information about the application). The "Regulations for Making a Decision on an Application for a Breeding Achievement Patent", approved by the State Commission of the Russian Federation for testing and protection of breeding achievements on February 10, 1997, No. 12-04/01, mentions this document under the name of a "claim regarding the novelty of the claimed variety".

Uniformity, distinctness and stability are checked by tests carried out by the State Sort Commission and other Russian organizations that have agreements with the State Sort Commission. The results of the tests carried out by the competent authorities of other states with which there are agreements and the data provided by the applicant can also be used.

Should all the requirements be met, including the name requirement, a decision to issue a patent for a selective breeding achievement is made, a description of the breeding achievement is given and the selective breeding achievement is included in the State Register of Protected Breeding Achievements.

At the same time, even with a patent for a breeding achievement, it should be borne in mind that the patent holder must see to it that the plant variety or the animal breed maintains the characteristics specified in the description of the plant variety or animal breed contained in the State Register of Protected Breeding Achievements during the full term of the patent for a selective breeding achievement. The patent holder must also, at their own expense, send seeds or breeding material for control tests and provide conditions for an on-site inspection. The case for early termination of the patent may occur if:

1 the breeding achievement no longer meets the criteria for uniformity and stability;

2 the patent holder failed within 12 months to provide seeds or breeding material, submit documents and information necessary to verify the safety of the breeding achievement or failed to provide conditions for an on-site inspection of the selective breeding achievement at the request of the federal executive body for breeding achievements.

Furthermore, the Civil Code provides for the possibility of issuing a compulsory licence for breeding achievements. After 3 years from the date of issuing a breeding achievement patent, any person who is willing and ready to use the selective breeding achievement, and if the patent holder refuses to conclude a licence agreement for the production or sale of seeds or breeding material on conditions consistent with the established practice, has the right to apply to the court with a claim to the patent holder for the provision of a compulsory simple (non-exclusive) licence to use such a breeding achievement in the territory of the Russian Federation. In the claim, this person must indicate the conditions proposed by them for obtaining such a licence, including the scope of use, the amount, procedure and terms of payments. If the patentee does not prove that there are valid reasons preventing them from granting the right to use the selective breeding achievement to another person, the court decides on the grant of said licence and the conditions for the grant. The total amount of payment for such a licence established by a court decision cannot be lower than the price of the licence determined under comparable circumstances.

Thus, obtaining a patent for a breeding achievement does not imply the possibility of completely blocking other persons' actions in terms of the achievement and it does not mean that the person who carried out the registration will fully control the registered object.

The Civil Code also provides for the possibility of registering computer programs, databases and topographies of integrated circuits. However, unlike the above situations, it is not mandatory but is carried out at the request of the right holder.

Thus, to register the topographies of integrated circuits, an application containing a request form and the deposited materials identifying the topography, including an abstract, should be submitted to Rospatent (the rules for filling out an application are regulated by Order of the Ministry of Economic Development of the Russian Federation No. 699 of September 30, 2015).

As a rule, the state registration and issuance of a certificate can take up to 62 working days from the date of receipt of the application. The topography of an integrated microcircuit is entered into the register, a certificate is issued and corresponding information is published in Rospatent's official bulletin in the case of a positive decision about the application.

The decision is positive if:

- the two-year term from the date of first use of the topography of the integrated circuit for the submission of the application is met or if the first use took place before the submission of the application;

- the necessary documents and materials of the application meet the requirements;
- the state fee has been paid.

As stated earlier, the public registration of such objects of IP rights is not mandatory. For instance, the registration of a computer program is carried out at the request of the right holder; it is not mandatory for providing judicial protection of the legitimate interests of the respective copyright holder (Resolution of the Eighteenth State Commercial Court of Appeal of July 18, 2012, on case No. A07-23757/2011).

In this case, the presumption of the reliability of the information entered in the register of computer programs or the register of databases applies. The applicant is responsible for the accuracy of the information provided for the state registration.

Rospatent carries out the registration of computer programs and databases. The following documents are required:

- a state registration application,
- materials identifying a computer program or database, including an abstract.

A substantive examination is not carried out. Rospatent is not required to verify the identity of the computer programs submitted for the state registration (Resolution of the Ninth Commercial Court of Appeal of April 24, 2019, on case No. A40-188731/18).

The submitted documents are checked for their sufficiency and compliance with the requirements, and unless any inconsistencies are found, the object is entered into the register.

When entered into the register, the relevant information becomes public. However, it should be borne in mind that no deposit, registration, or other formalities are required to recognise and exercise copyright (Review of IP Judicial Practice, 2015).

As for other objects of copyright, they are not subject to state registration. However, they can be deposited; it is a procedure for the voluntary, non-state registration of copyright objects by entering them into the non-state register. However, there is no special single register. Organizations that provide depositing have independent registers that contain necessary information about the copyright object and issue a confirmation certificate to the copyright holder. The deposit procedure is also determined by these organizations independently.

The deposit of a work is voluntary and not required by law; the occurrence of any consequences is thus not specified either (Resolution of the Presidium of the Intellectual Property Court of February 17, 2020, on case No. SIP-598/2019).

As pointed out by the Supreme Court, the fact of depositing only confirms the existence of copyright objects at the time of depositing; it does not confirm the authorship right to these objects (Ruling of the Judicial Collegium for Economic Disputes of the Supreme Court of the Russian Federation of September 17, 2020, on case No. A40-46622/2019).

A deposit certificate does not prove the existence of any rights to the work. For example, hearing a case based on the claim for the protection of exclusive property rights, the court rejected the plaintiff's argument that his copyright to the script in question being a subject matter of IP is confirmed by a registration certificate of a work of art, since the mentioned organization is not an authorized body for registration, establishment or confirmation of anyone's copyright (Resolution of the Intellectual Property Court of November 26, 2019, on case No. A40-230948/2016); it can be taken into account along with other evidence. The authorship is only confirmed by the evidence proving the creation of the work by a specific person (for example, testimony, evidence based on the establishment of the author's creative style, etc.) (Resolution of the Presidium of the Intellectual Property Court of February 17, 2020, on case No. SIP-598/2019). It is noteworthy that a similar position arises concerning optional state registration. So, in the judgement, it was noted that the plaintiffs' arguments that their authorship of computer programs confirmed by certificates of state registration of computer programs were not taken into account, since by virtue of Article 1262 of the Civil Code of the Russian Federation, such registration is of a declarative nature (Review of IP Judicial Practice, 2015).

If the registration was unlawfully carried out by another person who, in reality, is not the author, then the authorship should be disputed, not the validity of the deposit (Resolution of the Intellectual Property Court of May 4, 2018, on case No. A40-98194/2017).

Thus, regardless of whether the registration stipulates the legal protection of the IP subject matter, this procedure helps to inform an indefinite group of people about its existence. Given that the relevant data is public, anyone can access it. In the Russian Federation, this is implemented through official bulletins, by granting public access to registries on the internet and via information requests.

The importance of information for modern society cannot be overemphasized. Paraphrasing the well-known expression, it can be said that "Information is power". The person who has information can identify risks, make predictions and determine a plan for further action, which is crucial in any business. A lack of information seriously hinders further development and operation.

In accordance with the Law on Information, information is data regardless of the form of the presentation. One of the legal principles regulating the relations in the information field is the freedom of search, receipt, transfer, production and distribution of information in any legal way. The corresponding provision is also enshrined in part 4, Article 29 of the Constitution of the Russian Federation. Thus, by having the information entered into the register, the person automatically agrees to make the information publicly available.

At the same time, information openness can have several attitudes to it when it comes to the private interests of the author/right holder. On the one hand, this allows the author/right holder to be identified and indicates the existence of the appropriate rights, warning third parties against possible violations. On the other hand, it allows the creation of similar IP subject matter. It does not violate the law if the IP subject matter is not simply copied but rather serves as a prototype. From the standpoint of public interest, this circumstance can hardly be called negative since society needs development, ideas that allow new things, improve old ideas and apply new approaches to long-known phenomena. However, for the author/right holder, the loss of uniqueness threatens to devalue the object and, as a result, decreases the effectiveness of its use. The lack of registration also has well-known negative consequences. In order to avoid the dissemination of information about the IP subject matter, but at the same time protect it, one often refers to know-how, which will be described in section "Intellectual resources and human capital".

Notes

1 The Public Services Portal is a part of the infrastructure that provides data exchange and technological interaction of information systems used for rendering state and municipal services in electronic form. It can be accessed here: https://www.gosuslugi.ru/.

2 Universal succession can be defined as the transfer of the totality of the rights and obligations (inheritance, reorganization of a legal entity).

3 The stages and boundaries of the production of the goods, as well as the characteristics of the goods or special properties of the goods, for which a geographical indication or appellation of origin is used, must comply with the requirements established by federal laws and other regulatory legal acts of the Russian Federation. Control over compliance with the established requirements shall be carried out in accordance with federal laws (Article 1516 of the Civil Code).

6 Intellectual resources and human capital

Most modern business entities need to attract skilled people. Even the most automatized production site requires human supervision. It is not the mere presence of a person that is important, but their qualification and the ability to perform one's duties properly. Thus, when searching for a potential employee, their knowledge, competences and skills, as well as their ability to implement them efficiently, play a crucial role. At the same time, from the standpoint of business processes, it is not a single individual's capital that will be of particular interest, but rather the total human capital, and that is the staff's collective set of personal qualities that are used in the production process in one way or another.

The creation of intellectual property (IP) subject matter is a perfect example of activities in which the participation of people with a certain set of intellectual qualities and skills is necessary.

Surely, one can argue and draw attention to so-called artificial intelligence, with the help of which IP subject matter can also be created. Despite the fact that artificial intelligence can be considered as a simulated (artificially reproduced) human intellectual activity,[1] it has not yet become a full-fledged replacement for traditional intellectual activity, although its ever-growing role can hardly be denied. Nevertheless, the lack of ubiquity or complete autonomy from human supervision does not allow one to equate artificial with traditional types of intelligence.

Unresolved legal issues also do not add to its consolidation as a complete alternative to traditional intelligence; for example, there are problems such as the need to separate objects created by artificial and traditional intelligence, authorship of the objects created using an artificial intelligence technology, the normative establishment of their turnover, etc. In addition, the secondary nature (dependence) of artificial intelligence should be recognized because it has originated from the human mind and human specialists are required for its creation. Thus, in the near future, an alternative to traditional human intelligence, including in the field of IP, is unlikely to be found.

IP subject matter can be created by employees as a part of their labour duties, that is, within the framework of labour relations, which are regulated by the Labour Code of the Russian Federation No. 197-FZ of December 30, 2001 (hereinafter the Labour Code).

It is important to differentiate labour and civil relations. Labour relations are regulated by the Labour Code whereas civil relations are managed by the Civil Code. As it was explained, within the context of labour relations the employee didn't act as an independent economic entity and didn't bear corresponding risks (Resolution of the Eighth State Commercial Court of Appeal of May 6, 2019, on case No. A70-19660/2018). The aim of the employment contract is to specify the peculiarities of the labour process, while the civil contract is intended to define the certain result of the work. The conclusion of civil contracts instead of employment ones is prohibited.

Labour relations arise between the employee and the employer on the basis of an employment contract that is an agreement between the employer and the employee, according to which the employer undertakes to provide the employee with work according to the specified labour function, to ensure the work conditions provided in the labour legislation and other regulatory legal acts containing labour law norms, collective agreements, contracts, local regulations and this agreement, pay a salary to the employee promptly and in full, and the employee undertakes to personally perform the labour function defined by this agreement in the interests, under the management and control of the employer, to comply with the internal labour regulations set by the given employer.

Fulfilling one's labour duties in good faith (subclause 2, clause 2 of Article 21 of the Labour Code) is required from all employees. These requirements can be specified in the local regulations adopted by the employer, including job descriptions (Ruling of the Constitutional Court of December 19, 2019, on case No. 3361-O). Despite the fact that the Labour Code does not contain any mention of the job description, it is an important document that contains not only the employee's job function, range of job duties and limits of responsibility, but also the qualification requirements for the position held. The job description can be an appendix to an employment contract or can be approved as an independent document (Letter of Federal Service for Labour and Employment (Rostrud) No. 4412-6 of October 31, 2007).

In the process of performing their labour function, an employee may create some protectable results of intellectual activity. The Civil Code provides the following list of items:

- work created under an employment contract (Article 1295 of the Civil Code),
- performance created as a part of the job duties established for the employee (performer) (Article 1320 of the Civil Code),
- invention, utility model or industrial design made under an employment contract (Article 1370 of the Civil Code),
- selective breeding achievement made under an employment contract (Article 1430 of the Civil Code),
- topography of an integrated circuit made under an employment contract (Article 1461 of the Civil Code),

- production secret (know-how) created under an employment contract (Article 1470 of the Civil Code).

The main criterion that allows one to classify any of the above as made under an employment contract is their emergence as the result of the employee's performance of their job duties. In this regard, the following issues can be studied: the relation of the employer's job and the field to which the corresponding object belongs; the limits of the employee's work duties; the place where the protected objects were being created; the source of equipment and tools used to create them; the employer's possible control over the work processes as a part of which the protected object was created; the purpose of creating the protected object; the behaviour of the employee and the employer after the creation; the documents compiled in the course of the employee's labour activity, which, put together, can evidence the development of the objects in the course of fulfilling one's labour duties (Resolution of the Intellectual Property Court of August 18, 2020, on case No. A40-256611/2017).

If the object was not created during the performance of work duties, the created result cannot be considered as achieved under an employment contract. In this case, the relations between the parties will be regulated on a general basis, without applying special rules.

The obligation to prove that the intellectual activity result originated during and within the limits of an employee's work duties belongs to the employer.

As a rule, the main source of information is the employment contract and the job description, if the latter exists at all.

Resolution of the Plenum of the Supreme Court No. 10 specifically clarifies that, with regard to inventions, utility models and industrial designs, the recognition of a technical solution as one made under an employment contract does not require that the document defining the employee's labour obligations (labour contract, job description) indicate the creation of a particular patentable object or the improvement of a known technical solution. The crucial factor for the recognition of a technical solution as the one made under an employment contract is its creation within the framework of one's labour duties which proceed from the labour function or a specific task given by the employer.

At the same time, as noted in the Review of IP Judicial Practice, 2015, a work assignment can be given by the employer only within the limits of the labour duties established for the employee (author).

However, the performance of an assignment beyond one's working hours does not indicate that the achieved result shall not be considered as made under an employment contract. The employee's use of their own material resources to fulfil the task cannot be irrefutable evidence against the above, either (Appeal Ruling of the Penza Region Court of June 16, 2015, on case No. 33-1578/2015).

It should be noted that a dispute about the origin of a created intellectual result often becomes the basis for making an application to the court to invalidate the issued patent due to the incorrect indication of the right holder.

However, the result of intellectual activity being conducted under an employment contract or not is secondary as regards the issue of its recognition as protectable. For example, in one case, claims to recover compensation were denied because the project documentation produced by the plaintiff was not subject to copyright. As it was explained, the copyright object did not include the construction documentation in general, but only the architectural project, that is to say, the architectural part of the documentation, which described the architectural solution. The documentation produced by the plaintiff was part of the design documentation for the object and was not an architectural project. It also did not contain the description of the architectural solutions (Ruling of the Supreme Court of the Russian Federation of November 11, 2014, on case No. A40-97747/12).

It is noteworthy that the use of the employer's resources cannot be recognized as unambiguous evidence that the object was created under an employment contract.

At the same time, for some objects, there are specific legal instructions as regards the consequences of an employee creating IP subject matter using the employer's financial, technical or other material resources, but not in connection with the fulfilment of one's work duties or specifically assigned task. Such results will not be recognized as made under an employment contract, and the right to obtain a patent on and the exclusive right to such objects belongs to the employee. However, in this case, the guarantee that the employer's interest is taken into account is demonstrated through their right to demand a gratuitous simple (non-exclusive) licence to use the created result of intellectual activity for their own purposes for the entire duration of the exclusive right or the reimbursement of the expenses incurred in connection with the creation of such objects.

If the intellectual result is recognized as created under an employment contract, then the issues concerning the distribution of the emerging rights and the possibility of remuneration will inevitably arise.

With regard to the exclusive rights, the Civil Code establishes the following procedure for the distribution of rights: personal non-property rights belong to the author, and the exclusive right, as a general rule, goes to the employer. At the same time, the law does not require the conclusion of a licence agreement or an exclusive rights alienation agreement between the employee and the employer (Resolution of the Intellectual Property Court of June 1, 2015, on case No. A45-8050/2014).

However, another variant of the exclusive right distribution can be agreed. For example, special rules have been established by law to regulate the relationship between the parties to an employment contract in a situation where the exclusive right remains with the employee who created the work. In this case, the employer has the right to use that work under the terms of a simple (non-exclusive) licence with the remuneration paid to the copyright holder (a similar rule applies to the topography of an integrated circuit). The limits of the use of a work created under an employment contract, the amount, conditions and procedure for the payment of remuneration are determined by the agreement between the employer and the author or by the court in the event of a dispute.

The existence of an agreement that defines these aspects of the relationship between the parties may also become a subject of legal proceedings. For instance, an employer tried to invalidate the civil contract concluded with the employee because, in the opinion of the employer, according to said contract, the employee was paid for the work that was expressly stipulated in his employment contract. The court considered that it was not a case of duplication since identical duties were not found in the employment contract (Appeal Ruling of the Moscow City Court of August 22, 2016, on case No. 33-27167/2016).

With regard to the inventions, utility models, industrial designs and selective breeding achievements created under an employment contract, the employees shall follow the algorithm enshrined in the Civil Code unless otherwise agreed.

The employee is obliged to notify the employer in writing about the creation of a protectable IP subject matter in connection with the performance of their labour duties or a specific task assigned by the employer. However, the law does not describe the fulfilment of this obligation in detail, which once even served as the basis for a complaint to the Constitutional Court of the Russian Federation. The applicant pointed out that the legal provision did not contain an exact list of data to be included in a written notification to the employer about the creation of a protectable result, placing the employer in a privileged position and leading to an arbitrary decision of the question whether the employee did fulfil this obligation. However, the Constitutional Court of the Russian Federation did not receive a complaint for consideration, indicating that the contested norm per se, aimed at ensuring a balance of interests of the employer who possesses the exclusive right to the created under an employment contract invention, utility model or industrial design and the right to obtain a patent (clause 3 of Article 1370 of the Civil Code), and the employee who created the invention, utility model or industrial design as a part of their work duties or a specific task, cannot be regarded as violating the applicants' constitutional rights in the way indicated in the complaint (Ruling of the Constitutional Court of the Russian Federation No. 1204-O of May 28, 2020).

At the same time, the employee's failure to notify the employer about the created solution has no legal significance for recognizing the solution as made under an employment contract, given that other conditions are necessary to establish the nature of a technical solution, namely the fact of its creation during the performance of labour duties (Resolution of the Presidium of the Intellectual Property Court of June 3, 2014, on case No. SIP-253/2013).

The employer who received the corresponding notification has 4 months to decide on further action as regards the obtained intellectual result. As noted in Ruling of the Constitutional Court of the Russian Federation of May 28, 2013, No. 876-O, it is the employer that the legislator provides with the right to choose the methods of protection and use of the result of intellectual activity achieved under an employment contract.

The employer can exercise this right in the following ways:

- apply for a patent,
- transfer the right to obtain a patent on an employee's invention, utility model or industrial design to another person,
- notify the employee about keeping information about the corresponding result of intellectual activity in secret.

If they do not take any of the actions, the right to obtain a patent shall be returned to the employee. In this case, the employer, during the term of the patent, has the right to use the result obtained under an employment contract in the production on the terms of a simple (non-exclusive) licence paying remuneration to the patent holder; the amount, conditions and procedure for the remuneration payment are determined by the agreement between the employee and the employer, or by the court in the event of a dispute.

With regard to the works and performances created under an employment contract, the exclusive right can also be returned to the employee. This can happen if, within three years from the day when the work was placed at the employer's disposal, they have not started to use it, have not transferred the exclusive right to it to another person or informed the author about keeping the work secret.

As explained in Resolution of the Plenum of the Supreme Court No. 10, if the exclusive right to the work originally belongs to the author (employee) under an agreement with the employer or on the basis of subclause 2, clause 2 of Article 1295 of the Civil Code, the employer has the right to use such a work under a simple (non-exclusive) licence paying remuneration to the author, as well as transferring this right to a third party. The limits of the use of such a work, the amount, conditions and procedure for the remuneration are determined by an agreement between the employer and the author and by the court in the event of a dispute. In this case, the author also has the right to use said work or to transfer the exclusive right belonging to them at their own discretion, while the employer retains a non-exclusive licence on the same conditions.

The author's right to remuneration for the work created under an employment contract emerges when the employer begins to use it. However, other cases in which it may take place are also provided in the Civil Code. For example, for works and performances, the transfer of the exclusive right to another person and the employer's decision to keep the result secret can cause the emergence of such a right. The amount of remuneration, conditions and procedure for its payment are set by the contract between the employer and the employee and by the court in the event of a dispute.

With regard to an invention, utility model and industrial design, the grounds to receive renumeration are: receipt of a patent and non-receipt of a patent for reasons that depend on the employer,the transfer of the exclusive right and keeping it secret. The details of the remuneration shall also be determined by an agreement between the parties and by the court if a dispute arises.

For example, the court rejected an argument about the inclusion of the author's remuneration in the employee's salary, pointing out that no specific clause of the employment contract that shall stipulate the amount, conditions and procedure for the payment was cited. The citation of the general provision that stated the possibility of such an inclusion was not taken into account, since this provision of the employment contract did not disclose the exact amount, conditions and procedure for the payment (Ruling of the Civil Collegium of the Supreme Court of the Russian Federation of June 5, 2020, on case No. 2-5974/2018). On the contrary, in another case, it was established that the remuneration for the works created by the employee was included in the employee's salary (Ruling of the Constitutional Court of the Russian Federation of April 25, 2019, on case No. 1016-O).

It should be noted that in the Russian Federation, there are special "Rules for the Payment of Remuneration for Inventions, Utility Models, Industrial Designs Created under an Employment Contract", approved by Resolution of the Government of the Russian Federation No. 1848 of November 16, 2020. These rates, procedure and terms shall be applied if the employer and the employee have not entered into an agreement establishing the amount, conditions and procedure for the remuneration paid to the employee for their invention, utility model and/or industrial design created under an employment contract.

This document deals with two types of remuneration: for the creation of the result and for its use. The one for the creation of an invention is paid to the employee who is the author of such an invention in the amount of 30 per cent of their average salary, and for the creation of a utility model or an industrial design, the employer shall pay 20 per cent of the worker's average salary. If the employer uses an employee's invention, the employee is paid remuneration in the amount of three average salaries for the last 12 calendar months when the invention was used; for a utility model or industrial design, the remuneration amounts to two average salaries for the last 12 calendar months when the utility model or industrial design was used. In the event of the termination of the labour relations between the employer and the employee, the employer shall be obliged to pay remuneration to the author of such an invention, industrial design or utility model in accordance with the rules.

Resolution of the Plenum of the Supreme Court No. 10 explicitly stipulates that the obligation to pay remuneration to the employee (author) does not depend on the actual use or non-use of the invention, utility model or industrial design created under the employment contract. At the same time, the amount of remuneration agreed by the employee (author) and the employer may depend on the actual use due to the nature of the work. The remuneration payment to the employee (author) shall be carried out within the term of the patent (clauses 132–133).

In relation to a selective breeding achievement, the payment of remuneration for its use is also established. The Civil Code directly provides that the employee has the right to receive remuneration from the employer for the use of the created, derived or identified selective breeding achievement in the amount and on the terms determined by the agreement between them, but not less than the amount of two per cent of the annual income from the use of the selective breeding achievement, including the income from granting of licences. The disputes about the payment of remuneration shall be resolved in court.

With regard to the topography of an integrated circuit, the Civil Code also entitles the employee (author) to receive remuneration from the employer. All the details are set by the agreement or, in its absence, by the court.

In all cases, the right to remuneration is inalienable.

Among the results of intellectual activity, a special place is occupied by know-how (production secret), which is understood as a secret of production created by an employee in connection with the fulfilment of their job duties or a specific assignment. Know-how is an internal business tool that allows one to keep commercially relevant information secret from third parties. In fact, this represents a special legal regime that performs a protective function. Unlike several other IP subjects matter, for which publicity is an integral feature (for example, information about a subject matter that will be entered into special registers), in case of know-how, the information is kept secret.

Previously, it was obligatory to recognize know-how as a commercial secret (a commercial secret is a confidentiality mode that allows the information owner, under the existing or possible circumstances, to increase income, avoid unjustified expenses and/or maintain a position in the market of goods, works and services or obtain another commercial benefit) (Federal Law No. 98-FZ of July 29, 2004, "On Commercial Secrets"). Since October 1, 2014, it has become optional, but the owner of such information shall take reasonable measures to maintain its confidentiality, e.g. adopting internal acts regulating the work with know-how, signing a non-disclosure obligation, including corresponding provisions in the employment contract, establishing a special regime for the work with confidential data, for example, a ban on external email address data transfer, etc. (Ruling of the Constitutional Court of the Russian Federation of February on case No. 457-O 28, 2019; Appeal Ruling of the Voronezh Region Court of August 6, 2019, on case No. 2-1763/2019).

Information can be recognized as a production secret on two conditions that shall arise simultaneously: the information shall not be known to third parties, and it shall have actual or potential value for the owner (Ruling of the Third Cassation Court of General Jurisdiction of July 20, 2020, on case No. 88-9350/2020).

It is noteworthy that with regard to know-how, the transfer of the exclusive right to a production secret to the employee is not mentioned in the legislation. There are also no provisions on the payment of remuneration. In general, there are no norms that are dedicated to personal non-property rights. The absence of the author may indicate that know-how is inherently close to the means of individualizing goods, works, services and enterprises, although it is not directly related to them by the Civil Code.

Discussing the absence of the author figure, Victor A. Dozortsev noted that the original right (in the absence of the right of authorship) was assigned to those who have the resources for the creation of the solution, thanks to which the object arose at all, and the right was not attributed to those who actually created the IP subject matter (Dozortsev, 2003, pp. 253–254). With regard to the know-how achieved under employment contracts, the exclusive right shall belong to the employer.

Despite the rather thorough regulation of this area, the number of disputes arising in connection with intellectual results created under employment contracts is quite large. That is why one should take into account the risks that may accompany the creation and use of such solutions and also make an attempt to manage them. In accordance with GOST R 56823-2015 "National Standard of the Russian Federation. Intellectual Property. Results of Intellectual Activity Created under an Employment Contract", approved and put into effect by Order of Rosstandart No. 2102-st of December 3, 2015, the risk management (identification, minimization, control) of the results of intellectual activity created under employment contracts is the process of making and implementing managerial decisions on such intellectual results' life cycle, aimed at achieving a relative balance of the interests of the customers, the employer and the author(s) of the intellectual results, reducing the likelihood of an unfavourable outcome when using an intellectual activity result and the management of the rights to the intellectual result, thereby minimizing the losses related to various stages of the life cycle of the intellectual results created under employment contracts.

In the most general form, the main risks arising in this area (in relation to a specific IP object) are:

- the employer's risk consists of the inability to use the IP subject matter. This risk can be caused by various reasons related to the IP subjects matter themselves, the behaviour of the participants in the relationship or other events and third parties' actions;
- the employee's risk consists of the lack of fair compensation for the work done. In relation to the employee, doubts may emerge due to the inability to get fair compensation for the work. In this case, it covers both the material profit and moral compensation that can be manifested in the possibility to become well-known, receive a response from the people who have gained access to the created object, etc. However, in many cases, disputes arise over the payment of remuneration, and the existence of the employer's right to leave the intellectual activity result in secret does not contribute to the obtainment of moral satisfaction.

Thus, when deciding to create an intellectual activity result under an employment contract, all parties should think about the risks that accompany this process, since failure to take them into account can negatively affect the relationship between the parties and lead to the next level of risks that do not relate to a specific intellectual result, but to the interaction between the parties in general, namely, the risk of the loss of the specialist and the risk of the impossibility of creating an intellectual result due to the author's state.

Creativity is a challenging and contradictory process. It is deservedly considered an extremely complex form of mental activity because a huge number of factors affecting the author are involved in this process, the available algorithms cannot always be applied and the author has to find appropriate forms of expression for their ideas, thoughts and views. The author is an individual, that is, a person who is able to feel, suffer and experience different emotions that affect the ability to create.

Despite serious differences between the objects that can be made under employment contracts, the process of creating each of them is based on personal experience, skill, knowledge and the abilities of a particular person or a group of people.

At the same time, not everyone is capable of using their potential to the utmost and achieving the desired result of intellectual activity.

This can be caused by both an objective lack of qualification and some subjective factors, which are often collectively referred to as "lack of inspiration". It can be argued that the lack of inspiration is more typical of copyright and related right relations, but considering it from a broader perspective makes it obvious that this same phenomenon is applicable to other intellectual fields as well. A scientist, writer, performer are all creators, people who realize their knowledge, skills, competences and abilities. Despite their obvious differences, they have a similar goal, which is transforming a certain set of initial data into something that has not been created by anyone before, realizing the available potential.

Perhaps, in a broader sense, this is how creative intellectual activity can be explained. And minimizing the risks associated with its implementation appears to be possible through a complex approach.

The employee and the employer should settle all issues related to the legal registration of their relationship. The more aspects are taken into account, the smaller the risk of having to go to court to settle the dispute. In addition, detailed regulation will avoid the risk of disillusionment and uncertainty, which, unfortunately, are inseparable companions of any insufficiently regulated relations. The previously mentioned GOST R 56823-2015 suggested that, as a measure to prevent risks, labour and civil contracts that include provisions on the intellectual activity results achieved under employment contracts, the adoption of local regulations on such results and the determination of those responsible for regulating them shall be concluded.

This approach, of course, is correct, but it is more concerned with the organizational and legal basis for regulating the relations between the employee-author and the employer. However, taking into account the peculiar character of this field, establishing effective communication with all the employees involved in this area seems to be extremely significant. In this regard, the Recommendations for the Management of Rights to the Results of Intellectual Activity in Organizations (2017), which were developed by the Ministry of

Economic Development of the Russian Federation together with Rospatent and interested agencies, seem to be helpful.[2]

This document discusses the management of the personnel working with the results of intellectual activity. Among the measures that can increase the efficiency of the staff's management, there are material and non-material incentives for employees and the creation of a corporate culture that supports relevant activities, employee training, etc.

It is extremely important to create comfortable conditions for the author's work, taking into account their needs and requirements, providing the necessary resources for the work and listening to their views and reward for success in work.

These measures, of course, can be beneficial, but it is necessary to highlight one important point. Speaking about the creation of intellectual results, all the attention is paid to the authors, although in reality, the creation often involves those who do not directly participate in the process, e.g., supporting the project or generating ideas.

According to the Civil Code, individuals who have not made a personal creative contribution to the creation of such a result are not recognized as the authors of the result of intellectual activity, including those who provided only technical, consulting, organizational or material assistance, or only contributed to the registration of the rights to such a result or its use, as well as those who supervised the performance of the work.

The person who has brilliant ideas but does not physically implement them is not always recognized as the author either, taking into account that creative labour is mandatory. What is more, copyright does not apply to ideas.

However, imagining the staff as a single organism, it is hardly possible to provide support to the authors, putting aside everyone else, since in this case, the organism will not be able to function properly. Therefore, if the creation and use of the results achieved under employment contracts is an integral part of business, it is necessary to organize the work with the personnel in such a way as to provide the most comfortable conditions for both the authors and the people indirectly involved in this process but who are no less significant. Only in this case can the human capital become as efficient as possible.

Notes

1 For more information, see "GOST R 43.0.8-2017. National Standard of the Russian Federation. Information Support of Technology and Operator Activities. Artificially Intellectualized Human–Information Interaction. General Provisions", approved and put into effect by Order of Rosstandart No. 757-st of July 27, 2017.

2 Recommendations are posted on the official website of the Ministry of Economic Development: http://old.economy.gov.ru/minec/about/structure/depIno/2017031001.

7 Intellectual property in corporate relations

Corporate relations in Russia are defined in clause 1 of Article 2 of the Civil Code as relations associated with the participation in corporate-type organizations or the management thereof. A corporation in the Russian Federation is a legal entity based on participation (membership) (clause 1 of Article 65.1 of the Civil Code).

Corporations for which business is their main activity are called commercial corporations (paragraph 2, Chapter 4 of the Civil Code). However, non-profit corporations do not pursue profit-making as the main goal and do not distribute the received profit among its participants (Article 123.1 of the Civil Code). They can be created to achieve social, charitable, cultural, educational, scientific and managerial goals to protect people's health, develop physical culture and sports, satisfy the moral and other intangible needs of the public and protect people's and organizations' rights and legitimate interests and resolve disputes and conflicts and provide legal assistance as well as for other public purposes (clause 2 of Article 2 of Federal Law No. 7-FZ of January 12, 1996, "On Non-Profit Organizations" (hereinafter Law on Non-Profit Organizations). Some issues on non-profit organizations have already been touched upon throughout the text of the book; see Part 1.

A commercial corporation has such an asset as a company name. This intellectual property (IP) subject matter has already been partially touched upon in sections "Intellectual property: concept and types", "The state regulation of IP" of this book, including in the context of the Federal Tax Service's competence.

It is worth noting that in the Russian Federation, a strict regime is established for the company name of any commercial organization, not just of corporate ones. However, besides commercial corporations, only unitary state (municipal) enterprises are considered as commercial organizations. Clause 1 of Article 114 of the Civil Code establishes that a unitary enterprise is created on behalf of a public entity by the authorized state or municipal authorities' decision. Thus, a unitary enterprise is not created for business purposes per se; the company name of a unitary enterprise has no business value.

In Russia, non-profit organizations, including corporations, have names, but these are not company names. The company name requirements do not apply to the names of non-profit organizations. It is not important whether the non-profit organization is corporate or unitary.

Since it is the company name that possesses business value and at the same time is IP subject matter, it will be described in more detail.

The right to a company name is regulated by paragraph 1 of Chapter 76 of the Civil Code. A commercial corporation acts in civil circulation under its company name.

The company name of a legal entity must contain an indication of its organizational and legal form and the name of the legal entity itself, which constitutes the company name's arbitrary part. This part of the company name should not consist only of words denoting the type of activity. A commercial corporation should have one full company name and is entitled to have one abbreviated company name in Russian (Article 1473 of the Civil Code). It also has the right to have one full company name and (or) one abbreviated company name in any language of the peoples of the Russian Federation and (or) in a foreign language. At the same time, the possibility for a legal entity to have an abbreviated company name in a language spoken in the Russian Federation and a foreign language is not due to the company having an abbreviated company name in Russian. A commercial corporation's company name in Russian and in the languages of the peoples of the Russian Federation may contain borrowings from foreign language transcribed in Russian or, accordingly, in the language of an ethnic group within Russia, except for terms and abbreviations reflecting the organizational and legal form of the legal entity.

As indicated in section "The state regulation of IP" the company name has restrictions associated with using the official names of states, authorities, etc., in the arbitrary part of the company name.

The following example can demonstrate the implementation of the established restrictions.

A citizen of Russia (a founder) decided to establish a legal entity called *Kitaysko-russkaya torgovaya investitsionnaya ploshchadka* Limited Liability Company (LLC) (in English, China-Russian Trade Investment Platform).

The Leninsky District Inspection of Federal Tax Service in Vladivostok denied state registration to the holder of the mentioned name. The normative basis for the denial was clause "g (sounds like a "ж" in Russian) of Article 23 of the Law on State Registration of Legal Entities and Individual Entrepreneurs. It states that the grounds for denying state registration of a legal entity may be a discrepancy between the company name of the legal entity and federal law requirements.

However, the founder did not agree with the Inspection of Federal Tax Service's refusal and went to court. The judicial acts provided that, in the case under consideration, the company name of the LLC contains the word "*Kitay*" (in English, "China"), which is the short name of a foreign state, the People's Republic of China. The founder's insistence that the name of the country China is not the abbreviated official name of the People's Republic of China was not considered by the court based on an erroneous interpretation of the norms of the Civil Code and the All-Russian Classifier of the Countries of the World (Resolution of the Fifth State Commercial Court of Appeal of May 16, 2017, on case No. A51-30021/2016).

As noted in clause 4 of Article 1473 of the Civil Code, the inclusion of the official name of "the Russian Federation" or "Russia", as well as words derived from them in a company name of a legal entity shall be allowed by special permission.

The permission is granted by the Ministry of Justice of the Russian Federation. The issuance procedure was established by Government Resolution No. 52 of February 3, 2010, "On Approval of the Rules for Including the Official Name 'Russian Federation' or 'Russia' as well as Words Derived from this Name in the Company Name of a Legal Entity".

According to clause 2 of the rules, permission to include these words in the company name of a legal entity can be obtained if the legal entity has branches and (or) representative offices in more than half of the constituent entities of the Russian Federation, or the legal entity, in accordance with the legislation, is classified as a large taxpayer, as well as in the event that more than 25 per cent of the voting shares of a joint stock company (JSC) or more than 25 per cent of the authorized capital of an LLC is owned by the Russian Federation or an organization that the Russian Federation created based on a special federal law, the name of which includes the official name "Russian Federation" or "Russia", as well as words derived from this name (in terms of using the name of this organization in the company name of the specified legal entity).

At the same time, the founder of the legal entity, the name of which will include these words, submitted a range of documents to the Ministry of Justice:

- a statement of intent to include the official name "Russian Federation" or "Russia" as well as words derived from this name in the company name,
- copies of the constitutive documents of the legal entity (the originals shall be provided in the absence of notarized copies),
- the decision of the founders to apply to the Ministry of Justice to include the specified words in the legal entity's company name,
- the documents on the compliance of the legal entity with one of the requirements listed above, in particular, a copy of the notice issued by a tax authority of the registration of the legal entity as a large taxpayer and an extract from the register of shareholders of a JSC or an extract from the Unified State Register for Legal Entities (USRLE).

If permission is revoked, the legal entity is obliged to make the appropriate changes to its constitutive documents within three months. It is necessary to change the arbitrary part of the company name and register changes to the constitutive documents so that the commercial corporation can do business under a new name.

Thus, in the absence of permission, a legal entity shall not use the words "Russian Federation" or "Russia" or any derived words in its company name.

At the same time, as follows from the provisions of Article 1473 of the Civil Code, it is not the registration authority but the legal entity itself that must ensure compliance of its name with the requirements for the company name (Resolution of the Intellectual Property Court of December 20, 2019, on case No. A17-7437/2018).

The restriction on the arbitrary part of the company name that prohibits the use of signs that are contrary to public interests is the most noteworthy. For example, as stated in one of the acts of the Constitutional Court, the sign can be considered as contradicting public interests if it misleads consumers and business entities and creates unacceptable competitive advantages for the holder of the company name (Ruling of the Constitutional Court of the Russian Federation No. 2594-O of November 23, 2017).

For example, the courts recognized that the use of the words "*Mikhaylovskaya munitsipal'naya upravlyayushchaya kompaniya*" (in English, "Mikhailovskaya Municipal Management Company") in the arbitrary part of the company name of an LLC gives it an unreasonable advantage over competitors (business entities performing similar services in the Volgograd region), since the name *Mikhaylovskaya munitsipal'naya upravlyayushchaya kompaniya* makes consumers think they are dealing with the municipality's managing company. This can enhance public trust in the organization as well as its attractiveness to consumers due to the perception of the organization as a state or municipal company specializing in the management of multi-apartment buildings (Resolution of the Intellectual Property Court of November 28, 2019, on case No. A12-5301/2019).

As already said in section "The state regulation of IP " the company name implies its obligatory fixation in a special register (USRLE). In Russia, the exclusive right only applies to the company names that are included in the USRLE. The right arises from the date of state registration of the legal entity and is terminated when the company name is excluded from the USRLE due to the termination of the legal entity or a change of its company name. In other words, as indicated in clause 146 of Resolution of the Plenum of the Supreme Court No. 10, the Civil Code does not imply any special registration of the company name; the name is specified in the commercial corporation's charter and thus registered. Suppose the arbitrary part of the company name is changed. In that case, the right to a new company name arises from the date of state registration of the changes made to the constituent documents of a legal entity. All this also applies to the names in the languages of the peoples of the Russian Federation or foreign languages.

At the same time, in the Russian Federation, the exclusive right to a company name, including foreign legal entities, is subject to protection (clause 153 of Resolution of the Plenum of the Supreme Court No. 10).

A commercial corporation has the exclusive right to use its company name as a means of individualization in any way that does not contradict the law (exclusive right to a company name), including by indicating it on signs, print forms, invoices and other documentation in advertisements, on goods or their packages or the internet. Abbreviated company names, as well as company names in the languages of the peoples of the Russian Federation and foreign languages are protected by the exclusive right to a company name, if they are included in the USRLE (clause 1 of Article 1474 of the Civil Code).

For example, the JSC, *Gruppa Kompaniy "Maksima"* (in English, "Maxima" Group of Companies) (the plaintiff), applied to the State Commercial Court of the Moscow Region with a claim against the *MAKSIMA* LLC (the defendant) in order to legally oblige it to stop using not only the full company name but also the abbreviated one, which is confusingly similar to the plaintiff's company name in relation to the following activities: other auxiliary activities related to transportation, warehousing and storage activities, airport activities and transport handling of goods.

Opposing the stated requirements, the defendant referred to the fact that the organizational and legal form of the two companies, as well as the full names of the parties, are different, according to extracts from the Unified State Register of Legal Entities, which does not allow identifying the names of *GK MAKSIMA* JSC (abbreviated company name of the plaintiff) and *MAKSIMA* LLC as identical to the point of confusion.

Taking into account the above legal norms for the individualization of a legal entity, its name is of primary importance, and it is precisely the similarity of the arbitrary parts of the company names that creates the confusion between the legal entities. At the same time, the difference in the organizational and legal forms as parts of a company name does not itself indicate the absence of a violation of the right to a company name. As the court indicated, since, according to the case materials, the plaintiff's right to a company name arose earlier than that of the defendant and the fact that the plaintiff carried out similar activities is confirmed by the materials of the case, this creates a high probability of confusion between the plaintiff and the defendant in economic circulation when they carry out similar activities (Resolution of the Tenth State Commercial Court of Appeal of August 29, 2019, on case No. A41-99101/2018).

It should be borne in mind that clause 3 of Article 1474 of the Civil Code establishes a ban on the use of a company name identical to the company name of another legal entity or similar to it to the point of confusion, if said legal entities carry out similar activities and the company name of the another legal entity was included in the USRLE earlier than the company name of the former legal entity. However, it does not usually matter which of the entities was the first to embark on certain economic activities. The protection of the right to the company name of a legal entity that was included in the USRLE earlier than the other commercial organization can be denied on the basis of Article 10 of the Civil Code if it is found that this entity began to engage in a specific type of activity in order to take advantage of the reputation of the entity who began to carry out such activities earlier.

It should be noted that giving a commercial corporation a company name similar to the company name of another legal entity carries risks arising from the regulatory framework described. In particular, there is a risk that the right holder will be dissatisfied with the current situation and will defend their right to the company name.

The right holder could demand cessation of the use of the company name that is identical to its company name or similar to it to the point of confusion in relation to similar types of activities, the changing of the company name and compensation for the caused losses. All of the above risks can be realized in the course of doing business.

However, in Russia, the risks of choosing a company name similar to the name of another commercial legal entity are not limited to those specified earlier.

There is the risk of not being able to carry out the selected type of activity under the chosen company name even at the initiation stage. For example, there are types of activities in Russia for which one needs to obtain a special permit (licence). It is prohibited to carry out such types of activities without it. An example of such an activity is the management of apartment buildings.

According to subclause 1.1, clause 1 of Article 193 of Housing Code of the Russian Federation No. 188-FZ of December 29, 2004, one of the licencing requirements is the lack of identity or similarity to the extent of confusion between the company name of the licence applicant or licensee with the company name of another licensee, whose right to carry out business activities in the management of apartment buildings emerged earlier.

In this regard, according to Letter of the Ministry of Construction of Russia No. 26618-ACh/04 of June 21, 2018, "On the Evaluation of the Identity or Similarity of the Licensees' Company Names", when evaluating the possible identity or similarity to the extent of confusion of the licensees' company names, it is recommended to compare both the full and the abbreviated company names of the legal entity, which are indicated in the constituent documents of the legal entity and in the "Name" section of the USRLE. A name should be considered identical to another legal entity's name if one coincides with the other in all elements, and similar to the extent of confusion if the distinction between them is constituted by some minor individual features.

The graphic similarity of names is determined based on the following features:

- the use of signs of different alphabets to denote the same or similar phonemes (e.g., *ДОМ* LLC and DOM LLC where both designations are pronounced the same way in Russian);
- the use of the same letters with different letter cases, e.g., the use of uppercase or lowercase letters: URAL LLC UK and Ural LLC UK ("UK" is an abbreviation for the words "*Upravlyayushchaya Kompaniya*" meaning management company);
- the use of different symbols, punctuation marks, spelling marks in the same phrases or words (e.g., Comfort – Service LLC and Comfort Service LLC; Etalon LLC MC and Etalon + LLC MC; *Razvitie* LLC UK and UK *Razvitie* LLC);

- the use of additional single letters or syllables in the same phrases or words, e.g., Alex LLC and Alex i K LLC; *Kommunalschik* LLC and *Kommunalschik* LLC DO ("DO" is an abbreviation for the words "*Domoupravlyayushchaya Organizatsiya*", in English, house management organization).

Thus, choosing a company name is an important matter. It is necessary to take into account the existing regulatory restrictions to understand that in case of non-compliance with the requirements of the law, the state registration of a legal entity with the chosen company name could be refused.

In addition, no matter how attractive a competitor's company name may seem, it is worth considering the risks that are entailed by giving the corporation the same or similar name. Extensive Russian judicial practice shows that no matter how pure the founders' motives were, they are likely to lose the case. And while at the initial stage of business it is possible to simply change the arbitrary part of the company name, at the later stages, the previously described situations may entail not only litigation, but also the loss of customers and the loss of one's business reputation closely related to the name that the corporation used.

Article 1476 of the Civil Code establishes the correlation of the rights to the company name with the rights to the commercial name and the trademark and service mark. The right holder may use a company name or its elements as part of a commercial name belonging to them. In this case, the company name included in the commercial name is protected regardless of the protection of the commercial name.

Also, the company name or its elements can be used by the right holder in the trademark and service mark belonging to them. And accordingly, the company name included in the trademark or service mark is protected regardless of the protection of the trademark or service mark.

The last thing that should be noted is that the disposal of the exclusive right to the company name (including by alienating it or granting another person the right to use the company name) is not allowed in Russia (clause 2 of Article 1474 of the Civil Code).

This means that no transfer of rights to the company name as a separate object is possible. At the same time, the company name is not absolutely excluded from the economic turnover. A person who wants to create a legal entity with a specific company name, the rights to which belong to another commercial corporation, can acquire a 100 per cent stake in said corporation. So, the company name of such a corporation will indirectly affect the value of the acquired stake.

The transfer of the company name is also possible in the process of reorganizing the legal entity (Article 57 of the Civil Code). For example, as noted in Resolution of the Intellectual Property Court of March 19, 2015, on case No. A36-376/2014, if there is transformation, exlusive rights to means of individualization, including the company name of the reorganized legal entity, are transferred to another one by universal succession.

Also, one can keep the preferred company name when one corporation merges with another. When carrying out such reorganization, it is recommended to choose the entity whose company name is of interest as the main legal entity that survives. In such form of reorganization as a division, the company name can be perceived as an asset by the participants of the reorganized corporation. Hence, they could agree whose corporation will preserve the rights to the company name and, taking this into account, redistribute other assets of the reorganized legal entity.

Besides its company name, the authorized (joint) capital is of particular importance for a commercial corporation in Russia.

There are various regulatory requirements as to its formation procedure. In accordance with clause 1 of Article 66.2 of the Civil Code, the minimum size of the authorized capital of business companies (LLC, JSC) is determined by special laws. So, for an LLC, the minimum size of the authorized capital is established by Article 14 of Federal Law No. 14-FZ of February 8, 1998, "On Limited Liability Companies" (hereinafter Law on LLC). The size of the authorized capital of an LLC shall amount to at least 10,000 rubles.

When paying for the authorized capital of a business company, the deposited funds shall not be lower than the minimum size of the authorized capital. The remaining part of the authorized capital, should the amount of capital exceed the required minimum, can be paid for in non-monetary assets, including IP. When the exclusive right, another intellectual right (for example, the right to obtain a patent) or a right under a licencing agreement is added to the authorized (joint) capital of a business partnership or a company, and if this is documented in the decision to contribute property to the authorized (joint) capital or to create a partnership or a company, and if such a decision contains all the essential conditions to be included in the agreement on the transfer of the exclusive right or in the licence agreement, the conclusion of a separate agreement on the transfer of an exclusive right or a licence agreement that meets the requirements established by Part IV of the Civil Code (clause 1 of Article 1233) shall not be required.

In this case, the state registration of the transfer of the exclusive right to the result of intellectual activity, means of individualization, as well as the granting of the right to use them, can also be carried out at the request of the founder, subject to the submission of the relevant part of the decision on the creation of a partnership or a company (clause 45 of Resolution of the Plenum of the Supreme Court No. 10).

As the contributing rights to IP subject matter to the authorized capital of a business company is a non-monetary contribution, an independent valuation is required as expressly stipulated in Article 66.2 of the Civil Code.

In Russia, such independent valuation, including that of IP subject matter, is carried out by specialized valuators. These are members of one of the self-regulatory organizations of valuators with their liability insured in accordance with the established procedure. The valuators may perform valuating activities independently, in private practice, as well as on the basis of an employment contract between a valuator and a legal entity that meets a number of legal requirements.

In any case, a valuator should have a qualification certificate that specifies the area where they can carry out valuating activities (Article 4 of Federal Law No. 135-FZ of July 29, 1998, "On Valuation Activities in the Russian Federation"; hereinafter Law on Valuation Activities).

According to Article 16 of said law, the valuation of an object (asset) cannot be carried out by a valuator who, at the same time, is a founder, owner, shareholder, official or employee of a customer legal entity, as well as a person who has a property interest in the object to be evaluated or is closely related to these people. This requirement ensures the independence of the valuation.

According to Article 20 of the Law on Valuation Activities, the valuation procedure in Russia is regulated by special standards.

The Order of the Ministry of Economic Development of the Russian Federation No. 385 of June 22, 2015, establishes the Federal Valuation Standard "Valuation of Intangible Assets and Intellectual Property (No. 11)" (hereinafter Federal Valuation Standard).

IP valuation includes:

- analyzing the market of the object of valuation and the market of the goods, works and (or) services (produced and sold) involving said IP subject matter, as well as other external factors affecting its value;
- analyzing the economic situation in the country, industry and region, as well as other factors affecting the market of the object of valuation and the market of the products (goods, works, services) produced and sold with the use of the above IP object;
- identifying the object of valuation, including rights, privileges and other economic benefits associated with it;
- analyzing the current use, production forecasts and sales of the products (goods, works, services) that require the object of valuation.

The valuator shall collect information from various sources that is sufficient to identify the object of valuation. The factors considered in the process of collecting and analyzing information may include:

- rights, privileges or other economic benefits associated with the valuation object;
- duration of the exclusive right to IP;
- the ability of the valuation object to bring economic benefits and the sources of these benefits;
- the state and prospects of the industry where the valuation object was created and (or) used;
- licencing agreements or agreements on the alienation of the exclusive right to IP (if any);
- other factors that are directly related to the valuation object.

IP valuation can be conducted with the use of income-based, cost-based and market-based approaches.

The income-based approach implies discounting cash flows (future economic benefits) generated by the object of valuation or the capitalization of the annual net income (benefits, effect) from the object of valuation, including the possibility of providing paid access to economic benefits from the use of the IP subject matter to other persons.

When using the income-based approach, the valuator shall consider the following provisions (clauses 12–13 of the Federal Valuation Standard):

1 the valuator shall determine the future cash flows formed from the economic benefits generated by the object of valuation. In general, benefits could arise from cost savings, royalty exemptions, profit benefits, actual licence fees, royalty payments, excess income or other benefits;
2 the period during which the object of valuation can bring economic benefits, as a rule, is limited by the duration of legal protection or the duration of the licence agreement. The duration of the useful life of the object of valuation can be reduced based on the economic inexpediency of its further use;
3 the discount rate is calculated using one of the following methods:
   - analysis of the market indicators reflecting the profitability of objects similar to the one to be valued;
   - the weighted average cost of the capital of the organization (business) that uses the object of valuation;
   - the cumulative method that includes determining the risk-free rate of the funds use, the expected rate of inflation and the amount of a premium for the risks associated with an investment in the object of valuation;
4 the capitalization rate can be used when applying valuation ratios such as price/earnings multipliers or when adjusting the discount rate to reflect any future cash flow growth from the use of the object of valuation in the post-forecast period;
5 besides the capitalization of the intangible asset use income, it is necessary to take into account any tax benefits and advantages available to the owner of the IP object being assessed, including the effects of the amortization of the estimated intangible asset, in accordance with the norms of the current legislation, and make appropriate adjustments to the cash flows.

When applying the cost-based approach, the valuator shall consider the following provisions (clause 15 of the Federal Valuation Standard):

1 it is advisable to apply this approach to the valuation of an IP asset:
   - when the valuation object is created by the right holders themselves;
   - when there is not sufficient data to apply the market-based and income-based approaches;

2 the value of the object is determined by the cost-based approach when it can be recreated by determining the costs of its reproduction or replacement;
3 costs for the development of the valuation object may include labour costs and other types of remuneration, payment for materials, overhead expenses, as well as fees for legal protection, taxes and (or) business profit paid during the development of the valuation object;
4 historical (initial) costs of the valuation object creation, should they be used, shall be indexed to correspond to the current date;
5 when determining the cost of reproduction of the valuation object, the valuator shall determine the cost of the creation of the new exact copy of the object. The costs, in this case, shall be determined based on the prices for services valid on the valuation date using the knowledge, experience and skills of the authors/creators (if any) of the valuation object;
6 when determining the costs of creating an object with similar useful properties, the valuator shall determine the cost of creating the valuation object of the same utility, which is an analogue of the valuation object in terms of functionality and use. In this case, the costs shall be determined based on the current prices for raw materials, goods, services, energy resources and the cost of labour in the region and (or) the sector of the economy in which objects similar to the one subject valuation are created.

When applying the market-based approach, the value shall be determined using the following information (clause 16 of the Federal Valuation Standard):

- on the terms of deals, as well as offers for the sale and purchase of analogue objects on the market as of the valuation date or the date preceding the valuation date, if such information is available on the valuation date;
- on the influence of pricing factors of analogue objects on their market value.

Price multipliers can be used to determine the influence of the pricing factors of analogue objects on their market value.

In some cases, the price of analogue objects offers can be reasonably adjusted.

The following comparison elements are commonly used to compare the valuation object with other items that have been or are to be involved in transactions:

- the regime of the provided legal protection, including transferred IP rights and terms of use;
- financing terms of intangible assets deals, including the ratio of owned and borrowed funds;
- changes in prices for intangible assets for the period from the date of the deal involving an analogue object to the date of the valuation;
- the industry in which the intangible assets have been or will be used;
- the area covered by the rights that are assessed;

- functional, technological and economic characteristics of the selected analogue items similar to the corresponding characteristics of the valuation object;
- demand for products that can be produced or sold with the use of the valuation object;
- period of use of the valuation object, during which it can bring economic benefits;
- other characteristics of the intangible asset that affect the value.

The procedure for the formation of the authorized capital assumes that the value of the participant's non-monetary contribution to it is determined on the basis of the valuation report (the final document that is drawn up based on the determined value of the valuation object). This rule also applies when the intellectual rights are used as a contribution to the capital. Moreover, the participants of a business company are not entitled to determine the value of the non-monetary contribution to the authorized capital in an amount exceeding the amount of the valuation determined by an independent valuator (clause 2 of Article 66.2 of the Civil Code).

It should be noted that from the tax point of view, the transfer of IP rights from one subject to another is a sale, and in accordance with clause 1 of Article 146, Chapter 21 "Value Added Tax" of the Tax Code, operations for the sale of goods (works, services) are subject to VAT in Russia.

At the same time, considering the norms of the Tax Code in a systemic connection, it could be concluded that the transfer of exclusive rights to IP subject matter, including a service mark and (or) trademark from Russian and foreign shareholders or participants, as a contribution to the authorized capital of a Russian legal entity, shall not be subject to VAT (Letter of the Ministry of Finance of Russia No. 03-07-08/26423 of April 19, 2018; Letter of the Tax and Customs Policy Department of the Ministry of Finance of Russia No. 03-07-08/50926 of July 20, 2018).

The functioning of corporations involves deals with various counterparties. The deals can be made in relation to any objects, including IP, the circulation of which is not prohibited in Russia.

However, Russia has general requirements for certain types of corporate deals. So, according to Russian legislation, requirements are established for so-called "major deals" and "related-party deals" concluded by business companies.

As indicated by the Constitutional Court in Ruling No. 1678-O-O of December 8, 2011, these deals requirements contribute to maintaining the necessary level of the legal certainty of corporate relations, the stability of civil turnover and, besides, ensure that the property interests of the business company's participants should be reasonably balanced. In other words, these requirements are due to the need to protect the interests of those persons who invest their capital by participating in a corporation.

The major deals regime is determined by Article 46 of the Law on LLC and Articles 78–79 of Federal Law No. 208-FZ of December 26, 1995, "On

Joint Stock Companies", containing similar legal regulation (hereinafter Law of JSC).

Qualitative and quantitative tests can be used to assess a major deal. The qualitative test is to assess if the deal steps outside the ordinary course of business.

Deals that are not beyond the ordinary course of business are those that are customary for the company itself or other business entities carrying out similar activities. In today's Russia, it does not matter whether such deals have been made by the company before unless such deals lead to the termination of the company's activities, a change in its type or a significant change in its scale.

Such deals entail transferring property into temporary possession and (or) use of a third party or providing the right to use the result of intellectual activity or means of individualization under the terms of a licence to a third party or are associated with the company's property acquisition, transfer or transfer possibility (direct or indirect), e.g., loan, credit, pledge or surety.

The quantitative test is carried out on the basis of the ratio of the deal price to the book value of the company's assets, calculated based on its accounting (financial) statements as of the latest report date (hereinafter the book value of assets). For a deal to be considered major, it must be 25 per cent or more of the book value of the company's assets.

Several interrelated deals can be considered as one major deal. Such deals have a single economic purpose, there is a common economic objective of the sold property or there is the consolidation of all the property transferred into the ownership of one person, and so on.

According to Russian legislation, a major deal can be agreed with the business company's management bodies before it has been made; they can also approve it after that moment.

In an LLC, as a general rule, the decision on major deals falls under the competence of the general meeting of participants. The decision is made by the majority of votes from the total number of the company's participants (clause 8 of Article 37 of the Law on LLC).

In a JSC, the decision on the deal is made by the general meeting or by the board of directors. For example, a decision on a major deal amounting to more than 50 per cent of the book value of the assets is made by a general meeting of shareholders by a three-quarters majority of votes of the voting shareowners participating in the meeting.

The participants are provided in advance with the conclusion on the deal issued by the board of directors, and in the absence of such a body in the JSC management system, the conclusion issued by the sole executive body, indicating the intended results of the deal for the company, an assessment of its feasibility.

Related-party deals are regulated by Article 45 of the Law on LLC and Articles 81–84 of the Law on JSC.

The conclusion of this deal is determined by the interest of the persons who are members of or perform the functions of the management bodies of a company, the controlling person of a company or a person who has the right to give binding instructions to a company.

Such persons are considered interested if they, their spouses, parents, children, full and half brothers and sisters, adoptive parents and adopted children and (or) persons (organizations) under their control:

- are a party, beneficiary, intermediary or representative in the deal;
- are the controlling person of a legal entity that is the other party, beneficiary, intermediary or representative in the deal;
- hold positions in the management bodies of the legal entity that is the other party, beneficiary, intermediary or representative in the deal, as well as positions in the management bodies of the management organization of such a legal entity.

A related-party deal does not require prior consent.

However, the following entities can apply for preliminary approval of the deal: the sole executive body, a member of the collegial executive body, a member of the board of directors and participants who collectively own at least one per cent of the authorized capital (voting shares) of the company.

The named articles of the laws establish the procedure for approving related-party deals. Without going into details of the procedure, it is, nevertheless, worth noting that the rules somewhat vary for LLCs and JSCs.

In an LLC, the rules are simpler. Generally, the decision is made by the general meeting of the LLC participants by a majority of votes of the company's participants who are not interested in the transaction or controlled by the people interested in it.

When the business company concludes both major and related-party deals, the normatively established procedure for their approval shall be observed so that the deal will not be invalidated in court afterwards.

An interesting case from judicial practice highlights this issue.

Miksologist (LLC 1) was registered as a legal entity in 2003. The company participants are Participant V and Participant R with equal shares, each of which is 50 per cent of the authorized capital. Participant V became the director of LLC 1. The court found that the main activity of LLC 1 is the production of soft drinks and other mineral waters. At the same time, the company has since 2012 registered the trademarks "BARLINE", "*MAMIN RETSEPT*" and "BARLINE BARLINE" and patents used in the production of soft drinks. Later in 2014, another LLC called *Miksologist* (LLC 2) was registered as a legal entity, the address of which, as well as the main type of its production activity, coincides with the address of the location and the main type of activity (production of soft drinks) of LLC 1.

Based on the agreement on the transfer of exclusive rights dated December 23, 2015, LLC 1 transferred the trademarks and patents to its direct competitor, LLC 2. At the same time, on November 7, 2016, an entry about Participant V as the owner of 100 per cent of shares in the authorized capital of LLC 2 was made in the USRLE.

From the auditor's financial report on LLC 1, it follows that in 2013–2015 the company had satisfactory economic activities that involved the use of its trademarks, while in 2016, the economic activities of the company were terminated. According to the report, the actual termination of the company's activities was caused, among other things, by the stripping of assets (trademarks and patents) in 2015. Evidence that the deal for the sale of the company's only asset was economically expedient was not presented to the court. The court also found that LLC 1, represented by general director Participant V, made a deal on the transfer of the only economic asset during a corporate conflict over the company's management (there were other legal disputes). Considering the above, the court ruled that Participant V's and LLC 2's actions aimed to strip LLC 1's assets.

Thus, the court concluded that the contested deal violated the rights of Participant R as the second participant of the LLC 1 (Resolution of the State Commercial Court of the Moscow District of September 4, 2018, on case No. A40-219146/2016).

It should be noted that the acquisition of an IP subject matter as an asset by a business company can be challenged in court.

This happened in the following case, where the arbitration (bankruptcy) manager contested the deal due to bankruptcy. The challenging grounds were, among other things, non-compliance with the requirements of the approval procedure for a major deal.

The court established that Jump LLC acquired the right to use the JUMP trademark under a licence agreement. The arbitrary part of the company name was in Russian (*Джамп*), and the trademark is actually identical to the company name; the spoken part was an English transcription of the company name. Moreover, the specified trademark coincides with the commercial name used by Jump LLC in its main activity (JUMP kids club) from the beginning of this activity, which was earlier than the date of the purchase of the trademark.

At the same time, there was no evidence regarding the economic feasibility and validity for concluding the licence agreement between Jump LLC and the right holder. In addition, it is noted that the right holder was an affiliated person in relation to Jump LLC, i.e., it was a related-party deal.

Evidence that a general meeting of Jump LLC adopted the decision to conclude the licence agreement or approve the deal afterwards was not presented, which proves that the licence agreement was concluded in violation of the requirements of the law.

Besides, in accordance with the judicial act, when having to determine signs of a major deal, it is the purchase price of the right to use the trademark that is relevant and not the amount of the actual payment made under the contract. As for the case, the purchase price of the right to use the trademark was higher than the actual payments that had been made. The court determined the purchase price of the right to use the trademark for the entire period of the agreement, and it was found that it exceeded 25 per cent of the book value of assets of Jump LLC at the time of the agreement conclusion. The deal was invalidated (Resolution of the State Commercial Court of the North-Western Circuit of June 26, 2020, on case No. A56-61416/2018).

Thus, when making deals involving IP subject matter, it is necessary to take into account the provisions of the corporate legislation on certain types of deals, pay attention to possible affiliations and correlate the cost of the deals with the book value of assets of the business entities that are parties to said deals that can involve both transfer and obtainment of the rights to IP subjects matter. In Russia, there is a rule according to which a deal that is both major and related-party has a more complex approval mechanism. For example, in an LLC, the decision on such a deal is considered adopted if it is approved as a major deal by both the majority of the participants' votes and the majority of votes of all participants who are not interested in it (clause 6 of Article 46 of the Law on LLC). On the one hand, the above complicates the circulation of IP subject matter, but, on the other hand, it is aimed at protecting public interest (these include the interests of the participants (shareholders) of a business company).

References

Annual Report of Rospatent, 2019. [Otchet o deyatel'nosti Rospatenta za 2019 god]. (https://rospatent.gov.ru/content/uploadfiles/otchet-2019-ru.pdf).

Berezin, D.A. Price of a Commissioning Agreement [Tsena dogovora avtorskogo zakaza]. *Jurist [Yurist].* 2018. No. 12. P. 45–51. doi:10.18572/1812-3929-2018-12-45-51

Dozortsev, V.A. *Legislation and scientific and technical progress [Zakonodatel'stvo i nauchno-tekhnicheskiy progress].* Moscow, Yuridicheskaya literatura, 1978.

Dozortsev, V.A. The Concept of a Secret of Production ('Know-How') [Ponyatie sekreta promysla («nou-khau»)], in V.A. Dozortsev (ed.) *Intellectual Rights. Concept. System. Codification Tasks: Collection of Articles [Intellektual'nye prava. Ponyatie. Sistema. Zadachi kodifikatsii: Sbornik statey].* Moscow, Statut, 2003. P. 238–276.

Intellectual Property Law: Textbook. Vol. 1: General Provisions. [Pravo intellektual'noy sobstvennosti: Uchebnik. T. 1: Obshchie polozheniya]. Edited by Novoselova, L.A. Moscow, Statut, 2017a.

Intellectual Property Law: Textbook. Vol. 2: Copyright. [Pravo intellektual'noy sobstvennosti: Uchebnik. T. 2: Avtorskoe parvo]. Edited by Novoselova, L.A. Moscow, Statut, 2017b.

Ioffe, O.S. *Soviet Civil Law (Course of lectures). [Part III]: Legal Relations Associated with the Products of Creative Activity; Family law; Inheritance law [Sovetskoe grazhdanskoe pravo: Kurs lektsiy.Ch. 3. Pravootnosheniya, svyazannye s produktami tvorcheskoy deyatel'nosti. Semeynoe pravo. Nasledstvennoe parvo].* Leningrad, Izdatel'stvo Leningradskogo universiteta, 1965.

Lazareva, N. Intellectual Rights in Court Decisions [Intellektual'nye prava v sudebnykh resheniyakh]. *EG-Jurist [EZh-Yurist].* 2015. No. 3.

Mikryukov, V.A. *Limitations and Encumbrances of Civil Rights [Ogranicheniya i obremeneniya grazhdanskikh prav].* Moscow, Statut, 2007.

Nefediev, E.A. *Commercial Law: Lectures by Professor Nefediev [Torgovoe pravo: Leksii] Professora Nefed'eva)].* Moscow, Tipo-Litografiya V.R. Kellera, 1900.

Raygorodskiy, N.A. *Invention Law of the USSR [Izobretatel'skoe pravo SSSR].* Moscow, Gosudarstvennoe izdatel'stvo yuridicheskoy literatury, 1949.

Ring, M.P. *Agreements for Research and Development Work [Dogovory na nauchno-issledovatel'skie i konstruktorskie raboty].* Moscow, Publishing House Legal Literature, 1967.

Sagdeeva, L.V. The Rights of Prior and Posterior Use as the Limitation on Exclusive Rights [Prava prezhdepol'zovaniya i poslepol'zovaniya kak obremeneniya isklyuchitel'nogo prava]. *Journal of Russian Law* [*Zhurnal rossijskogo prava*]. 2018. No. 8. P. 69–76. doi:10.12737/art_2018_8_7.

Scientific and Practical Commentary on Judicial Practice in the Field of Intellectual Property Rights Protection. Edited by Novoselova, L.A. Moscow, Norma, 2014.

Vaksberg, A.I. *Publisher and Author: Legal Relationships [Izdatel'stvo i avtor. Pravovye vzaimootnosheniya].* Moscow, Iskusstvo, 1958.

Yaichkov, K.K. *Invention and its Legal Protection in the USSR [Izobretenie i ego pravovaya okhrana v SSSR].* Moscow, Izdatel'stvo Akademii nauk SSSR, 1961.

Part Three

Competition, monopolism and cooperation in the field of IP

8 The main ways IP is used in business

The ways of using intellectual property (IP) are determined by the IP's essence and the role that the results of IP play in modern society. There are plenty of ways to use IP and the method is chosen according to the IP's intended purposes. Both business and IP are in constant development. The more they evolve, the more intertwined they become. Today, IP is an integral part of business.

So, IP is actively used in business. Moreover, all relations in this area are based on a combination of three fundamental principles:

- the principle of competition,
- the principle of monopoly,
- the principle of cooperation.

In accordance with Article 2 of the Civil Code, business activity is an independent activity carried out at one's own risk, aimed at the systematic receipt of profit from the use of property, sale of goods, performance of works or provision of services.

On the one hand, Article 34 of the Constitution of the Russian Federation indicates the free use of one's abilities and property for business and any other economic activities not prohibited by law, but, on the other hand, economic activities aimed at monopolization and unfair competition shall not be allowed.

As stated in the "Review of the Appeals of Citizens, Representatives of Organizations (Legal Entities), Public Associations Received by the Ministry of Economic Development of Russia and the Solutions" approved by the Ministry of Economic Development of the Russian Federation,[1] competition is a necessary condition and the most important way to conduct business effectively. The introduction of new technologies and efficient distribution of resources are an integral part of market relations, one of the tools of which is free competition.

Article 10 of the Civil Code establishes a general rule on the inability to exercise civil rights in order to restrict competition and abuse of a dominant position in the market. As noted in the Decision of the Intellectual Property Court of April 9, 2019, on case No. SIP-458/2018, as per the above norm, acts of unfair competition, including those related to the acquisition and use of the exclusive right to a means of individualization in conformity with the norms of Federal Law No. 135-FZ of July 26, 2006, "On Protection of Competition" (hereinafter Law on Protection of Competition), shall also be considered as an abuse of right.

This law contains definitions of a number of significant concepts, such as:

- competition is a rivalry between economic entities in which their independent actions exclude or limit the ability of the other to unilaterally influence the general conditions for the circulation of goods in the market;
- unfair competition implies any actions of business entities (groups of persons) aimed at gaining advantages in business, contradict the legislation of the Russian Federation, business customs, the requirements of integrity, reasonableness and fairness and have caused or may cause damages to competing business entities or have caused or may harm their business reputation;
- monopolistic activity means abuse of a dominant position by an economic entity, a group of persons, agreements or concerted actions prohibited by antimonopoly legislation, as well as other actions (inaction) recognized as monopolistic activities in accordance with federal laws.

In addition, this regulatory legal act also contains several prohibitions, for example, a ban on unfair competition related to the acquisition and use of the exclusive right to the means of individualization of a legal entity, to unfair competition associated with the use of results of intellectual activity and the prohibition of unfair competition associated with the creation of confusion.

Resolution of the Presidium of the Intellectual Property Court of May 20, 2019, on case No. SIP-527/2018 explained that in order to recognize the right holder's actions aimed at acquiring and using the exclusive right to a trademark as an act of unfair competition within the framework of the state commercial court proceedings, the following circumstances must be established:

- the fact that other people had used the controversial sign before the defendant applied for registration of that sign as a trademark,
- the defendant is aware of the fact that others had used the sign before the defendant applied for registration of that sign as a trademark,
- competitive relations between the defendant and the plaintiff had already existed by the time the defendant applied for registration of that sign as a trademark,
- the defendant intended to harm the plaintiff or push them out of the market by acquiring the exclusive right to such a sign (acquiring a monopoly on it) and making demands aimed at preventing the use of the controversial sign,
- the defendant caused or was likely to cause harm to the plaintiff by filing claims to terminate the use of the disputed sign.

The Decision of the Intellectual Property Court of November 11, 2020, on case No. SIP-276/2020 points out that in order to resolve the issue of good faith, it is necessary to study the circumstances related to the acquisition of the exclusive right itself and the subsequent behaviour of the right holder, indicating the purpose of such an acquisition. The bad faith of the right holder should, first of all, be established at the stage of filing an application for registration of the sign as a trademark, since it was then that the intention to unfairly compete with other market participants was realized through the use of the exclusive right to a trademark, providing for the ban on the use of identical or similar signs to individualize goods and services.

It is noteworthy that the requirements of the law and articles containing the prohibition on the abuse of a dominant position by an economic entity and a ban on agreements restricting competition between economic entities do not apply to the exercising of the exclusive rights to the results of intellectual activity and equivalent means of individualization of a legal entity, products, works or services.

The Intellectual Property Court explains that clause 4 of Article 10 of the Law on the Protection of Competition ("Prohibition of Abuse of Dominant Position by an Economic Entity") establishes that the requirements of this article do not cover the exercising of the exclusive rights to the results of intellectual activity and means of individualization. This rule, among others, discloses the essence of the exclusive right, which is the right owner's legal monopoly to use the protected subject matter, as well as the possibility to protect this right from third parties using it in the absence of legal grounds (Resolution of the Intellectual Property Court of November 1, 2018, on case No. A36-10122/2017).

It should be noted that IP rights are often referred to as legal monopoly (Ruling of the Constitutional Court of the Russian Federation No. 171-O of April 22, 2004; Ruling of the Constitutional Court of the Russian Federation No. 741-O of April 23, 2015), but this approach is not supported by everyone. In particular, Aleksei Y. Ivanov draws attention to the fact that the right holder's economic rights take place within the framework of ordinary subjective rights and the exclusive right does not imply the presence of market power (Ivanov, 2020). Andrei E. Shastitko explains the complexity of using the term "legal monopoly" based on the economic understanding of monopoly. In his opinion, the uniqueness of the results of intellectual activity undoubtedly encourages their recognition as a monopoly, but it should be borne in mind that the results can be interchangeable, and the rights to them can belong to different right holders (Shastitko, 2018).

Probably, this discussion per se would not be so interesting if it were not for the removal of IP from the legal scope of some provisions of the Law on Protection of Competition. Thus, Resolution of the Presidium of the Intellectual Property Court of April 22, 2016, on case No. SIP-661/2015 directly says that the exclusive rights themselves represent a legal restriction of competition and a legal form of monopoly (exclusive right).

It is likely that the non-application of several provisions of the legislation on the protection of competition is due to the need to ensure a balance between the interests of exclusive rights holders and the public and private interests of developing competition in commodity markets. As explained further, it is carried out on the basis of a reasonable combination of the legislative prohibitions on monopolization, abuse of rights and unfair competition in economic activity and restrictions on their application in the field of IP, optimization of approaches to determining the list of forbidden practices recognized as unfair competition in the field of IP, including abuse by right holders ("GOST R 58223-2018. National Standard of the Russian Federation. Intellectual Property. Antimonopoly Regulation and Protection Against Unfair Competition", approved by Order of Rosstandart No. 597-st of September 13, 2018; hereinafter – GOST R 58223-2018).

There are certain restrictions on recognizing IP as a legal monopoly, particularly the exhaustion of the right holder's rights to the trademark, which represents a legal limitation of the legal monopoly on the use of the exclusive right to a trademark. This issue has raised numerous discussions. However, putting aside all the arguments for and against, it appears to represent an attempt to find a balance of interests of all the persons involved in the relationship.

The position of the Constitutional Court of the Russian Federation, set forth in Resolution No. 8-P of February 13, 2018, seems to be extremely significant. The legal action brought before the court concerned the demand that the defendant be prohibited from storing, importing or offering for sale or otherwise introducing goods marked by a trademark used without the permission of the right holder into civil circulation on the territory of the Russian Federation. The appeal to the Constitutional Court of the Russian Federation was due to the fact that, in the applicant's opinion, the provisions of the Civil Code of the Russian Federation:

- contradict Articles 1, 7, 17–19, 35 and 55 of the Constitution of the Russian Federation and violate the constitutional principles of legal certainty and fairness to the extent that these provisions, the way the courts interpret them, classify goods with a trademark lawfully placed on them, produced, marked and sold by the right holder himself or with his consent outside the Russian Federation as counterfeits;
- apply such civil liability measures as withdrawal from circulation and destruction of goods that have not yet been put into circulation (in particular, not released for free circulation by the customs authorities), as well as the recovery of compensation in relation to such goods, while they do not contain objective signs of a threat to public interests and their circulation does not infringe on the public order;
- apply the same sanctions to both counterfeits marked without the right holder's consent and original goods;
- do not take into account the cost of such goods when determining the amount of compensation to be recovered;

- allow the application of these sanctions in the absence of the statutory goal to protect the exclusive right to a trademark, i.e., when the signs placed on the goods do not create confusion or mislead the consumers.

This appeal had to do with parallel imports, which means the import of original goods marked with the trademark of the right holder in the absence of the right holder's permission from outside Russia to Russia. In such cases, import is carried out not by the right holder or the official distributor but by other legal entities, importers. Such a distribution system creates a conflict of interest between importers and the right holders claiming absolute powers to control parallel imports. The Constitutional Court recognized that the national principle of the exhaustion of exclusive rights, enshrined in the Russian Federation, which prohibits importing goods with trademarks used without the permission of the right holders into Russia, does not contradict the Constitution.[2]

At the same time, as noted in the mentioned Resolution by the Constitutional Court, the Civil Code of the Russian Federation does not provide any constitutional and legal grounds for the imposition of such liability measures for the violation of the exclusive right to a trademark as withdrawal from circulation and destruction of goods previously introduced by the right holder into civil circulation on the territory of another state and imported into the territory of Russia without their consent (parallel import), in contrast to the consequences of importing counterfeit goods, which shall be able to avoid seizure and destruction only as an exception (if the introduction of such goods into circulation is dictated by the need for protection of socially significant interests). This means that goods imported into the territory of Russia in the order of parallel import can be withdrawn from circulation and destroyed only if their inadequate quality is established and (or) to ensure safety, protect human life and health and protect nature and cultural values, which, however, does not exclude the application of other legal measures for violation of the exclusive right to a trademark, taking into account the constitutional and legal interpretation of the provisions of clause 4 of Article 1252, Article 1487, clauses 1–2 and subclause 1 clause 4 of Article 1515 of the Civil Code of the Russian Federation contained in the Resolution.

This position was also reflected in Resolution of the Plenum of the Supreme Court No. 10.

There are other means of restricting the rights of the right holder in the field of IP, for example, compulsory licences, free use and the right of prior use and subsequent use. They are all aimed at achieving a balance of interests of the right holder and third parties.

However, relations in the field of IP are not limited to resolving issues dealing with monopoly or competition. The principle of cooperation cannot be ignored either. It takes place at the earliest stage when the object of intellectual rights is not yet available, but its creation is planned. The right holder may provide other persons with the opportunity to use it for a fee or free of charge in the future.

When determining the methods of use, it must be borne in mind that all options have their pros and cons. So, if a person wants to do this on his own, then, on the one hand, he will fully control all the processes, but on the other hand, responsibility for the decision and also business risk falls on him. Business risk, in this case, suggests that there can be a positive effect from the use of the IP subject matter, and there is a possibility of obtaining a negative result. In the context of business activity in Russia, it is customary to talk about general business risk since risk is one of the legitimate features of the mentioned activity (Article 2 of the Civil Code). However, it is also possible to single out certain types of risk that can be distinguished from this general one. But even the risks associated with the use of the IP subject matter in business will affect the overall entrepreneurial risk. It is imperative that the business entity is aware of the presence of risk in its activities. Recognition of this fact allows the possibility of minimizing the risk. It is possible to reduce business risk, inter alia, by analyzing the necessary information, including on the implementation and protection of intellectual rights.

So, entrepreneurs must pay special attention to the protection of IP to identify violations and choose the right method of protection.

For instance, in a situation where a competitor registers one's commercial name as a service mark, the injured holder of the commercial name may try to claim that the actions of the competitor should be recognized as an act of unfair competition (Articles 14.4 and 14.8 of the Law on Protection of Competition). However, it is rather difficult to prove the existence of an act of unfair competition. In one case, the court noted that the evidence presented by a plaintiff does not prove the following circumstances:

- the defendant was aware of the fact that the plaintiff used the controversial sign prior to the date on which actions to register the exclusive right to the service mark were taken;
- the defendant had the intention, by acquiring the exclusive right to the sign (acquiring a monopoly on it), to harm the plaintiff or to oust the plaintiff from the commodity market by making claims aimed at preventing the use of the controversial sign;
- infliction or the likelihood of causing harm to the plaintiff by filing claims to terminate the use of a commercial name.

At the same time, the court drew attention to the plaintiff's argument that the state registration of the service mark violates the plaintiff's exclusive rights to the commercial name as the significant one. However, the identification of the service mark with the commercial name, the exclusive right to which, according to the plaintiff, belongs to them, may be the basis for challenging the granting of legal protection to this mark in accordance with clause 8 of Article 1483 of the Civil Code. In this case, it is necessary to comply with the administrative procedure for protecting one's rights (see section "Protection of IP rights") (Resolution of the Presidium of the Intellectual Property Rights Court of November 11, 2020, on case No SIP-585/2019).

If the person does not want to act on his own, he can find a partner with which to cooperate. But the potential risk of termination of joint activities and, as a result, disputes over the subsequent use of IP must be taken into account.

For example, an individual entrepreneur filed a lawsuit to prohibit the use of a commercial name in any form. Previously, the plaintiff and the defendant were in a registered marriage. The marriage contract was concluded between them, but the question of the commercial name was not resolved in it. Based on the case materials, the courts concluded that during the period of being married, the parties jointly used the controversial sign in their business. The courts also found that there is no evidence of the use of the controversial sign exclusively by the plaintiff and only for the individualization of her activities, and there is also no evidence that the controversial sign is associated by consumers exclusively with the plaintiff's activities (Resolution of the Intellectual Property Court of October 27, 2015, on case No. A60-934/2015)

The transfer of rights to another person can be regarded as the fastest way to receive remuneration for it, on the one hand, and to get ready-to-use IP subject matter, on the one hand. However, in this case, there are several risks: the risk of delay in payment, incomplete payment or even non-payment (for the right holder), the risk of reduced economic attractiveness (both partners), the risk of inability to use the IP (both partners) and the risk of failed expectations for the use of IP (for the transferee).

Moreover, speaking about business, such an aspect as the commercialization of IP shall also be mentioned.

IP commercialization is an extremely significant aspect of any IP-related business entity's activity. In the most general sense, it can be defined as the use of an IP subject matter and the disposal of the rights to it for the purpose of making a profit.

GOST R 58223-2018 on intellectual property and antimonopoly regulation offers a more detailed definition according to which the commercialization of an IP subject matter implies activities to obtain economic income from the implementation of exclusive rights to IP subject matter both when using them in the creation, production and sale of goods (works/services) by the participants of the product market, and in the civil circulation of IP, including purposes to attract additional investment and additional capitalization of assets by business entities as right holders.

However, commercialization is impossible without effective IP management, which is understood as an area of management activity focused on the effective management of the exclusive and other property rights to IP subject matter and the relations emerging in the course of their distribution between entities and their use in the economic activity of an enterprise/organization, including:

- state regulation of the management activities carried out primarily through a system of taxes, restrictions, benefits, orders;

- establishment of the rules for the selection, distribution and registration of intellectual rights, their use and disposal, as well as protection in the course of economic activity (including at the level of local regulations and organization standards);
- organization of accounting, evaluation and use of IP, including for the purposes of capitalization, taxation and commercialization;
- creation of a risk management system in the field of IP;
- development and application of a system of indicators for auditing the effectiveness of legal protection, circulation and legal protection of IP;
- training/retraining of personnel in the field of IP;
- ensuring effective coordination and control at all stages of the life cycle of IP.

GOST R 56273.4-2016/CEN/TS 16555-4: 2014. National Standard of the Russian Federation. Innovation Management. Part 4. Intellectual Property Management, was approved and put into effect by Order of Rosstandart No. 1937-st of May 12, 2016 on this issues.

IP management can be carried out both by the right holder and authorized persons. An example of the management by authorized persons is organization activities that manage copyright and related rights collectively.

Collective management organizations may be created to manage rights related to one or more types of copyright and/or related rights objects, one or more types of such rights in relation to certain uses of the IP subject matter or any copyright and/or related rights. They are non-profit organizations whose activities are regulated by the Civil Code (Part I), Law on Non-Profit Organizations and the charter of a particular organization.

For the transfer of authority, an agreement shall be concluded in writing,[3] being the basis for the emergence of such authority. An exception to this rule is collective organizations with state accreditation. They can manage rights and collect remuneration for those right holders with whom they do not have such agreements (see section "The state regulation of IP").

An organization's authority to manage rights on a collective basis may also proceed from an agreement with another organization, including a foreign one, that administers rights on a collective basis.

A collective management organization:

- concludes licencing agreements with users;
- enters into agreements with users on the payment of remuneration and collects funds for these purposes;
- collects remuneration, subject to the conclusion of the contract, directly by the right holder and the presence of an indication thereof in the contract;
- collects reports on the use of copyright and related rights objects;
- distributes remuneration for the use of copyright and related rights objects among the right holders, and also pay it to them;

- submits a report containing information on the use of their rights, including the amount of the collected remuneration and the amount withheld from it, to the right holder;
- creates registers containing information about the right holders, the rights transferred to the organization in question for management, as well as about copyright and related rights objects;
- places information about the rights transferred to it for management, including the name of the copyright or related rights object, the name of the author or another right holder in a publicly accessible information system;
- protects the rights transferred to it for management.

The organization itself is not entitled to use objects of copyright and related rights, the exclusive rights to which have been transferred to it for management.

Another option for the transfer of management is the conclusion of a fiduciary management agreement. Under this contract, one party (the founder of the management agreement) transfers the property to the other party (the trust manager) for a certain period of time in trust, and the other party undertakes to manage this property in the interest of the founder of the management agreement or the person indicated by them (beneficiary).

As a general rule, a trust manager can be an individual entrepreneur or a commercial legal entity, with the exception of a unitary enterprise. A citizen who is not an entrepreneur and a non-profit organization, with the exception of an institution, may act as a trustee only in cases provided by law, for example, as a consequence of the need to manage the inherited property.

This agreement must contain the following conditions:

- the list of the property transferred for trust management;
- the name of the legal entity or the name of the individual in whose interest the property is managed (the founder of the management or the beneficiary);
- the amount and form of remuneration to the trust manager, if the contract stipulates the payment of remuneration;
- duration of the contract.

A fiduciary management agreement shall be concluded in writing. Its term, as a general rule, does not exceed 5 years.

The trust manager has the right to perform any legal and actual actions in relation to this property should they be in the interest of the beneficiary in accordance with the trust agreement. The agreement can specify actions required, e.g., in relation to the protection of the exclusive right: identifying violations, maintaining correspondence with the violator and filing an application to the court.

In this case, the trust manager must indicate their status thereof. If they fail to notify the counterparty about this, then they shall be answerable to the third parties personally and the property belonging to them.

The collection of the management founder's debts on the property[4] they transferred to trust is not allowed unless this person is insolvent (bankrupt).

Indicating the existence of the two above-described management options, clause 48 of Resolution of the Plenum of the Supreme Court No. 10 gives explanations that help to distinguish between them. As noted above, a non-profit organization, as a general rule, cannot be a trust manager. At the same time, only non-profit organizations can be empowered to manage rights on a collective basis. Carrying out trust management of property in the interest of the founder of the management agreement (beneficiary), the trust manager has the right to exercise the powers of the owner of the exclusive right within the limits stipulated by law and the contract (clause 1 of Article 1020 of the Civil Code) and to dispose of the exclusive right unless otherwise provided by the contract. At the same time, unlike a licence agreement, the use of the result of intellectual activity or means of individualization can be carried out only in the interests of the beneficiary. An agreement authorizing the management of rights on a collective basis shall not contain a condition on the use of copyright and related rights objects by the manager. The granting of such powers can be the subject matter of a licence agreement.

Despite the possibility of transferring the exclusive rights to a management organization, right holders often choose to determine the usage of the IP subject matter by themselves. They can use IP in their major activities, alienate their exclusive rights, transfer the right to use the corresponding result of intellectual activity or means of individualization and attract funding. For example, to obtain a loan, a pledge is significant. Under a pledge agreement on the exclusive right to a result of intellectual activity or to means of individualization (non-property rights cannot act as a subject of pledge), the pledger has the right to use such a result of intellectual activity or such means of individualization and to dispose of the exclusive right to such a result or to such a means during the term of this agreement and without the consent of the pledgee, except in the case of alienation of the exclusive rights, unless otherwise provided by the contract. The pledger is not entitled to alienate the exclusive right without the consent of the pledgee, unless otherwise provided by the contract.

As indicated in Resolution of the Plenum of the Supreme Court No. 10, a pledge agreement may establish:

- restriction on the pledger's independent use of the result of intellectual activity or means of individualization;
- restriction on the independent disposal of the exclusive right to the result of intellectual activity or means of individualization in ways other than concluding an agreement on the alienation of an exclusive right (for example, a ban may be imposed on a public statement which is provided in clause 5 of Article 1233 of the Civil Code, or on the conclusion of licence agreements, including the rules of Article 1286.1 of the Civil Code);

- the right of the pledger to conclude an agreement on the alienation of the exclusive right to the result of intellectual activity or means of individualization.

The pledger protects the exclusive right that is the subject of the pledge.

At the same time, the pledge of intellectual rights shall consider the risks of devaluation of rights to these objects, as well as the risk of their loss or limitation ("GOST R 58590-2019. National Standard of the Russian Federation. Intellectual Property. Management in a Credit Institution", approved and put into effect by Order of Rosstandart No. 950-st of October 10, 2019; hereinafter GOST R 58590-2019).

GOST R 58223-2018 includes the methods and forms of commercialization of IP, in which antitrust regulation and protection from unfair competition are required.

The methods of IP commercialization are:

- use of IP in their own activities,
- use of IP as a mechanism to create added value when granting the right to use IP on a contractual basis,
- use of IP for capitalization of assets through intangible assets,
- use of IP to attract investments (pledge),
- use of IP in the formation of authorized capital, etc.

The following forms of commercialization are mentioned: alienation and granting of exclusive rights, cross-licencing, return on investment and pledge of exclusive rights.

Similar methods and forms are also envisaged for a credit institution (GOST R 58590-2019).

At the same time, it seems that the named forms and methods are quite universal and can be used by various business entities.

It should also be noted that commercialization is not the only purpose of IP management. If a business sticks to a socially-oriented concept, then IP can be used not only for profit-making, but for pursuing other society-related goals too, e.g., activities aimed at organizing recreation and health improvement for children; provision of services in the field of preschool education and general education; additional education for children; psychological, pedagogical, medical and social assistance to learners experiencing difficulties in mastering basic general educational programs, development and social adaptation; training activities for employees and volunteers of socially-oriented non-profit organizations aimed at improving the quality of services provided by such organizations; cultural and educational activities (including the activities of private museums, theatres, libraries, archives, studio schools, creative workshops, botanical and zoological gardens, houses of culture, houses of folk art), etc. (Federal Law No. 209-FZ of July 24, 2007, "On the Development of Small and Medium-Sized Businesses in the Russian Federation"). For example, money received from the use of IP can be aimed at achieving the above goals.

The gratuitous provision of the opportunity to use an IP object by itself can be considered as achieving public interest. At the same time, a commercial entity will not be put at a disadvantage, since such activities tend to form a positive image of the entity, which nowadays seems to be extremely important for entrepreneurial activity.

In general, it can be noted that more ways of using IP can be added to the above.

In this regard, its intangible nature and other specific features provide the right holder with a wide range of opportunities, e.g., its joint use, its contribution to the authorized capital, cross-licencing, etc. Other options can be mentioned too, e.g., educational organizations of higher education can create business societies and business partnerships whose activities consist of the practical application (implementation) of the results of intellectual activity. They can also take part in business societies and business partnerships (Federal Law No. 273-FZ of December 29, 2012, "On Education").

However, proceeding from the goals of building a successful business, a significant number of issues should be taken into account. IP can serve as a significant competitive advantage; it can generate great profit if it is properly commercialized and contribute to the creation of a favourable reputation if it is effectively managed (for example, the use of IP in socially significant projects), but it must not be overestimated. Unreasonable expectations can ultimately have a negative impact on business performance.

Notes

1 The document is posted on the official website of the Ministry of Economic Development: http://old.economy.gov.ru/minec/references/regulations/201831075.
2 Information of the Constitutional Court of the Russian Federation on Resolution of the Constitutional Court of the Russian Federation No. 8-P of February 13, 2018, is posted at: http://www.ksrf.ru/ru/news/pages/ViewItem.aspx?ParamId=3389.
3 The rules on agreements on the alienation of exclusive rights and on licencing agreements do not apply to these agreements.
4 It is worth noting that the Civil Code provides the peculiarities of the forced collection of IP. For example, such an action on an author's exclusive right to a work is not allowed, except in the case of collection under a pledge agreement, which was signed by the author, and the subject matter of which is the exclusive right to a particular work specified in the agreement and owned by the author. The author's right to place claims against other people under an exclusive right alienation agreement or a licence agreement, as well as on income received from the use of a work, may be recovered. The exclusive right that does not belong to the author themselves, and the right to use a work belonging to the licensee, may be subject to collection (Article 1284 of the Civil Code).

9 The transfer of intellectual property rights

The transfer of intellectual property (IP) rights is an integral element of IP market relations. The transfer of rights can be carried out through civil contracts on the basis of employment contracts and other grounds established by law. At the same time, all these grounds have their own peculiarities that shall be taken into account for an appropriate transfer of rights. In addition, it should be borne in mind that not all IP rights are subject to transfer. For instance, the rights of authorship and to a name are inalienable and non-transferable.

The contractual model for the transfer of IP rights is considered to be the most common. It provides ample opportunities to determine the rights and obligations of the parties.

Among the civil contracts used to transfer IP rights, contracts that are specifically designed for this field (regulated by Part IV of the Civil Code) and contracts that are common and not mentioned in Part IV of the Civil Code (regulated by Part II of the Civil Code) shall be distinguished.

The most frequently used IP contracts are the alienation of the exclusive right and the licencing agreement. At the same time, in addition to the norms of Part IV of the Civil Code, general provisions on obligations (Articles 307–419 of the Civil Code) and a contract (Articles 420–453 of the Civil Code) apply to them, as otherwise they are not established by the rules of the corresponding section of the Civil Code and do not proceed from the content or the nature of the exclusive right.

Under an agreement on the alienation of the exclusive right, one party (the right holder) transfers or undertakes to transfer its exclusive right to the result of intellectual activity or to the means of individualization in full to the other party (transferee/purchaser) (Article 1234 of the Civil Code).

The essential terms of this contract include the subject of the agreement and the agreement being gratuitous or non-gratuitous. As a general rule, the transferee/purchaser undertakes to pay the right holder the contractual remuneration, the form of which can vary: fixed one-time or periodic payments, percentage of revenues (proceeds), etc.

However, the parties can agree on the gratuitous character of the contract, with the exception of commercial legal entities, which are created to make profits, since this can be qualified as a gift. In accordance with Article 575 of the Civil Code, a gift is not allowed in relations between commercial legal entities, with the exception of ordinary gifts, the value of which does not exceed 3,000 rubles.

If the parties disregard the issue of the non-gratuitousness/gratuitousness of the contract, then the contract will be recognized as not concluded.

The contract must contain an indication of the full transfer of exclusive rights. In its absence, the contract will be considered a licence agreement. An exception is an agreement concluded in relation to the right to use the result of intellectual activity created for inclusion in a complex subject matter.

The contract must be concluded in writing. Otherwise, it shall be deemed invalid.

For IP subject matters that require mandatory state registration or subject to voluntary registration, it is also necessary to register the transfer of the exclusive right. In this case, Rospatent deals with the exclusive rights to inventions, utility models, industrial designs, trademarks, service marks, topographies of integrated circuits, computer programs and databases.

Registration is regulated by:

- "Rules for the State Registration of the Disposal of the Exclusive Right to an Invention, Utility Model, Industrial Design, Trademark, Service Mark, Registered Topography of Integrated Circuits, Computer Program, Database under a Contract and the Transfer of the Exclusive Right without a Contract", approved by Resolution of the Government of the Russian Federation No. 1416 of December 24, 2015
- "Administrative Regulations for the Federal Service for Intellectual Property's State Service for the State Registration of the Agreement-Based Disposal of the Exclusive Right to an Invention, Utility Model, Industrial Design, Trademark, Service Mark, Registered Topography of Integrated Circuits, Computer Program, Database", approved by Order of the Ministry of Economic Development of the Russian Federation No. 371 of June 10, 2016

Registration includes the following administrative procedures:

1) acceptance and registration of documents;
2) verification of fees payment and documents examination;
3) entering information into the relevant register, issuing (sending) a notice of the state registration to the applicant, publishing information about the state registration in Rospatent's official bulletin.

To register the transfer of the exclusive right, an application must be submitted to Rospatent. The application can be signed by both parties or by only one of the parties to the contract. In case of the latter, the application must be accompanied by a document confirming the contractual relationship between the parties, for example, a contract, notarized extract from the contract or notice on the disposal of the exclusive right signed by the parties to the contract. The alienation agreement does not have to be attached to the application if both parties sign it (Resolution of the Intellectual Property Court of January 15, 2020, on case No. A40-295350/2018).

Thus, an interested party to the contract has the right, without the other party's participation, to apply for state registration (clause 3 of Article 1232 of the Civil Code; clause 37 of Resolution of the Plenum of the Supreme Court No. 10). This rule minimizes the risk of an unfair counteragent evading state registration.

State registration of the disposal of the exclusive right and transfer of the exclusive right is carried out when all the necessary documents have been submitted fully in the form that is specified and contain reliable information. In addition, the rights that are the subject of the contract shall not go beyond the rights of the parties, and the alienation of the exclusive right to a trademark, service mark or industrial design under the contract cannot serve as a possible justification for misleading the consumer about the product or its manufacturer.

The grounds for refusing state registration are:

- failure to pay the fees,
- failure to respond to Rospatent's notification on the provision of missing or corrected documents within three months from the dispatch date,
- failure to comply with the conditions of the state registration.

Suppose the transfer of the exclusive right under an exclusive right alienation contract is subject to state registration. In that case, the exclusive right to such a result or means of individualization shall be passed from the right holder to the transferee/purchaser at the moment of state registration.

Failure to comply with the requirement for state registration does not entail the invalidity of the contract itself. By virtue of clause 6 of Article 1232 of the Civil Code, the transfer of the exclusive right, its pledge or the granting of the right to use are deemed as not to have taken place (clause 37 of Resolution of the Plenum of the Supreme Court No. 10).

When it comes to tax disputes (i.e., tax liability cases), the absence of registration can be evidence that the agreement is only formal and has not been intended to have appropriate legal consequences since the use of an exclusive right is fully possible only subject to state registration of the transfer of rights (Resolution of the Eighteenth State Commercial Court of Appeal of November 6, 2020, on case No. A76-6266/2020).

General provisions on this type of agreement are the same for all types of IP; however, there are special rules for some of them.

The alienation of the exclusive right to an industrial design or trademark is not allowed if it can mislead the consumer about the product or its manufacturer (Articles 1365 and 1488 of the Civil Code). The Intellectual Property Court states in the Resolution of December 16, 2019, on case No.

A56-114236/2017, that cases in which information about a product included in a trademark transferred to a new owner creates a distorted view of the product or its manufacturer, thus affecting the consumer's decision, are misleading.

According to "Recommendations on the Verification of Agreements on the Disposal of the Exclusive Right to the Results of Intellectual Activity or Means of Individualization", approved by Order of Rospatent No. 186 of December 29, 2009, the alienation of the exclusive right to a trademark may be considered misleading if a trademark contains:

- a sign representing the state's coat of arms, flag or another state symbol and sign, the official name of a state, emblem, the abbreviated or full name of an international and intergovernmental organization, their emblems, flags, other symbols, official control and guarantee marks, fineness stamps, seals, an award or another distinction or a sign similar to them to the point of confusion, which was included as an unprotected element following the consent of the competent authority or its right holder if the trademark is assigned to a person who has not been given such approval;
- a sign indicating the place of production or distribution of goods and included in the trademark as an unprotected element if the trademark is assigned to a person located in a different geographical area;
- a sign that is identical or similar to the point of confusion to the official names and images of especially valuable objects of cultural heritage to the peoples of the Russian Federation or objects of the world cultural or natural heritage, as well as to images of cultural value stored in collections and funds if the trademark is assigned to a person that does not have the owner's consent.

When the exclusive right to a production secret is alienated, the person who has disposed of the right is obliged to maintain the confidentiality of the production secret until the exclusive right to the production secret expires (Article 1467 of the Civil Code). The exclusive right to a production secret is terminated for all right holders from the moment the confidentiality of the relevant information is lost.

It should be noted that in relation to an invention and selective breeding achievement, the right to the public offer to conclude a patent alienation agreement is provided for by law. In this case, it is also about the alienation of the exclusive right. This opportunity is provided to the applicant, who is the sole author of the invention or selective breeding achievement. They can submit a statement that, should the patent be issued, they shall conclude a patent alienation agreement on conditions consistent with the established practice with any citizen of the Russian Federation or any Russian legal entity that is the first to express such a desire and notify the patent owner and relevant registration authority. If such a statement exists, patent fees both for the patent application and the patent obtained under it shall not be paid (this obligation shall pass to the person with whom the contract will be concluded). The number of applications (related to inventions) filed by one applicant during a year, in respect of which they are exempt from paying patent fees, is ten.

This information is published in the official bulletin. Suppose no one has applied with a written notification of the desire to conclude a contract on the patent alienation within 2 years from the publication date. In that case, the patent owner may submit a petition to the indicated federal body to withdraw the application. In this case, they will be obliged to pay all the fees from which they were previously exempt.

The Civil Code also provides for the possibility of alienating the right to obtain a patent. It originally belongs to the author of the invention, utility model, industrial design or selective breeding achievement, who can transfer it under an agreement on the alienation of the right to obtain a patent. The right to obtain a patent may pass to another person (assignee) or transferred in cases and on the grounds established by law, including by way of universal succession or by contract, including an employment contract (Article 1357 of the Civil Code). The contract must be in writing. It is important that, according to the general rule, the risk of non-patentability in relation to an invention, utility model, industrial design and the risk of non-protection in relation to selective breeding achievement shall be undertaken by the purchaser of such a right. However, had the parties agreed otherwise, this provision can be changed.

Licence agreements are of no less importance. Under a licence agreement, one party – the owner of the exclusive right to the result of intellectual activity or to the means of individualization (licensor) – grants or undertakes to provide the other party (licensee) with the right to use such a result or such a means within the scope stipulated by the contract. In this case, it is not about the transfer of the exclusive right but about the indication of specific ways to use the IP subject matter. For example, as directly stated in Resolution of the Plenum of the Supreme Court No. 10, each method of using a creative work is an independent part of the exclusive right belonging to the author (other right holder). The right to use a work via each of these methods may be the subject of an independent licence agreement (clause 89).

The transfer of the exclusive right to the result of intellectual activity or to a means of individualization to the new right holder is not a basis for modification or termination of the licence agreement concluded by the previous right holder. The new right holder becomes the licensor on the terms of the previously concluded licence agreement. The licensee's consent to conclude an agreement on the alienation of the exclusive right is not necessary (clause 40 of Resolution of the Plenum of the Supreme Court No. 10).

The essential terms of this agreement are:

- the subject matter. The contract must contain an indication of the result of intellectual activity or means of individualization, of which the right to its use is granted under the contract, stating the document number certifying the exclusive right to such a result or means where necessary (patent, certificate);

- the compensation or the gratuitous nature of the agreement. Granting the right to use the result of intellectual activity or means of individualization free of charge in relations between commercial legal entities throughout the world and for the entire duration of the exclusive right under the terms of an exclusive licence is not allowed unless the Civil Code provides otherwise (Article 1235 of the Civil Code);
- ways of using the result of intellectual activity or the means of individualization. The licensee can use the result of intellectual activity or means of individualization only within the limits of those rights and in the ways provided for by the licence agreement. The right to use the result of intellectual activity or a means of individualization, which is not directly indicated in the licence agreement, shall not be granted to the licensee.

In this regard, the proper formulation of these terms seems to be extremely important since the opposite can have negative consequences. For example, the court recognized a licence agreement as not concluded due to the absence of sufficient individualization of non-exclusive rights in relation to specific software products in the licence agreement and any bilateral documents. Given that the parties did not agree on the price and procedure for transferring each specific software product nor sign the bids, all the facts indicated that the parties had not reached an agreement on the subject and price of the contract (Resolution of the State Commercial Court of Moscow Circuit of December 17, 2019, on case No. A40-17125/2017).

The absence of an agreed condition on compensation or gratuitousness is also the basis for recognizing the contract as not concluded; however, when solving this issue, it shall be carried out as per the principle of good faith. So, a party that has accepted full or partial fulfilment from the other party under such a licence agreement or otherwise means it is not entitled to demand this agreement to be recognized as not concluded if the statement of such a requirement, taking into account specific circumstances, contradicts the principle of good faith (clause 3 of Article 1 and clause 3 of Article 432 of the Civil Code). Good faith is one of the fundamental principles of the Russian legal system. According to Article 1 of the Civil Code, in the establishment, exercise and protection of civil rights and the performance of civil obligations, participants in civil legal relations must act in good faith. This term does not have a legal definition, but its essence is explained in Resolution of the Plenum of the Supreme Court No. 25. It states that assessing the actions of the parties as being in good or bad faith, one should proceed from the behaviour expected from any participant in civil turnover, taking into account the rights and legitimate interests of the other party and helping it, including obtaining the necessary information. Bad faith behaviour entails a refusal to protect the right belonging to a party in whole or in part and the use of other measures to ensure the protection of the interests of the bona fide party or third parties from the bad faith behaviour of the other party.

The terms of the exclusive right territory and duration, which are determined by the parties, are of great importance for the licence agreement.

However, if these conditions are not agreed, then the rules provided by the Civil Code will apply.

If the agreement does not specify the territory within which the use of such a result or means is allowed, the licensee has the right to use them within the whole territory of the Russian Federation.

If the licence agreement does not specify its duration, the agreement is considered to be concluded for 5 years unless the Civil Code provides otherwise. The period for which the licence agreement is concluded cannot exceed the duration of the exclusive right to the result of intellectual activity or means of individualization.

In case of the expiration of the exclusive right, the licence agreement shall be terminated. A written form is mandatory for a contract. It is also subject to the state registration requirement.

The licence agreement can be concluded on the terms of an exclusive or non-exclusive licence.

An exclusive licence grants the licensee the right to use the result of intellectual activity or means of individualization without the licensor retaining the right to issue licences to other persons.

With regard to an exclusive licence, the following should be considered:

- the licensor does not have the right to use the result of intellectual activity or means of individualization to the extent that said right had been granted to the licensee under an agreement on the terms of an exclusive licence unless otherwise provided by the agreement. The exclusive licence does not allow the possibility of granting the right to use the corresponding subject matter to third parties, while the licensor may either preserve the rights to use the subject matter or fail to preserve them, depending on the agreement of the parties (Decision of the State Commercial Court of the Sverdlovskii Region of August 6, 2018, on case No. A60-6645/2018);
- suppose a third partie's violation of the exclusive right to the result of intellectual activity or means of individualization, for which an exclusive licence has been issued, affects the rights of the licensee obtained on the basis of the licence agreement. In that case, the licensee may, along with other methods of protection, protect their rights in the ways specified for the protection of intellectual rights and exclusive right. The basis for the licensee's claim to recover compensation for violation of the exclusive right is the violation of the licensee's rights obtained from the licence agreement, not the right holder's.

A non-exclusive (simple) licence grants the licensee the right to use the result of intellectual activity or the means of individualization, while the licensor retains the right to issue licences to other persons.

Unless otherwise provided by the licence agreement, the licence is assumed to be simple (non-exclusive). At the same time, an error in the qualification of the contract may lead to the incorrect application of the legislation. For example, the court indicated that given the fact that the defendant was granted a non-exclusive right to use a trademark and invention (a simple non-exclusive licence), the plaintiff's arguments that he was not able to use the trademark and invention in his activities, or grant the right to use them to third parties, was rejected as it contradicted the evidence presented and the provisions of the current legislation (Articles 1235 and 1236 of the Civil Code of the Russian Federation) (Resolution of the Ninth State Commercial Court of Appeal of March 12, 2020, on case No. A40-184340/2019).

Considering the peculiarities of the licence agreement, its fulfilment is also important since this agreement is concluded for a certain period of time. The law stipulates the licensee's obligation to submit reports on the use of the result of intellectual activity or means of individualization to the licensor; however, the parties may agree otherwise. If the agreement specifies such an obligation for the licensee, then it seems reasonable to clarify the procedure for submitting reports. Otherwise, the licensee shall be obliged to submit such reports to the licensor at their request. Contracts often establish penalties for failure to fulfil this obligation.

It should also be noted that a licensor's disregard for the licence control right can be significant in licence-related disputes. For example, the court pointed out that in a case of contract renewal, the licensor, exercising the standard of care that would be expected of a reasonable and prudent person, had to make sure (in the purpose on licence control) that the defendant had complied with the conditions of the licence agreement for the use of computer programs in the prescribed ways, taking into account the restrictions established by the contract (Resolution of the Intellectual Property Court of November 2, 2020, on case No. A29-5935/2019).

The use of the result of intellectual activity or the means of individualization shall be carried out in strict accordance with the contract and only when it is valid. Otherwise, the licensee may be held liable for the violation of the exclusive right provided by law. However, the contract may also explicitly entail liability for such a violation.

As explained in clause 41 of Resolution of the Plenum of the Supreme Court No. 10, if the licence agreement contains a condition on the legal liability for the violation of the exclusive right to the result of intellectual activity or means of individualization, expressed in the use of such a result or means outside the scope of the rights granted by the agreement, the licensor has the right to demand recovery of damages or payment of compensation for the part that is not covered by the contractual penalty terms established for the above violation (offset penalty).

Should the contract allow the recovery of the contractual penalty only, the licensor cannot demand the recovery of compensation (losses) (exclusive penalty).

Suppose the agreement allows the application of liability at the discretion of the licensor. In that case, the licensor, if they choose so, have the right to demand the recovery of a penalty or compensation for losses (payment of compensation) (alternative penalty).

Taking into account the terms of the contract, it is possible to collect additional penalties besides the amount of compensated losses (compensation paid) (surcharge penalty).

Provided that the contract is non-gratuitous, the licensee is also obliged to pay remuneration to the licensor. A material breach of this obligation gives the licensor the right to unilaterally terminate the licence agreement and demand compensation for the losses caused by its termination. In this case, the contract is terminated upon the expiration of a 30-day period from the date of receipt of the relevant notice if the licensee has failed to fulfil the obligation to pay remuneration during this period. The remuneration payment demand shall not depend on the use or non-use of the corresponding result or means by the licensee, although in court practice, there are examples when the debtor points out this circumstance (Resolution of the Intellectual Property Court of February 26, 2020, on case No. A56-141067/2018).

If the parties agree on a fixed payment for the right to use the result of intellectual activity or means of individualization, and also additionally agree on the amount of remuneration in the form of percentage deductions from the revenue (proceeds) (subclause 3, clause 5 of Article 1235 of the Civil Code), provided the result of intellectual activity or means of individualization is not used by the licensee, only the fixed amount is subject to payment. At the same time, the licensor shall not be deprived of the right to demand compensation for the losses caused by non-use of the result of intellectual activity or the means of individualization, and to terminate the contract.

When the parties to the licence agreement agreed on the amount of remuneration only in the form of percentage deductions from the revenue (proceeds), the use of the result of intellectual activity and means of individualization is not-existent and the licensor has the right to demand compensation for the losses caused by non-use of the result of intellectual activity or means of individualization, as well as to terminate the contract. The amount of damages can be determined based on the price that is usually charged for the legitimate use of this or similar results of intellectual activity or means of individualization under comparable circumstances.

The publishing licence agreement (Article 1287 of the Civil Code Civil Code) is another type of licence agreements. Its parties are the author/copyright holder and the publisher, that is, the person who, in accordance with the contract, is obliged to publish the work.

An integral element of this agreement is that the licensee (publisher) shall start using the work no later than the term specified in the agreement. If this obligation is not fulfilled, the licensor has the right to terminate the contract without reimbursing the licensee for the losses caused by such a refusal.

If the contract does not contain a specific date for the start of the use of the work, then such use must be started within the universal period for the given type of work and the method of their use. The licensor can terminate such an agreement on general grounds for termination of contracts, which are defined in Article 450 of the Civil Code (Part I).

The licensor has the right to demand the full payment of the remuneration stipulated by the agreement.

Forcing the licensee to publish the work is not provided in the Civil Code, although there are examples of such claims in court. In these situations, it is indicated that an inappropriate way of protecting the violated right has been chosen (Appeal Ruling of the Moscow City Court of June 22, 2017, on case No. 33-23198/2017).

It is noteworthy that, sometimes the licensee tries to make claims for the recovery of lost profits. However, it must be proven that it really arose as a result of the actions of the licensor; otherwise, the case will be denied. (Appeal Ruling of the Moscow City Court of August 26, 2020, on case No. 33-30100/2020).

The Civil Code also specifies an open licence, a public licence and a compulsory licence (see section "Creation and registration of IP").

An open licence and a public licence provide an opportunity for an indefinite number of persons to use IP subject matter, but there are significant differences between them.

A public licence (Article 1233 of the Civil Code) is the right holder's permission to free use of a work of science, literature or art belonging to them or an object of related rights on the conditions determined by the right holder and within the specified period.

If there is no indication in the statement of the right holder of:

- the term, then it shall be considered to be of 5 years,
- the territory, then it shall be considered to be the territory of the Russian Federation.

A statement about the opportunity provided must be made public by posting on the official website of the Ministry of Culture of the Russian Federation ("Rules for Posting the Statements of Rights Holders on the Granting of the Right of Free Use of Science, Literature or Art Works on Certain Conditions and for a Period Specified by Them", approved by the Decree of the Government of the Russian Federation No. 745 of June 8, 2019).

During the validity period, the statement cannot be withdrawn, and the conditions of use provided cannot be limited.

The corresponding statement cannot be made if the right holder has concluded another agreement for the provision of an exclusive licence for the use of a creative work or object of related rights within the same legal limits.

Suppose the right holder is a party to a valid contract with a paid simple licence. In that case, the placement of a statement informing about granting a similar scope of rights will terminate such an agreement. In this case, the right holder who made the corresponding statement in the presence of a licence agreement in force shall compensate for the losses caused to the licensee.

Had the statement been made unlawfully, e.g., by a person who does not have the corresponding right, the author or another right holder has the right to demand to apply measures to protect the exclusive right against the violator.

An open licence also implies the possibility of granting any person the right to use a work and objects of related rights within the limits provided for by the contract (Articles 1286.1 and 1308 of the Civil Code) under the terms of a non-exclusive licence. If the open licence does not indicate the territory where the use of the work is allowed, such use is allowed throughout the world. Suppose the validity period of an open licence is not determined in respect of computer programs and databases. In that case, the contract is considered concluded for the entire period of validity of the exclusive right, and in respect of other types of works, the contract is considered concluded for 5 years.

This agreement is an accession agreement, that is, an agreement with predetermined conditions that are fully accepted by the counterparty. Its terms must be available to an indefinite circle of persons and placed in such a way that the licensee should be able to read them before beginning to use the subject matter.

As a general rule, an open licence is free of charge, but it can also be for a fee if it contains a corresponding indication.

The licensor can refuse to fulfil the terms of the agreement unilaterally (wholly or in part) if the licensee provides third parties with the rights to use the work belonging to the licensor or to use a new result of intellectual activity created by the licensee on the basis of this work, beyond the scope of the rights and (or) on terms that are different from those provided for by the open licence.

The licensor may grant the licensee the right to use the work belonging to him to create a new result of intellectual activity. In this case, unless otherwise provided by an open licence, it is considered that the licensor made an offer to conclude an agreement (clause 2 of Article 437 of the Civil Code) on the use of the work to any persons wishing to use a new result of intellectual activity created by the licensee on the basis of this work, within the limits and on the terms provided by the open licence. Acceptance of such an offer is also deemed to be an acceptance of the licensor's offer to conclude a licencing agreement with respect to this work.

In the event of an unlawful provision or use of an open licence, the author or right holder can apply exclusive rights protection measures to the violator.

In addition, open licences are also provided for inventions, utility models and industrial designs (Article 1368 of the Civil Code).

In this case, the patent owner informs Rospatent about the possibility of granting any person the right to use an invention, utility model or industrial design (open licence). Information on the subject is published in Rospatent's bulletin.

If an interested person applies to the patent holder with a proposal to conclude an agreement, they will be obliged to do so under the terms of a simple (non-exclusive) licence. At the same time, the size of the patent fee for maintaining a patent on an invention, utility model or industrial design shall be reduced by 50 per cent from the year following that of the open licence publication.

As pointed out in "Recommendations on the Implementation of the Administrative Procedures and Actions for the Consideration of a Statement by a Right Holder on Granting any Person the Right to Use an Invention, Utility Model or Industrial Design (Open Licence), or a Petition to Withdraw an Open Licence Statement", approved by Order of the Ministry of Economic Development of the Russian Federation No. 552 of August 12, 2015, the publication of information on the provision of an open licence indicating the correspondence address in Rospatent's official bulletin gives an additional opportunity to the patent owner to draw attention to the invention, utility model or industrial design to which they own the exclusive right. This opportunity is of particular importance for individuals who cannot independently use, and therefore really implement, an invention, utility model or industrial design.

The patent holder has the right to file a petition to withdraw their statement for an open licence if, within 2 years from the open licence publication date, they have not received proposals in writing to conclude a licence agreement on the terms contained in the statement. In this case, they shall pay all the fees by themselves.

An open licence is also provided for selective breeding achievements (Article 1429 of the Civil Code). The patent holder applies to the Ministry of Agriculture of the Russian Federation with a corresponding statement and acquires the right to reduce the fees by 50 per cent starting from the year following that of the open licence publication.

The withdrawal of the statement can be carried out no matter the existing licence agreements under the open licence terms. The condition is the expiration of a 2-year period from the statement publication date. If there were no proposals to conclude licencing agreements, then upon withdrawal of an open licence, the patent owner is obliged to pay all unpaid fees.

If prior to the withdrawal of the open licence, open licence agreements were concluded, the licensees retain their rights for the entire duration of these agreements. In this case, the patent owner is obliged to pay the fee for maintaining the patent in full from the open licence withdrawal date.

The Civil Code provides for the possibility of concluding a sublicence agreement with the written consent of the licensor. Under the sublicence agreement, the sublicensee can be granted the rights to use the result of intellectual activity or means of individualization only within the scope of those rights and methods of use provided by the licence agreement for the licensee.

As a general rule, it is the licensee that bears responsibility for the actions of the sublicensee to the licensor. However, the licence agreement may specify a different procedure.

At the same time, as noted by the court, actions that go beyond the sublicence agreement's scope are an illegal use of the result of intellectual activity. Liability for the violation of such rights occurs on a general basis, i.e., the offender themselves becomes responsible for such a violation (Appeal Ruling of the Moscow City Court of December 24, 2013, on case No. 11-42063).

It should be noted that the rule of joint disposal applies both to the contract for the alienation of the exclusive right and to the licence contracts. The disposal of the exclusive right to the result of intellectual activity or to the means of individualization shall be carried out by the right holders jointly unless otherwise provided by the Civil Code or an agreement between right holders (Article 1229 of the Civil Code). That is, in the presence of several right holders, their will to dispose of the right must be agreed upon, unless otherwise provided by the Civil Code or an agreement between them. For example, the court clarifies that in order to prove the transfer of the exclusive right, it is necessary to establish the will of each original right holder (members of the musical group) to such disposal (Resolution of the Intellectual Property Court of July 31, 2018, on case No. A46-3927/2016). In another case, it was noted that disposal of the exclusive right made by one of the authors regarding a jointly created work was not sufficient and did not give rise to a transfer or granting of the right to such a work (Resolution of the Ninth State Commercial Court of Appeal of September 18, 2020, on case No. A40-210460/2019).

Furthermore, there is a normative ban on the terms of an exclusive right alienation agreement or a licence agreement that restricts the right of a person to create results of intellectual activity of a certain kind or in a certain field of intellectual activity or to alienate the exclusive right to such results to other persons (Article 1233 of the Civil Code). Such conditions are considered invalid. For example, the court indicates that the condition on the alienation of the exclusive rights to all literary, artistic, photographic and other works that the author will create in the future to the purchaser is invalid on the grounds of clause 4 of Article 1233 of the Civil Code. Any restrictions on the author's legal capacity are inadmissible based on Article 44 of the Constitution of the Russian Federation (Resolution of the Intellectual Property Court of May 26, 2020, on case No. A40-121738/2019).

It should also be considered that the author's liability under the contract on the alienation of the exclusive right to a work and under a licencing agreement is limited by the amount of real damage caused to the other party unless the agreement provides for a lower amount of the author's liability (Article 1290 of the Civil Code). So, for example, the court considers that imposing on the authors the obligation to compensate the publisher for lost profits infringes on the authors' rights guaranteed by law (Appeal Ruling of the Moscow City Court of February 10, 2017, on case No. 33-4884/2017).

As noted earlier, the disposal of intellectual rights can also be carried out by contracts that are not mentioned in Part IV of the Civil Code; that is, they are not part of the group of IP agreements but belong to contracts of a general scope.

For example, Part II of the Civil Code contains norms on enterprise (property complex, see section "Intellectual property: concept and types"), sale and purchase contract, according to which, as a general rule, the buyer acquires exclusive rights to the means of individualization of the enterprise, products, works or services of the seller (commercial name, trademark, service mark), as well as the rights to use such means of individualization on the basis of licence agreements. However, the contract may provide otherwise. Special attention should be paid to the fact that the right of prior use and subsequent use can be transferred under this agreement.

In turn, under an enterprise lease agreement, the lessor grants the lessee the rights to the signs that individualize the activities of the enterprise and other exclusive rights in temporary possession for consideration.

A commercial concession agreement is of great importance too. According to Article 1027 of the Civil Code, under a commercial concession agreement, one party (right holder) undertakes to provide the other party (user) the right to use a set of exclusive rights belonging to the right holder, in business, including the right to a trademark or service mark, and the rights to other objects of exclusive rights mentioned in the agreement, in particular, to a commercial name and (or) a production secret (know-how), for a specified or unspecified period of time and on the basis of payment.

The parties to this agreement are commercial legal entities and natural persons registered as individual entrepreneurs.

The contract is a reimbursable one, and the parties can determine the form of remuneration, for example, fixed one-time and (or) periodic payments, deductions from the proceeds, a mark-up on the wholesale price of goods transferred by the right holder for resale, etc. Failure to pay the remuneration within the period established by the contract allows the right holder to refuse to fulfil the commercial concession agreement wholly or in part.

The right holder is obliged to transfer technical and commercial documentation and provide other information that the user requires to exercise the rights granted to them under the commercial concession agreement and instruct the user and their employees on any issues related to the exercise of these rights.

Unless otherwise agreed, the right holder must ensure the state registration of the grant of the right to use a complex of exclusive rights under a commercial concession agreement, provide advisory and technical assistance and control the quality of goods (works, services) produced (performed, rendered) by the user.

The user's obligations are reduced to the proper use of the provided set of exclusive rights. The violation of the terms about the quality of the goods produced, the work performed, the services rendered or a gross violation of the right holder's instructions gives the right holder the opportunity to refuse to fulfil the contract.

Upon the expiration of the commercial concession, the user who has properly fulfilled their obligations has the preferential right to renew the agreement.

The agreement shall be concluded in writing and transfer of rights is registered in Rospatent. If this requirement fails to be met, the granting of the right is considered to not have taken place.

In practice, there are cases of confusion between a commercial concession agreement and a licence agreement. For example, the court noted that a plaintiff believed that instead of a licence agreement, he was entering into a commercial concession agreement for the acquisition of a franchise (Resolution of the Eleventh State Commercial Court of Appeal of September 11, 2018, on case No. A65-11063/2018).

The rules on the licence agreement are applied to the commercial concession agreement if this does not contradict the provisions of the Civil Code and the essence of the commercial concession agreement. However, as noted by the court, the stipulated peculiarities of the legal regulation under a commercial concession agreement do not form the basis for its qualification as a licence contract (Resolution of the Intellectual Property Court of May 20, 2020, on case No. A56-24852/2019).

The transfer of IP rights can also be carried out in the order of inheritance. The necessary explanations on this issue are contained in Resolution of the Plenum of the Supreme Court No. 9 of May 29, 2012, "On Judicial Practice in Inheritance Cases".

The exclusive rights to the results of intellectual activity and the means of individualization are transferred to the heirs for the rest of the validity period, the duration of which is established by the Civil Code and depends on the type of IP, and after the expiration of the corresponding period, the results of intellectual activity being works of science, literature, art (both published and unpublished), computer programs, databases, performances, phonograms, inventions, utility models or industrial designs, selective breeding achievements or topographies of integrated circuits shall pass into the public domain and can be freely used in accordance with the Civil Code by any person without anyone's consent or permission and without the payment of royalties.

If there are several heirs, then they are subject to the rules of the plurality of right holders.

In addition to the exclusive right, the inheritance includes other property rights, for example:

- the resale right;
- the right to obtain a patent, the right to restore the validity of a patent on an invention, utility model or industrial design and the right to obtain a patent on a selective breeding achievement;
- the rights of the author being an employee under an employment agreement, the revenue not received by the author, as well as the author's right to remuneration, being the owner of the exclusive right to a work made under an employment contract, if the employer uses the work under a simple (non-exclusive) licence;
- the employee's right to remuneration for the results of intellectual activity, e.g., an invention, a utility model or an industrial design or a selective breeding achievement;
- the right to remuneration for the topography of integrated circuits. The right to remuneration paid to the author as the owner of the exclusive right to a topography of integrated circuits made under an employment contract if the employer uses such a topography of integrated circuits under the

> terms of a simple (non-exclusive) licence shall pass to the author's heirs on a general basis.

Special attention is paid to the inheritance of the exclusive right to a trademark and commercial name when the right holder is an individual entrepreneur. Suppose the exclusive right to a trademark is inherited by a person who is not an individual entrepreneur. In that case, it must be alienated within a year from the date of opening the inheritance (date of citizen's death) (except if they are registered as an individual entrepreneur during this period). Before the expiration of this period, the legal protection of a trademark or a service mark on the basis provided in subclause 4, clause 1 of Article 1514 of the Civil Code cannot be terminated.

An individual entrepreneur's exclusive right to a commercial name as a means of individualization belonging to the right holder of the enterprise (clauses 1 and 4 of Article 1539 of the Civil Code) is inherited only in cases where the heir is a legal entity or an individual entrepreneur.

In addition to the above, other options for the transfer of intellectual rights are also possible, for example, a transfer as a result of the reorganization of a legal entity, forced collection on the property of the right holder, etc.

10 IP in digital economy

Digital technologies play a crucial role in today's society. One can hardly imagine the modern world without computers, the internet, computer programs, databases, etc. On the one hand, all this greatly facilitates access to information, which is extremely important nowadays; on the other hand, a special approach to regulating this area, considering its peculiarities, is required. As a rule, social relations connected with digital technologies are called "digital". The economic area is no exception. So, the digital economy is understood as an economic activity in which the key factor of production is digital data. In comparison with traditional forms of management, the processing of large volumes of data and the use of the data analysis results lead to a significant increase in the efficiency of various types of production, technologies, equipment, storage, sale, delivery of goods and services (Decree of the President of the Russian Federation No. 203 of May 9, 2017, "On the Strategy for the Development of the Information Society in the Russian Federation for 2017–2030").

As stated in GOST R 58223-2018, during the transition to the digital economy, the share of added value from the intellectual property (IP) turnover in the pricing of manufactured goods, works/services and finances will only increase, which, in turn, will stimulate competition, including unfair competition, in this sphere.

All the above draws one's attention to the exercise and protection of intellectual rights in the information society.

For instance, electronic document management might have been an unusual phenomenon a few years ago. However, today, human activity is unthinkable without it. The business sphere is no exception. And it is not only about maintaining correspondence with counterparties by e-mail, posting information about the company and its products on a website but also about interaction with the state authorities.

Thus, as can be seen from the acts, regulating the activities of Rospatent, applications, requests and other documents can be filed on the internet through Rospatent's (Federal Institute of Industrial Property; FIIP) official website using the FIIP's information systems or by the public services portal (PSP).

For instance, if the application for the grant of a patent is submitted online, the formal requirements shall be the same as those submitted on paper, except the signature requirements.

The electronic application shall be signed with an enhanced qualified electronic signature. It must be mentioned that electronic signature issues are normatively regulated in Russia. An electronic signature is information in electronic form that is attached to other information in an electronic document (signed information), or is otherwise related to this information, and is used to identify the person signing the information (Article 2 of Federal Law No. 63-FZ of April 6, 2011, "On Electronic Signature"; hereinafter Federal Law on Electronic Signature).

In general, the interacting parties can use:

- a simple electronic signature,
- an enhanced electronic signature (enhanced unqualified electronic signature or enhanced qualified electronic signature).

A qualified electronic signature implies compliance with more requirements, but it also provides more opportunities. In accordance with clause 1 of Article 6 of the Federal Law on Electronic Signature, information in electronic form signed with a qualified electronic signature shall be recognized as an electronic document that is equivalent to a paper document signed with a handwritten signature and can be used in any legal relationship in accordance with the legislation of Russia, unless the federal laws or the corresponding regulatory acts establish that this type of document must be exclusively on paper. At the same time, such information signed by a simple electronic signature or an unqualified electronic signature shall be recognized as an electronic document equivalent to the paper document in cases specially established by regulatory acts or by the agreement between the participants of an electronic interaction.

It must be mentioned that in Russia, electronic signatures created according to the law of a foreign state and international standards shall be recognized as being the type to which they correspond on the basis of the Federal Law on Electronic Signature. The recognition of electronic signatures created in accordance with the law of a foreign state and international standards, as an enhanced electronic signature, and their application in legal relations in accordance with the Russian legislation shall be possible in cases established by the international treaties of the Russian Federation. Such electronic signatures are recognized as valid if their compliance with the requirements of the specified international treaties is confirmed by an accredited trusted third party, an accredited certification centre or another person authorized to do it by an international treaty of the Russian Federation, taking into account the Federal Law on Electronic Signature. The electronic signature and the electronic document signed with it cannot be considered invalid because the certificate of the electronic signature verification key was issued according to the norms of foreign law.

When a public service is provided in an electronic form, certain types of electronic signature permitted for use by the Russian legislation are used. The allowed types of electronic signatures for the mentioned purposes are established by Resolution of the Government of the Russian Federation No. 634 of June 25, 2012, "On the Types of Electronic Signatures, the Use of Which is Allowed when Applying for State and Municipal Services."

Another important aspect of an electronic interaction is as follows. In accordance with clause 4 of Article 11 of Federal Law No. 149-FZ of July 27, 2006, "On Information, Information Technologies and Protection of Information" (hereinafter Law on Protection of Information), for the purpose of concluding civil contracts or formalizing other legal relations that require electronic communication, the exchange of electronic messages signed with an electronic signature or another alternative to the sender's handwritten signature in the manner prescribed by regulatory acts or by the agreement between the parties, shall be considered an exchange of documentation.

In this case, a written contract can be concluded by drawing up one document (including electronic) signed by the parties or by exchanging letters, telegrams, electronic documents or other data, taking into account the following. The written part of the deal is also considered to be realized if the person concludes the deal using electronic or other technical means that allow the reproduction of the contents of the deal on a material carrier without changing them; the requirement for a signature is considered fulfilled if the method that is used allows the positive identification of the person who is expressing their will (clause 2 of Article 434 and clause 2 of Article 160 of the Civil Code).

Returning to online submission, its advantages should be mentioned.

As it appears in the acts regulating Rospatent's activities, in cases prescribed by them, the amount of the established fees for the consideration of an application is reduced by 30 per cent on the condition of corresponding in electronic form.

Furthermore, electronic communication does not require special working hours (registration can be carried out 24 hours a day, even at weekends and on holidays), and the exchange of information is easier and faster in comparison with traditional methods.

In the context of the ongoing digitalization, a recently introduced provision of the Civil Code is worth closer consideration.[1] In accordance with Article 309, the deal's terms may imply that the parties to the deal shall fulfil the obligations arising from it, although these are not expressly stipulated, upon the occurrence of certain circumstances using information technologies determined by the agreement. In other words, the current civil legislation mentions an automated execution of an obligation, subject to specified conditions, and, thus, allows legally enshrined possibility of using a smart contract. The above does not have any restrictions on the scope of obligations; therefore, it can be applied to IP.[2]

Nevertheless, electronic document management, with all its advantages, has not yet replaced the traditional version. So, despite the fact that Rospatent has issued a number of documents in electronic form (for instance, patents), at the request of an interested person, it remains possible to ask for a paper version. In the process of executing contracts, counterparties, transmitting documents by e-mail, duplicate them in the traditional form.

In the event that electronic images of evidence are sent to the court after the initiation of proceedings, the court may require the submission of the originals of this evidence, in particular, if:

- in accordance with federal law or other normative legal acts, circumstances are subject to confirmation only by such documents (for example, a bill of exchange);
- it is impossible to resolve the case without the original documents (for example, the borrower's receipt);
- submitted copies of the same document are different in their content;
- the judge has doubts based on the materials of the case about the reliability of the evidence presented and (or) the issue on their reliability was brought up for discussion by the participants of the case (Articles 67 and 71 of the Civil Procedure Code; Articles 71 and 75 of the State Commercial Procedure Code; Articles 70 and 84 of the Administrative Procedure Code) (clause 24 of Resolution of the Plenum of the Supreme Court of the Russian Federation No. 57 of December 26, 2017, "On Some Issues of the Application of Legislation Regulating the Use of Documents in Electronic Form in the Activities of Courts of General Jurisdiction and State Commercial Courts").

Despite the significant role of paper documents, the Russian normative regulation aims to maintain electronic interaction between subjects. Moreover, digitalization affects both public and private relations, including business.

It is also obvious that the internet and everything connected with it has become an integral part of the life of a modern person. In this regard, attention should be given to websites.

Article 2 of the Law on Protection of Information provides the definition of an internet site. This is a set of programs for electronic computers and other information contained in the information system, access to which is provided through the information and telecommunication network internet by domain names and (or) by network addresses that allow identifying sites on the internet. It is the site owner who determines the procedure for the site users.

Taking into account the provisions of Article 1260 of the Civil Code, an internet site is a composite work and, thus, is included in the list of copyright objects, although this issue has long been controversial. Until October 1, 2014, a website was not directly mentioned among copyright objects, so the question of whether it was IP subject matter used to be decided based on specific circumstances.

However, even the Resolution of the Presidium of the Supreme Commercial Court of April 22, 2008, on case No. A63-14046/2006-C1 indicated that a website consists of materials (texts, drawings, photographs, audiovisual works, etc.) that are selected and arranged in a certain way and that can be accessed with the help of a computer program (computer code), which is an element of the site. This combination, as programming experts put it, is the content of the site. As noted in this act, the court has to check whether the defendant's website, created by a third person under a contract, can be considered an independent composite work that shows a different selection or location of similar materials or whether a substantial part of the composite work, the rights to which belong to another business entity, was copied. Many courts adhere to this point of view too.

However, in judicial practice, the internet site has not always been recognized as an object of copyright. An example is the Appeal Ruling of the Kostroma Regional Court of September 25, 2013, on case No. 33-1578 that denied a claim for the recognition of copyright and the author's right to the name, restoration of the violated rights, compensation for moral damage and recovery of legal costs since internet sites are not subject to copyright protection. The individual elements (main pages) used by the defendant were for informational purposes only and their content did not correspond to the characteristics of works being objects of copyright.

Thus, the legitimate recognition of a website as a composite work in 2014 became a progressive measure of copyright regulation. Today's business is practically unthinkable without the use of websites. An internet site is often what makes business counterparties and consumers contact a particular organization to order (purchase) goods or services. A well-designed, user-friendly website should be considered a way to attract customers. Such a site forms the first positive impression of the business entity. The direct fixation of internet sites as IP subject matter, due to the written nature of Russian law, provides the legal basis for the protection of the rights to them.

For example, the court satisfied a legal claim on the obligation to stop using part of a website to recover compensation for a violation of the exclusive rights to a work in the amount of 2 million rubles. When monitoring medical institutions providing ophthalmological services, the plaintiff found that the defendant had copied a significant part of a website's content, being a composite work, the rights to which belong to the plaintiff. The claim was satisfied since the plaintiff had had exclusive rights to the controversial work before the defendant had entered into an agreement for the creation and development of the site; the fact of violation of the plaintiff's rights was proven, and the grounds for reducing the amount of compensation to be collected were not established. At the same time, the courts of all instances examined the contracts for the creation of websites provided by the parties. In the judicial act, the Intellectual Property Court, being a cassation instance, drew attention to the fact that the courts of other instances had established the following circumstances. Referring to the mentioned contract, the defendant failed to provide any evidence of its execution. At the same time, the plaintiff presented the acts of works performed as well as the payment orders confirming the fact of the payment for the work performed under the agreement on the creation of the website (Resolution of the Intellectual Property Court of December 23, 2019, on case No. A27-3997/2019).

The domain name is an extremely important part of an internet site. According to Article 2 of the Law on Protection of Information, the domain name is a sign intended for naming and addressing websites in order to provide access to information posted on the internet.

The main functions of the domain name are providing access to certain information and individualizing the information resource containing this information and its owner (Resolution of the Intellectual Property Court of September 4, 2018, on case No. A40-91339/2017).

The domain name is not recognized as IP subject matter; however, it is closely intertwined with IP.

It should also be noted that unless otherwise following from the circumstances of the case and the evidence presented, in particular, from the information posted on the site, it is presumed that the owner of the site is the administrator of the domain name referring to the site in question (clause 78 of Resolution of the Plenum of the Supreme Court No. 10).

Unfortunately, in Russian practice, the illegal use of domain names that prove identical or similar to the point of confusion to objects of IP rights, especially trademarks, can be found. That is why, based on the provisions of the Civil Code, a claim can be filed to prohibit the use of the domain name in a certain way (for example, to delete information about specific types of goods on the site in question or to stop addressing this site) (in case of IP rights protection, it is about the suppression of the actions that violate the right or pose a threat of its violation, see section"Protection of IP rights").

It is noteworthy that the concept of cybersquatting is reflected in judicial practice,[3] which is understood in a general sense as the registration of a domain name for the purpose of unfair competition, subsequent resale and advertising (Resolution of the Federal State Commercial Court of Moscow Circuit of December 31, 2010, on case No. A40-170684/09-26-1231; Decision of the State Commercial Court of Moscow City of June 8, 2011, on case No. A40-88268/10). Generally, it is used by the parties to substantiate their position.

As a rule, the violation of the exclusive right to a trademark includes the actual use of the domain name that is identical or similar to the point of confusion to the trademark in relation to goods similar to those for which this trademark has been granted legal protection. However, if they are not identical or similar to the point of confusion and their distinctiveness is great enough, and while using the compared signs, there will be no likelihood of their confusion in the minds of consumers, then the claim of the right holder will not be satisfied (Ruling of the Supreme Court of the Russian Federation of November 29, 2019, on case No. A41-77610/2017).

At the same time, the legal protection of a well-known trademark covers goods that are not homogeneous with those in respect of which it is recognized as well known if consumers associate the trademark used by another person in relation to these goods with the owner of the exclusive right to the well-known trademark, which can infringe on the legitimate interests of the right holder (clause 3 of Article 1508 of the Civil Code). Therefore, a violation of the exclusive right to a well-known trademark may not be only the use of the domain name but also the very fact of registering a domain name that is identical to this well-known trademark or similar to it to the point of confusion.

It should be borne in mind that, as indicated by the Intellectual Property Court, the use of a domain name itself may be considered a violation of the exclusive right to a trademark if it is registered as a well-known trademark or the court has established that the administrator's actions to acquire domain name rights are an act of unfair competition. The conclusion of the court of appeal on the violation of the exclusive right to a trademark by using it in a domain name was called premature, made with an incomplete study of the circumstances of the case to be established in this case (the trademark was not well-known and the circumstances indicating unfair competition were not determined). By virtue of clause 3 of Article 1484 of the Civil Code, the prohibition on the use of a trademark can only apply to specific goods in respect of which the court has established a violation of the exclusive right. Meanwhile, the appellate court forbade the defendant from using the trademark as a whole on the site, regardless of the specific goods (services). Taking into account these circumstances, the court of cassation considers that the decision of the court of appeal was adopted in violation of substantive law and, therefore, this judicial act cannot be recognized as lawful and must be cancelled; the case is then sent for a new consideration to the court of appeal (Ruling of the Intellectual Property Court of December 11, 2020, on case No. A40-247918/2019).

The administrator's actions aimed at acquiring the right to the domain name (taking into account the circumstances of its subsequent use) may be recognized as an act of unfair competition. In this case, based on the purposes of the domain name registration, such a registration itself may be considered a violation of the exclusive right to a trademark.

For example, the courts concluded that in the actions of the defendant, expressed in the use of a domain name in its business, a set of conditions formulated in the ICANN policy, which qualifies these actions as an act of unfair competition, existed (Resolution of the Intellectual Property Court of December 18, 2019, on case No. A40-84048/2018), namely:

- the disputed domain name is confusingly similar to the plaintiff's trademark, commercial name and company name. Using the domain name, the entrepreneur deliberately attracted internet users to the site by creating similarities with the plaintiff's means of individualization;
- it appears from the circumstances of the case and the evidence attached to the claim that the defendant could not have been unaware that the use of such a domain name would draw additional attention to the entrepreneur and his goods and services. Moreover, the entrepreneur set himself the

goal of obtaining additional benefits due to the visibility of the plaintiff and the services provided to him;

- the entrepreneur is a competitor of the plaintiff, a professional market participant, in connection with which consumers have a false impression that the site belongs to the plaintiff;
- the defendant has no rights and legitimate interest in relation to this domain name. At the same time, the defendant's argument that he has certain rights and legitimate interests in relation to the disputed domain name on the grounds that the entrepreneur is a co-founder of a legal entity affiliated with the plaintiff does not correspond to reality, since this legal entity and the entrepreneur were not and are not the owners of the self-titled trademark and the disputed domain name does not reflect the surname or name of the entrepreneur or the company name of such a legal entity.

Special attention should also be given to the use of ICANN policy in this case. As has been repeatedly pointed out by the Intellectual Property Court in disputes over domain names identical or confusingly similar to trademarks, when considering the issues of the bad faith of a person participating in the case, the court, in accordance with clause 1 of Article 5, clauses 1–2 of Article 10 of the Civil Code, clauses 2–3 of Article 10.bis of the Paris Convention to establish the content of fair practice in the registration and use (administration, delegation and other actions) of domain names and may use the provisions formulated in the ICANN policy, including in paragraphs 4 (a), 4 (b) and 4 (c) (Resolution of the Intellectual Property Court of May 16, 2019, on case No. A40-126845/2018; Resolution of the Intellectual Property Court of May 13, 2019, on case No. A40-77364/2018).

Suppose the acquisition of the right to the domain name is recognized as a violation of the exclusive right. In that case, the court can satisfy the requirement to annul the corresponding registration (clause 158 of Resolution of the Plenum of the Supreme Court No. 10).

At the request to suppress actions that violate the right to a trademark expressed in the illegal use of a domain name, interim measures can be taken in order to prevent significant damage to the applicant (for interim measures, see section "Protection of IP rights") specifically aimed at preserving the existing state of relations between the parties, in particular, the prohibition for the administrator to take any actions aimed at refusing or transferring the rights to administer the domain name, including changing the registrar, as well as prohibiting the registrar from annulling the domain name and transferring the domain name administration rights to another person (clause 160 of Resolution of the Plenum of the Supreme Court No. 10).

It is noteworthy that the use of an e-mail address in the presence of confusing similarity with the plaintiff's trademarks may be seen as a violation of exclusive rights. The court explained that an e-mail address is a way of sending electronic messages between users on the internet. By sending commercial offers, information, documents and other information to potential clients from e-mail addresses, if they are similar to the point of confusion with trademarks, the plaintiff contributes to the emergence of persistent associations related to the plaintiff among consumers. The court found the defendants' use of these signs as a violation of the plaintiff's exclusive rights (Resolution of the Intellectual Property Court of February 11, 2020, on case No. A41-7379/2019).

It should be noted that in some cases, the website turns from a copyright object into an instrument of IP rights infringement. This could involve not only an inappropriate domain name but also the content of the site.

As noted by the Intellectual Property Court, it is the domain administrator who is responsible for the content of the information on the website since it is impossible to use the site's resources without his control. This is because it is the domain name administrator who determines the procedure for using the domain and as such is responsible for the choice of the domain name and possible violations of the rights of third parties related to the choice and use of the domain name. They also bear the risk of losses associated with such violations. At the same time, responsibility for the violation of exclusive rights on the internet can be borne not only by domain administrators but also by persons who, with the consent of the administrator, use internet resources to post information about themselves as a manufacturer or seller of goods (services), i.e., actual users of the site (Resolution of the Intellectual Property Court of January 10, 2020, on case No. A57-16159/2018).

In connection with the above, the Supreme Court of the Russian Federation explained that in the event of IP litigation, the burden of proof that the material including the results of intellectual activity or means of individualization is posted on a site by third persons and not the owner of the site, and that the latter is therefore an information intermediary, lies on the site owner. In the absence of such evidence, the site owner is presumed to be the person using the results of intellectual activity or means of individualization (clause 78 of Resolution of the Plenum of the Supreme Court No. 10).

These explanations are important since there is a special ("lightweight") liability for an information intermediary (Article 1253.1 of the Civil Code).

First of all, an information intermediary is:

- a person transferring materials in the information and telecommunication network, including the internet;
- a person who provides the opportunity to post materials or information necessary to obtain them, using the network;
- a person who provides access to materials in this network.

An information intermediary is responsible for the violation of intellectual rights in the information and telecommunications network on the general grounds specified by the Civil Code if they are found guilty, but taking into account the following.

First of all, an information intermediary transferring materials in an information and telecommunications network shall not be responsible for the violation of intellectual rights that occurred as a result of this transfer, provided that the following conditions are met:

- the information intermediary is not the initiator of this transfer and does not determine the recipient of the specified material;
- the information intermediary does not change the specified materials during the provision of communication services, with the exception of changes made to ensure the technological part of the transfer;
- the information intermediary did not know and should not have known that the use of the corresponding result of intellectual activity or means of individualization by the person who initiated the transfer of the materials containing the corresponding result of intellectual activity or means of individualization was illegal.

An information intermediary posting material in the information and telecommunications network is not responsible for the violation of intellectual rights that occurred as a result of posting material by a third person or at such person's direction, while the information intermediary observes the following requirements:

- the information intermediary did not know and should not have known that the use of the corresponding result of intellectual activity or means of individualization contained in the material was illegal;
- in the case of receiving the right holder's written statement on the IP infringement with an indication of the website page and (or) the uniform resource locator (URL) of the materials posted, the information intermediary promptly took the necessary and sufficient measures to stop the infringement. The list of necessary and sufficient measures and the procedure for their implementation can be established by law.

At the same time, claims on the protection of intellectual rights that are not related to civil liability measures, including the removal of information that violates exclusive rights or about restricting access to it, can be brought against the information intermediary who, taking into account the above, shall not be responsible for the IP violation.

These rules apply to the persons providing access to materials or the information necessary for their obtainment, using an information and telecommunications network.

As explained by the Supreme Court in clause 78 of Resolution of the Plenum No. 10, if the owner of the site makes changes to the materials posted by third persons on the site containing the results of intellectual activity or means of individualization, the decision whether the owner is an intermediary depends on the role the owner played in the collection of the posted material and (or) whether the owner received income directly from the illegal placement of the material. Suppose the material has been substantially processed and the site owner has received some income from the material posted. In that case, the owner may not be an information intermediary but a user of the corresponding results of intellectual activity or means of individualization.

As indicated by the Intellectual Property Court, the defendant, while providing the services of an information intermediary, showing the due degree of care and discretion, should have foreseen the unfavourable consequences established by Article 1253.1 of the Civil Code of the Russian Federation in a case of timely failure to take necessary and sufficient measures to stop the violation of intellectual rights to disputed works. Within the meaning of the norms of Article 1253.1 of the Civil Code of the Russian Federation, in relation to liability for the violation of intellectual rights, the position of an information intermediary is determined by the fact that an information intermediary is liable only in the presence of fault, and in the presence in the aggregate of the conditions provided for by clauses 2–3 of Article 1253.1 of the Civil Code, the information intermediary is exempt from liability. After analyzing the evidence presented in the case materials, the court concludes that the defendant, being a person carrying out business activities at his own risk, did not exercise due diligence when introducing content on the site, without checking the presence of the plaintiff's consent to use the disputed works. The courts recognized the defendant as a person who violated the plaintiff's exclusive right (Resolution of the Intellectual Property Court of January 31, 2019, on case No. A56-108483/2017).

As for ensuring the rights of the right holder, the practice of blocking inadequate internet sites is particularly important nowadays. This measure allows the suspension and even termination of the infringement committed by means of the internet site.

The procedure for restricting access to internet sites that have repeatedly and illegally posted information containing objects of copyright and (or) related rights, or the information necessary to obtain them using an information and telecommunication network, including the internet, is provided in Article 15.6 of the Law on Protection of Information.

Within 24 hours from the moment Roskomnadzor received the decision of the Moscow City Court,[4] said authority:

1) sends the telecom operators a request through the interaction system to take measures to permanently restrict access to the site on the internet;
2) sends the operators of search engines distributing online advertising aimed at attracting Russian consumers' attention, an electronic request to terminate the spread of the information about the domain name as well as the indexes of webpages that posted the specified information.

Then, as a general rule, within 24 hours from the receipt of the request, the telecom operator providing access to the internet information and telecommunications network is obliged to restrict access to the corresponding site on the internet.

Within 24 hours from the date of receipt of the request, the operator of the search engine distributing advertising on the internet must stop spreading the information about the domain name and the page indexes of the sites, access to which is limited on the basis of the valid decision of the Moscow City Court.

Information about websites, access to which is limited by the Moscow City Court's decision, is posted on the Roskomnadzor official website.

It should be noted that it is possible to block both an individual site and also the illegal distribution of content on a search engine's resources, at least as a preliminary interim measure (Ruling of the Moscow City Court of August 8, 2018, No. 2i-1831/2018).

Digitalization is not possible without computer programs and databases (they are already described as IP objects in section "Intellectual property: concept and types"). As follows from the above, the existing normative regulation of these objects as IP works determines the peculiarities of their creation, circulation and protection.

The vast majority of violations in relation to computer programs, as a rule, concern their unauthorized use.

For instance, controversial programs were launched in the absence of a security key, i.e, the defendant used unlicenced copies of software products (Ruling of the Supreme Court of the Russian Federation of June 6, 2019, on case No. A28-13626/2017); confiscated software products modified by hacking the technical means of protecting software products, recording on a material carrier and subsequent storage, and storing the program in computer memory indicates the use of a material carrier until proven otherwise (Ruling of the Supreme Court of the Russian Federation of March 13, 2018, on case No. A20-2391/2013).

At the same time, such works have some peculiarities. For example, a violation of someone's rights can be established in the course of verification conducted by state authorities.

Thus, during verification activities, the representatives of a state authority found out that a business entity unlawfully used three copies of computer programs; therefore some objects and documents were seized, including four computers and a memory stick. In order to determine the type of computer programs installed on the seized items and the legality of their use, the law enforcement authority appointed a computer and technical examination. According to the expert's opinion, the provided equipment contained certain computer programs, the right holder of which is another business entity. Regarding these circumstances, the right holder applied to the defendant with a claim for compensation for the violation of the exclusive rights to the computer programs (for compensation, see section "Protection of IP rights"). The defendant's failure to comply with the pre-trial claim was the basis for the plaintiff's lawsuit (Resolution of the Intellectual Property Court of June 25, 2020, on case No. A43-13251/2019).

It should also be noted that the Civil Code of the Russian Federation provides for the possibility of using technical means of protection, which are understood as any technologies, technical devices or their components that control access to a work, prevent or restrict the implementation of actions that are not permitted by the author or other right holder in relation to the work. For example, they include a protection key, which is a means of protection against illegal copying of the program (Ruling of the Supreme Court of the Russian Federation of January 21, 2019, on case No. A33-16672/2017) and installing software without a corresponding key are the main signs of illegal installation and use (Resolution of the Intellectual Property Court of March 30, 2018, on case No. A32-19345/2016).

As noted earlier in section "Intellectual property: concept and types", since a database is not just a work, but a composite work (clause 2 of Article 1260 of the Civil Code), its legal regime is somewhat different from the legal regime of a computer program. It should be noted that the contents of a database can be a collection of any materials, including materials of an official and regulatory nature. In addition, by virtue of clause 6 of Article 1260 of the Civil Code, the copyright for derivative or composite works does not prevent other people from translating or reworking the same original work, as well as creating their own composite works by a different selection or arrangement of the same materials. In this regard, the existence of copyright to a database or a collection as a composite work does not imply the existence of the rights to the materials included in the database and collection and the prohibition for other people to use these materials (Resolution of the State Commercial Court of the Moscow Circuit of September 28, 2017, on case No. A43-13251/2019).

Speaking about databases, both the material itself and its structure are important. Special attention should be paid to the storage of data since the loss of data or its receipt by competitors entails the loss of the business entity's competitive advantage. Access to a database should not be haphazard; it should be well-thought by the organization.

Thus, a Limited Liability Company (LLC) filed a lawsuit against an individual entrepreneur to prohibit the use of an LLC's database, to suppress the entrepreneur's actions that violated the LLC's exclusive right and the right to the commercial secret related to the organization of a business forum. As established by the courts, the LLC carries out commercial activities in the field of consulting and organization of international conferences, seminars and masterclasses for specialists in the energy and information technology (IT) industry and others. The company uses a database that contains information about:

- the contacts of the partners, clients, potential clients of the company;
- held and planned events;
- the employees' activities;
- negotiations with counterparties.

The specified information is confidential. The order of the general director and the provision on the company's commercial secret established a commercial secret regime. The business contract and the agreement, according to which the entrepreneur undertook not to disclose information that constituted a commercial secret and became known during the provision of services, were concluded between the LLC and the entrepreneur.

As part of the business contract execution, the company granted the entrepreneur access to the database. As established by the courts, the entrepreneur carried out competitive activities in relation to the forum planned by the LLC, illegally using the database and information constituting the company's commercial secret (Resolution of the Intellectual Property Court of October 2, 2020, on case No. A56-37859/2019).

The analysis of this case indicates that business entities should put a great deal of effort into ensuring their intellectual rights. It will help to protect the rights to the databases used.

It must be also mentioned that according to Article 1280 of the Civil Code, as a rule, a person who legally owns a copy of a computer program or a copy of a database (user) has the right, without the permission of the author or other right holder and without paying additional remuneration to:

- carry out actions necessary for the functioning of a computer program or database (including during use in accordance with their purpose), including recording and storing in the computer memory (one computer or one network user), entering into a computer program or a database of changes solely for the purpose of their functioning on the user's technical means, correction of obvious errors (unless otherwise provided by an agreement with the right holder);
- make a copy of a computer program or database, provided that this copy is intended only for archival purposes or to replace a lawfully acquired copy in cases where such a copy is lost, destroyed or became unusable.

The person also can study, research, or test the operation of such a program in order to identify the ideas and principles underlying any element of a computer program and reproduce and transform the object code into source text (decompile a computer program) or instruct other persons to carry out these actions, if they are necessary to achieve the ability to interact with an independently developed computer program and other programs that can interact with the decompiled program, subject to the following conditions:

- the information necessary to achieve interoperability was not previously available to this person from other sources;
- the specified actions are carried out in relation to only those parts of the decompiled computer program that are necessary to achieve the ability to interact;
- the information obtained as a result of decompilation can only be used to achieve the ability to interact with an independently developed computer program with other programs, cannot be transferred to other persons, except for cases when it is necessary to interact with an independently

developed computer program and other programs, and also cannot be used to develop a computer program that is essentially similar in appearance to a decompiled computer program or to carry out another action that violates the exclusive right to a computer program.

The application of these provisions must not contradict the usual use of a computer program or database and must not unreasonably prejudice the legitimate interests of the author or other right holder(s).

Thus, building digital economic relations requires significant attention to the IP objects both on the part of the legislator and the authorities.

For example, the Board of the Eurasian Economic Commission developed Recommendations No. 21 of November 24, 2020, "On the Main Approaches in the Implementation of Activities to Protect Intellectual Property Rights on the Information and Telecommunication Network 'Internet' in the Member States of the Eurasian Economic Union". Even earlier, Russia adopted a national standard on the use of protected results of intellectual activity on the internet, which drew attention to the problems of infringement of IP rights on the internet, unified terminology and considered the features of their use on the internet and protecting rights to them (GOST R 56824-2015. National Standard of the Russian Federation. Intellectual Property. Use of Protected Results of Intellectual Activity on the Internet, approved and put into effect by Order of Rosstandart No. 2103-st of December 3, 2015).

Obviously, given the development of the digital space, society is getting more and more interested in it, but this interest should not lead to an infringement of the right holders' interests. Changing approaches to the offences, taking into account the opportunities offered by the internet, and the emergence and development of new technologies require a change in the approach to the implementation, provision and protection of IP rights by holders. That is why the IP infringements monitoring service is gaining popularity in Russia, reflecting the right holders' concern with this problem.

Notes

1 This regulatory provision was introduced by Federal Law No. 34-FZ of March 18, 2019.

2 Furthermore, the issues of the legal nature, application and other questions related to blockchain technology are being actively discussed (see, for example, Savelyev, A.I. Some Legal Aspects of Implementation of Smart Contracts and Blockchain Technologies under Russian law [*Nekotorye pravovye aspekty ispol'zovaniya Smart-kontraktov i Blokcheyn-tekhnologiy po rossiyskomu pravu*]. *Statute [Zakon]*. 2017. No. 5. Pp. 94–117).

3 For more information, see Ruling of the Supreme Court of the Russian Federation of October 29, 2020, on case No. A41-85820/2019; Decision of the State Commercial Court of Moscow City of November 14, 2019, on case No. A40-116198/18-105-577.

4 The Moscow City Court can adopt a ruling on interim measures, indicating the blocking of the site (see also section "Protection of IP rights"). This court can decide to permanently restrict access to the website (see, for example, Decision of the Moscow City Court of March 16, 2020, on case No. 3-273/2020).

11 Protection of intellectual property rights

Before proceeding directly to the protection of intellectual property (IP) rights, some theoretical aspects should be discussed.

First, there is an issue of differentiating between the security of a right and its protection. As noted in the legal literature, these concepts are often confused or the delineation between them is too vague.

There are different points of view. For example, some similarities of these concepts may be noted or one may argue that these are different names for the same concept. Some scholars suggest that the concept of security is broader than that of protection. There is also an opposite approach where protection includes security of rights.[1]

The position according to which security and protection are two different concepts (narrow approach to the 'protection') seems to be more reasonable. Security of rights should be associated with the need to ensure them. For example, the conclusion of an agreement between co-authors (Article 1258 the Civil Code) or right holders (Article 1229 the Civil Code) can be considered as a means of securing their rights, not their protection. Challenging the provisions of such an agreement implies the implementation of protective mechanisms. At the same time, in the literature, the protection of rights includes, for example, the publication of information about copyright (clause 1 of Article 1300 of the Civil Code) (Novoselova, 2017). Since this is controversial, this section of the book will focus specifically on the protection of IP rights in the previously specified narrow sense.

Second, the theory of Russian law offers different concepts of the independence of the right to protection. In accordance with the doctrinal approach, the protection of a right is a constituent element of the subjective right. The right to protection is also considered an independent subjective right.[2]

This issue is a complicated one. On the one hand, the Constitution of the Russian Federation states that there is the subjective right to protect one's rights. According to Article 2 of the Constitution, a person, their rights and freedoms are the supreme value. At the same time, recognition, observance and protection of human and civil rights and freedoms are the state's duty. In accordance with Article 45 of the Constitution, state protection of human rights and freedoms shall be guaranteed and everyone has the right to protect one's rights and freedoms in all ways that are not prohibited by law. By Article 46 of the Constitution, everyone is also guaranteed judicial protection of rights. Thus, there is a set of constitutional norms in the basic law, indicating the importance of subjective rights protection. And it is their combination that often leads researchers to the conclusion that the right to protection is independent of other subjective rights.

But at the same time, it is difficult to imagine the right to protection in isolation from other subjective rights, since the implementation of protective mechanisms is always performed for a reason: to ensure one's rights, recover one's rights, eliminate the violation, etc.

That is why the right to protection will always have an auxiliary function no matter how independent it can be. But at the same time, without such a right, its clear regulation and its guarantee and observance, it is impossible to properly exercise human and civil rights. After all, as Veniamin P. Gribanov said, "subjective right granted to a person but lacking necessary protection can only be a declarative right" (Gribanov, 2001).

Therefore, it seems difficult to unambiguously conclude the independence of the right to protection (or absence thereof). Both positions are equally justified. However, the truth can be seen at the junction of these approaches. The right to protection is dependent on the basic subjective right but has its own implementation mechanism, which ensures the relative independence of the right to protection. It should be noted that the implementation of the right to protection in the IP field, no matter how scientists understand it, holds particular interest for both doctrine and practice.

Leaving the controversial problems of the doctrine aside and referring to the applied aspects of IP, it can be concluded that the discussion of the applicable form and the methods of subjective rights protection is significant.

The relations in the field of IP are governed by civil law. At the same time, the protection of civil rights is possible both in a jurisdictional form and a non-jurisdictional one.

The jurisdictional form of protection is traditionally subdivided into administrative and judicial and involves resorting to the state authorities' help to protect one's subjective rights. Non-jurisdictional form implies the independence of a person's (entity's) actions to protect their rights, including self-protection.

On the one hand, the development of society presupposes a gradual improvement in the methods of rights protection. On the other hand, there is no effective protection mechanism that can be applied in all cases. That is why everyone has an opportunity to take independent action to protect one's rights in ways not prohibited by law. However, the practice of applying self-protection norms is contradictory, as self-protection is defined in general terms in Russia. Therefore, the Russian doctrine actively analyzes self-protection. The question of its legal nature, mechanism of implementation, methods, limits of self-protection and so on are being studied. It should be noted that self-protection is named as a method of rights protection in Article 12 of the Civil

Code; however, Russian theorists and practitioners often disagree with this approach. They think this is a form of protection (Gorbacheva, 2005, pp. 3–4).

When it comes to defining the self-protection of civil rights in Russian legal literature, two approaches are mainly used. The first is to follow Veniamin P. Gribanov's position, who pointed out that self-protection of civil rights should be understood in a way that an entitled person can take legally acceptable de facto actions aimed at protecting their rights and interests. Along with self-protection measures, there are legal, operational action measures that are inextricably linked with obligations (Gribanov, 2001). Holding a thing is a traditional example of operational measures. So, according to clause 1 of Article 359 of the Civil Code, the creditor, who has something that is to be transferred to a debtor or a person indicated by the debtor, has the right to hold this thing if the debtor fails to fulfil the obligation to pay for it or reimburse the creditor for associated costs and other losses until the obligation is performed.

The second approach attributes operational measures to self-protection.[3] Self-protection is understood as actions not only of de facto nature but also of a legal one.

The Civil Code provides a rather scarce regulatory framework for self-protection. A person whose right has been violated can resort to self-protection in accordance with the method and nature of the violation (Article 14 of the Civil Code).

As explained by the Supreme Court of the Russian Federation, the possibility of self-protection does not exclude a person's right to use other methods of protection provided for in Article 12 of the Civil Code, including its protection in court. The court noted that within the meaning of Articles 1 and 14 of the Civil Code, self-protection of civil rights may be expressed, inter alia, in a person's action on their own property or assets found in their legal possession. Self-protection may also consist of actions directed at the property of the offender if self-protection has signs of justifiable defence (self-defence) (Article 1066 of the Civil Code) or is performed in a state of extreme necessity (Article 1067 of the Civil Code) (clause 10 of Resolution of the Plenum of the Supreme Court No. 25).

That is to say that there are no clear criteria for the self-protection of civil rights in Russia. Nevertheless, in judicial practice, including the field of IP, this issue is being studied.

In the case of recovering compensation for the violation of exclusive rights to trademarks, the defendant believed the plaintiff's actions to be wrong. The defendant indicated that the plaintiff did not inform the defendant about the plaintiff's rights to the subject matter, warn about the need to stop selling the counterfeit goods, inform the defendant about the cost of the right to use the trademark based on the price that is usually charged for the lawful use of such objects under comparable circumstances and in the way that the offender (defendant) used and did not suggest that the defendant enter into civil legal relations with the plaintiff in order to regulate the relations connected with the lawful use of an object of intellectual activity. Instead, the plaintiff bought the counterfeit product and then used it in the claim for compensation. In this regard, the court noted that the plaintiff purchased the goods for the purpose of self-protection of civil rights. (Resolution of the Eighteenth State Commercial Court of Appeal of March 6, 2020, on case No. A76-36858/2019).

Common examples of self-protection in court are cases when the right holder or their authorized person takes photographs or records a video during the control purchase of goods infringing on IP rights. The Resolution of the Tenth State Commercial Court of Appeal of July 15, 2020, on case No. A41-100707/2019 indicated that the fact of the goods sale by the defendant can be confirmed by a cheque, the goods as well as a video recording made for the purposes and on the basis of self-protection of civil rights in accordance with Articles 12–14 of the Civil Code.

Clause 55 of the Resolution of the Plenum of Supreme Court No. 10 noted that the fact of illegal distribution of counterfeit material within a purchase and sale agreement can be proved not only by presenting a cash or sales cheque or another document confirming payment for the goods and by hearing testimony (Article 493 of the Civil Code), but also based on other evidence, such as audio or video recordings. No consent is required for audio or video recordings from the person in respect of whom they are made to be recognized as admissible evidence. Information on the distribution of counterfeit goods is not information about one's private life, including information on personal or family secrets.

Thus, the control purchase or filming more likely provides an opportunity to prove the defendant's illegal actions rather than represent a means of self-protection of the right holder's IP rights.

Thus, no matter how it is defined, self-protection cannot be considered a full-fledged form of protecting intellectual rights. Due to the object of protection's predominant intangibility, this is the sphere of relations that requires clear and detailed regulation. Such regulation implies determining the boundaries of the subjects' behaviour that are needed to initiate rights and the process of their implementation and protection. In many cases, it is impossible to understand the priority of rights without proper analysis. In the framework of self-protection, such proper analysis is not possible. Therefore, self-protection in these relations cannot be fully realized; it can only be of an auxiliary nature.

As for the jurisdictional form of protection, in accordance with clause 1 of Article 1248 of the Civil Code, as a general rule, IP disputes are resolved by the court. But, in accordance with clause 2 of Article 1248 of the Civil Code, administrative (non-judicial) procedure is required in some cases aimed at intellectual rights protection. Had one submitted to the court a claim subject to administrative (non-judicial) procedure, the court would refuse to accept the application (clause 1, part 1 of Article 134 of the Civil Procedure Code; clause 1, part 1 of Article 127.1 of the State Commercial Procedure Code).

When hearing cases on the violation of intellectual rights, the objections of the parties related to the matters that are subject to administrative procedure shall not be taken into account by the court and cannot be used as the basis for the court's decision (clause 52 of Resolution of the Plenum of the Supreme Court No. 10).

The non-judicial procedure is considered to be an exception to the general procedure of civil rights protection, in Russia. Thus, civil rights protection in the administrative procedure is carried out only in cases provided by law (clause 2 of Article 11 of the Civil Code). With regard to the protection of IP rights, the administrative procedure is provided for certain circumstances.

The administrative procedure for resolving IP disputes is provided for:

- state registration of certain results of intellectual activity and means of individualization, including when granting patents and (or) certificates on:
    - inventions,
    - utility models,
    - industrial designs,
    - selection achievements,
    - trademarks,
    - service marks,
    - geographical indications,
    - appellations of origin of goods,
- challenging the granting of legal protection to these results and means of individualization,
- termination of this legal protection.

Rospatent and the Ministry of Agriculture hear these administrative disputes in accordance with their competence.

For example, clause 3 of Article 1387 of the Civil Code establishes that Rospatent's decision to grant a patent on an invention, to refuse to grant a patent on an invention or to declare the application for the invention withdrawn can be challenged by the applicant by filing an objection to Rospatent within seven months from the date when the state authority sends the corresponding decision or copies of the materials requested to the indicated federal executive authority and those opposed to the application and indicated in the decision to refuse to grant the patent if the applicant has requested copies of these materials within three months from the date of sending the decision made on the application for the invention.

The direct procedure for hearing the administrative disputes mentioned earlier is established by special bylaws:

- Order of the Ministry of Education and Science of the Russian Federation No. 644, the Ministry of Economic Development of the Russian Federation No. 261 of April 30, 2020, "On Approval of the Rules for Consideration and Resolution of Administrative Disputes by the Federal Executive Body for Intellectual Property" (hereinafter Rospatent's Dispute Resolution Rules);

- Order of the Ministry of Agriculture of the Russian Federation No. 559 of October 31, 2007, "On Approval of the Rules for Consideration and Resolution of Disputes on the Protection of Infringed Intellectual Rights to Selective Breeding Achievements".

Hearing and the resolution of administrative disputes, as well as the administrative procedures related to the dispute resolution, shall be carried out by Rospatent itself or with the Federal Institute of Industrial Property (FIIP)'s help (also, see section "The state regulation of IP").

In accordance with clause 3 of Rospatent's Dispute Resolution Rules, the basis for the dispute consideration is an objection or application accepted in the manner prescribed by the Rules. The named document specifies the subject matters of the objections and applications (clauses 3.1, 3.2 and 3.3).

Objections can be filed against the decisions of Rospatent, including decisions on:

- issuing or refusal thereof of the patent on an invention, utility model or industrial design;
- recognition as withdrawn of an application for the patent on an invention, utility model or industrial design;
- recognition as withdrawn of an application for a trademark, a geographical indication or an appellation of origin of goods;
- state registration or refusal thereof of a trademark;
- granting or refusal to grant the exclusive right to a previously registered geographical indication, etc.

In addition, objections can be filed against:

- grant of the patent on an invention, utility model or industrial design if they do not comply with the conditions of patentability;
- grant of the patent on an invention, utility model or industrial design if they cannot be the subject of patent rights;
- granting legal protection to a geographical indication and (or) granting the exclusive right to a geographical indication;
- granting legal protection to an appellation of origin of goods and (or) granting the exclusive right to such appellation;
- other points determined by the named Rules.

Applications can be submitted for:

- early termination of the legal protection of a trademark or well-known trademark, on early termination of the legal protection of a sign under international registration in Russia;
- the termination of the legal protection of a well-known trademark if it has lost the features that were described earlier (see section "Intellectual property: concept and types");

- the termination of the legal protection of an appellation of origin and the validity of the certificate(s) of the exclusive right to the appellation;
- the termination of the certificate(s) of the exclusive right to it;
- the termination of the legal protection of a geographical indication and the exclusive right to it;
- the termination of the exclusive right to a geographical indication.

An objection, an application and other documents and materials can be submitted both in paper form by post or at a document reception window and online through the official website.

Within a period of up to five working days from the date of receipt, an objection or application is accepted, registered and transferred to a FIIP structural unit that carries out the formal verification of the objection or application.

In order for the application to be accepted and registered, the following requirements shall be met. The objection or application shall relate to one request, of one patent on an invention, utility model or industrial design, one industrial design by international registration, one means of individualization or one certificate of the exclusive right to a geographical indication or an appellation of origin of goods. The objection or application shall be printed in Russian, signed by the person submitting it (the representative) and be legible. In addition, there are requirements for the content of the objection or application. In particular, the subject of the application must be indicated in accordance with clauses 3.1–3.3 of Rospatent's Dispute Resolution Rules; the applicant's data and the arguments on which the objection or application is based, etc., shall be indicated (clause 5).

Suppose the requirements for the application or objection are not met. In that case, the person who filed it is sent a notice of refusal to accept and register the objection or application within five working days from the date of their receipt, indicating the reasons for the refusal.

Further, a formal check is carried out within five working days. Based on the results of this check, the application or objection can be accepted for hearing or their acceptance for hearing can be refused. Moreover, the list of reasons for refusal is exhaustive (clause 13 of Rospatent's Dispute Resolution Rules).

Direct hearing of the dispute is carried out at the meetings of the collegium, which is formed by persons included in a special list. Rospatent determines and publishes the list of specialists from which such collegia are formed to hear disputes on its official website. Each collegium consists of the chairman and other members of the collegium. The composition of the collegium is approved by the head of Rospatent or an authorized person. Information about the composition of the collegium is posted on the official website.

The dispute hearing shall be in Russian. Suppose a party to the dispute does not speak Russian. In that case, the collegium shall explain and ensure the right to read the case materials, explain the right to participate in the collegium meeting and give explanations on the circumstances of the case in their native language or a freely chosen language of communication if this party to the dispute has an interpreter.

The first meeting of the collegium shall take place no later than one or two months from the date of acceptance of the objection or application for consideration. The duration of this period depends on the reason (subject) of the appeal to Rospatent. The conclusions of the collegium on the satisfaction (partial or full) of the objection, application or refusal thereof are drawn up in the conclusion (clause 50–51).

Within two months from the date of the meeting of the collegium, at which its conclusion was formed, the head of Rospatent or an authorized person makes one of the following decisions, based on the results of the dispute hearing:

- on the satisfaction of the objection or application in whole or in part,
- on refusal to satisfy the objection or application.

The conclusion of the collegium shall be attached to the decision of the head of Rospatent or an authorized person and shall form an integral part of it (clause 52). The conclusions of the collegium can be rejected if they contain violations. In this case, a new collegium shall be formed and a new meeting shall be appointed.

The analysis of administrative practice shows the scrupulous work of the collegia in drawing conclusions on objections (applications) submitted to Rospatent.

Before recognizing legal protection granted to the trademark *Apteka EKONOMNAYa MATREShKA*,[4] (in English, Pharmacy ECONOMICAL *MATRYOSHKA*; the word "*Apteka*" (pharmacy) is an unguarded element) as completely invalid, the collegium analyzed its sound, graphic and semantic similarity with the trademarks *МАТРЕШКА* and *MATRESHKA*, owned by the applicant who objected to the protection of the trademark. The analysis carried out by the collegium showed that the contested and opposed trademarks are similar in general, despite their individual differences. At the same time, the similarity of the compared signs predetermines the possibility of their collision in civil circulation when they are used to mark similar services. As a consequence, the consumer can believe that the compared means of individualization belong to the same enterprise or come from the same commercial source (Decision of Rospatent of December 9, 2020, on application No. 2013723012). Thus, in the described situation, the right holder of the МАТРЕШКА and MATRESHKA trademarks was able to successfully defend his rights through the administrative procedure.

Less successful in protecting its rights with the administrative procedure was the entity (Limited Liability Company; LLC) that challenged Rospatent's refusal to register the trademark. The sign applied for registration as the trademark consisted of a label in the form of a battlement wall of an ancient fortress, into which a graphic image of a tower and word elements "*KAVKAZKAYa*" and "*KREPOST*" (in English, "CAUCASIAN" and "FORTRESS", respectively) were inscribed. The analysis carried out by the collegium showed that the applied sign is similar to the point of confusion with other trademarks already registered in Russia. Thus, Rospatent's conclusion that the declared sign did not comply with the requirements established for trademarks was recognized as legitimate by the collegium, decided that there were grounds for the refusal to satisfy the objection (Decision of Rospatent of December 9, 2020, on application No. 2019757818/33).

As was noted, the Ministry of Agriculture of Russia resolves administrative disputes over the protection of intellectual rights in the framework of the relations that include filing and consideration of the applications for the granting of patents on selective breeding achievements, the state registration of the results of intellectual activity, the issuance of the corresponding title documents and challenging the protection (or termination thereof) of these results.

For the administrative resolution of a dispute, an application shall be submitted to the mentioned authority. All incoming applications are sent to the Ministry's structural divisions, which are responsible for the preparation of the legal opinion. For the preparation of the legal opinion, positions of the competent structural units are requested. The requests shall include all the necessary documents (if any) attached thereto. The opinion shall be ready within five days.

Applications are considered collectively at a special meeting, with at least three people being present, including the chairman or their deputy (the dispute resolution board). The dispute resolution board meeting may be attended by the person who submitted the application and (or) their representative, the patent holder and, if necessary, the person who made the decision based on the results of the examination.

The decision shall be made within six months from the date of the submission of the application unless additional tests are required. The decision can be to accept the claim, refuse to accept the claim or terminate the dispute proceedings. It should be noted that the decision shall be published in the official bulletin of the Russian Ministry of Agriculture.

IP judicial protection offers more opportunities to right holders.

First, an administrative decision can be challenged in court (clause 2 of Article 11 of the Civil Code).

Second, in accordance with paragraph 1 of Article 1250 of the Civil Code, intellectual rights are protected by the methods provided for by the Code, taking into account the essence of the violated right and the consequences of the violation of this right. Moreover, Article 12 of the Civil Code establishes a wide range of methods for protecting civil rights as the articles of part IV of the Civil Code dealing with IP describe the special ways the rights shall be protected. All this provides the person whose rights have been violated with great opportunities to choose a desired method of protection, while the extensive judicial practice makes it possible to assess the risks of implementing a particular method and, if it is possible, to use alternative variants.

It should be noted that the methods of protecting intellectual rights can be applied by both the authors and right holders themselves and organizations for collective rights management. In addition, they can also be applied by other persons if it is specifically established by law (clause 2 of Article 1250 of the Civil Code). Despite the fact that in clause 2 of Article 1250 of the Civil Code, the trust manager is not directly indicated as a person who has the right to apply to the court for the protection of the violated exclusive right if the exclusive right has been transferred into trust, then the trust manager has the right both to exercise the rights transferred to them for management and to protect those rights in the same ways as the right holder can (Resolution of the Intellectual Property Court of May 22, 2020, on case No. A40-133741/2019).

First of all, the protection of personal non-property rights will be described. Article 1251 of the Civil Code says that if there is a violation of the personal non-property rights of the author, their protection is carried out through:

- recognition of the rights,
- restoration of the previous situation prevailing before the rights' infringement,
- suppression of actions that violate the right or create a threat of its violation,
- compensation for moral damage,
- publication of the court's decision on the violation.

The following situation can illustrate the recognition of a right to protect the author's personal non-property rights.

The employee (plaintiff) applied to the Intellectual Property Court with a claim against the LLC to declare the authorship part of the patent on *Elektricheskiy chaynik skladnoy* utility model (in English, Electric folding kettle) invalid. The director of the LLC was indicated as the author and the company was the patent holder. The statement of claim was motivated by the fact that the controversial *Elektricheskiy chaynik skladnoy* utility model was produced through the creative work of an employee. Since the director did not indicate the plaintiff as the author in the application, in order to restore his authorship rights to the utility model, the plaintiff who believed that he was the author of the utility model applied to the Intellectual Property Court with the claim. After examining the evidence, the Intellectual Property Court ruled that Rospatent should annul the patent on the utility model and issue a new patent indicating the employee as the author and the LLC as the patent holder (Decision of the Intellectual Property Court of February 21, 2019, on case No. SIP-477/2018).

It is also possible to challenge co-authorship in order to protect one's rights. Two people were indicated as the authors of an invention, *Tsirkulyatsionnyy perevodnik* (in English, circulation sub): an employee (the plaintiff) and the general director of the LLC; the patent was issued in the name of the LLC. The employee appealed to the Intellectual Property Court with a statement of claim to the general director and the LLC to declare the patent invalid in the part indicating the general director as a co-author. The employee argued that the invention was made only by his creative work, while the general director of the LLC did not take any part in the creation. The court noted that the presumption of authorship, enshrined in Article 1347 of the Civil Code, redistributes the general burden of proof established by the state commercial procedural legislation of Russia, imposing the obligation to prove that the controversial invention was not created by the creative work of the person indicated as the author in the patent, to the plaintiff who initiated the proceedings. However, the plaintiff did not submit evidence confirming the circumstances set forth by him in the statement of claim, refuting the co-authorship of the general director (Decision of the Intellectual Property Court of November 28, 2019, on case No. SIP-693/2019).

The compensation for moral damage implies the payment of a sum of money due to physical or mental suffering. The compensation for moral harm is regulated in Article 151 of the Civil Code. In accordance with this article, if a citizen is inflicted with moral damage by actions that violate their personal non-property rights or infringes on the intangible assets belonging to the citizen, the court can impose the obligation of monetary compensation for this harm on the violator. When determining the amount of compensation for moral harm, the court takes into account the degree of the offender's fault and other noteworthy circumstances. The court must also consider the degree of physical and mental suffering associated with the individual characteristics of the citizen who is harmed.

This compensation shall only be paid if the author's personal non-property rights are violated. For example, in one case, the Judicial Collegium for Civil Cases of the Supreme Court cancelled the judicial rulings on the case due to the following reasons. Hearing the dispute, the courts proceeded from the fact that the book distributed by the defendants contains work that copies the plaintiff's work, while fragments from the plaintiff's work constitute the major part of the text that forms the basis of the works that are placed in the collection. The plaintiff was not indicated as the author in this publication; evidence that the plaintiff's writings were used in accordance with the current legislation was not presented to the court. The court, guided by Articles 151 and 1251 of the Civil Code, decided in favour of the plaintiff, allowing him to recover compensation for moral harm for violation by the defendants of his rights to dispose of the result of intellectual activity, considering them to be personal non-property rights. However, the right to dispose of the result of intellectual activity is a property right and compensation for moral harm is not one of the means of exclusive right protection (clause 1 of the "Review of Judicial Practice on Cases Related to the Resolution of Disputes on the Protection of Intellectual Property Rights", approved by the Presidium of the Supreme Court of September 23, 2015).

Special attention should be paid to the issue of protecting honour, dignity and business reputation due to their importance for these relations. Protection of the honour, dignity and business reputation of the author is carried out in accordance with the general rules, which are established in Article 152 of the Civil Code. In particular, a citizen can demand the refutation of the information discrediting their honour, dignity or business reputation in court if the person who disseminated the information does not prove that it is true. The refutation shall be produced in the same or similar way in which information about the citizen was disseminated.

In cases where information discrediting the honour, dignity or business reputation of a citizen has become widely known and, in this regard, the refutation cannot be brought to the general knowledge, the citizen has the right to demand the removal of the information, as well as the suppression or prohibition of the further dissemination of this information by means of the seizure and destruction of copies of the material carriers containing the specified information made for the purpose of being introduced into civil circulation, without any compensation, if the removal of such information is impossible without the destruction of the copies of material carriers.

Suppose information defaming the honour, dignity or business reputation of a citizen turns out to be available on the internet after its dissemination. In that case, the citizen has the right to demand the removal of the information and the refutation of this information in a way that ensures that the refutation is brought to internet users.

Suppose the procedure for the refutation of the information discrediting the honour, dignity or business reputation of a citizen is not defined in the normative way. In that case, it is established by the court.

Apart from the refutation of the information or the publication of their answer, the citizen in respect of whom information discrediting the honour, dignity or business reputation has been spread has the right to claim damages and demand compensation for moral harm caused by the dissemination of this information.

By virtue of clause 4 of Article 1274 of the Civil Code, the creation of a literary, musical or another parody or a caricature based on another (original) lawfully published work and the use of this parody or caricature are allowed without the consent of the author or another holder of the exclusive right to the original work and without paying them any remuneration. The author of the original work has no right to prohibit this type of use of the work based on the provisions of part IV of the Civil Code. However, suppose the parody or caricature discredits the honour, dignity or business reputation of the author of the original work. In that case, one has the right to use other protection methods (for example, those that were discussed as regards the protection of honour, dignity and business reputation) (clause 99 of Resolution of the Plenum of the Supreme Court No. 10).

At the same time, protecting the honour, dignity and business reputation of a citizen even after his death (a request may be made by interested people) is allowed.[5]

Attention should be drawn to the fact that the citizens' right to protect their honour, dignity and business reputation is their constitutional right (clause 1 of

Resolution of the Plenum of the Supreme Court of the Russian Federation No. 3 of February 24, 2005, "On Judicial Practice on Cases of Protecting the Honour and Dignity of Citizens, as well as the Business Reputation of Citizens and Legal Entities").

The protection of the exclusive rights to the results of intellectual activity and to the means of individualization is of particular importance for business. As explained by the Supreme Court, in the event of a violation of the exclusive right, the right holder has the right to protect the violated right by any of the methods listed in Article 12 and clause 1 of Article 1252 of the Civil Code. It should be noted that clause 1 of Article 1252 explains the methods of rights protection as regards the relations in question and, in general, these are the measures that tend to be implemented.

First of all, the court decision on the committed violation can be published with the indication of the actual right holder. The claim shall be made against the infringer of the exclusive right. So, in accordance with Article 1407 of the Civil Code, the patent holder has the right to demand the publication of the court decision on the unlawful use of the invention, utility model, industrial design or on any other violation of their rights in the official bulletin.

As noted in clause 58 of Resolution of the Plenum of the Supreme Court No. 10, demanding to publish the court decision on the committed violation with the indication of the actual right holder, the plaintiff shall specify where the corresponding publication is required and justify the reasons for their choice. The defendant has the right to submit objections to the place of publication of the decision. Assessing the arguments of the plaintiff and the objections of the defendant to the proposed place of publication, the court shall determine the place of publication of the decision taking into account that the choice shall aim to restore the violated right (for example, in the same print publication where false information about the right holder was published; in the official bulletin of the federal executive body for IP; in a source, the place of distribution of which is determined by the place of production and distribution of counterfeit goods or the place of implementation and nature of the plaintiff's activities).

Apart from the abovementioned, it is possible to file a claim for the recognition of the right. The claim is made against a person who denies or otherwise refuses to recognize the right, thereby violating the interests of the right holder. Disputes over the recognition of rights should be distinguished from other claims made by interested people. The following case should be cited as an example of an inappropriate choice of protection method.

The court approved an amicable agreement between an individual entrepreneur and an LLC based on the entrepreneur's claim against the company for the early termination of the legal protection of a trademark. According to the terms of the agreement, the entrepreneur had to pay the company a sum of 100,000 rubles for the alienation of the exclusive right to the trademark by transferring funds to the company's current account, which the entrepreneur did. Later, the entrepreneur submitted an application for the registration of the alienated trademark to Rospatent, but Rospatent refused to register it. Referring to the fact that the company did not apply to Rospatent for registration of the transfer of the exclusive right to the disputed trademark, the plaintiff filed a claim with the state commercial court to recognize the agreement on the transfer of the exclusive right to the trademark between the entrepreneur and the company as concluded. The court refused to satisfy the claims, deciding that there are no grounds to confirm the conclusion of the deal, represented by the amicable agreement in respect of which the judicial act entered into force. The Intellectual Property Court noted that although filing a claim for recognition of a right is a means of protecting exclusive rights to the results of intellectual activity and the means of individualization, this very dispute does not concern the recognition of rights since it is about the interpretation of the terms of the deal concluded between the parties. Accordingly, the entrepreneur's method to protect the violated right is inappropriate (Resolution of the Intellectual Property Court of November 26, 2020, on case No. A60-7000 2020).

To protect IP rights, a lawsuit may be filed with the court for the suppression of actions that violate the right or create a threat of its violation. The claim shall be made against the person who commits the unlawful actions. An example of such a claim is the one demanding to prohibit some particular performer from performing certain works. The claim to suppress actions that violate the right or create a threat of its violation can be filed not only against the person who commits such illegal actions or makes necessary preparations for them, but also against other persons who can prevent the actions.

The claim can only be satisfied if the person's unlawful behaviour has not yet been ceased or there is a threat of the right violation. Thus, the claim to prohibit the offer for sale or to prohibit the sale of counterfeit goods cannot be satisfied if the defendant's goods have already been sold. Claims for a general prohibition for a person to use the result of intellectual activity or the means of individualization in the future will not be satisfied either (for example, on the prohibition of placing information on the internet). This prohibition is established directly by law (Article 1229 of the Civil Code) (clause 57 of Resolution of the Plenum of the Supreme Court No. 10).

It is possible to claim the seizure of a material carrier, too. In accordance with clause 4 of Article 1252 of the Civil Code, if the manufacture, distribution or another type of use, as well as the import, transportation or storage of material carriers containing the result of intellectual activity or the means of individualization, lead to a violation of the exclusive right to them, such carriers are considered counterfeit and are subject, by a court decision, to withdrawal from economic circulation and destruction without any compensation, unless other measures are provided for by the Civil Code. The claim shall be made to its manufacturer, importer, custodian, carrier, seller, other distributor or buyer acting in bad faith.

Tools, equipment or other means used or necessary to violate the exclusive rights to the results of intellectual activity and the means of individualization are subject, by a court decision, to withdrawal from economic circulation and destruction at the expense of the offender if the law does not provide their forced withdrawal to the income of the Russian Federation.

In accordance with Article 1252 of the Civil Code, the protection of exclusive rights to the results of intellectual activity and means of individualization is carried out by filing a claim for damages. This claim is against a person who unlawfully used the result of intellectual activity or the means of individualization without concluding an agreement with the right holder (non-contractual use) or otherwise violated their exclusive right and caused them damage. Article 15 of the Civil Code provides that a person whose right has been violated can ask for full compensation of the damages caused if the law or the contract does not provide for a smaller amount of compensation. Damages mean expenses that the person whose right has been violated has undergone or will have to undergo to restore the violated right, loss or damage to their property (real damage), as well as the lost income that this person would have received under normal conditions of civil turnover if their right had not been violated (loss of profits). Suppose the person who violated the right has received any income as the result of their actions. In that case, the person whose right has been violated can seek compensation, along with other damages, for the loss of profits in an amount not less than such income.

Considering the normative distribution of the burden of proof for the recovery of lost profits, the plaintiff shall prove what income they really (reliably) would have received if they had not lost the opportunity to use the exclusive right. Thus, when filing claims for the recovery of lost profits, the plaintiff has to provide evidence that receipt of profit was possible (the existence of conditions for generating income, making preparations, reaching agreements with counterparties, etc.) (Resolution of the Intellectual Property Court of September 8, 2020, on case No. A34-5796/2016).

For certain types of results of intellectual activity or means of individualization, the Civil Code establishes that in case of a violation of the exclusive right, instead of damages, the right holder can demand payment of compensation for the violation of this right from the violator.

The Constitutional Court, in its Resolution of December 13, 2016, No. 28-P, formulated the legal position, by virtue of which the recovery of compensation for an IP right infringement, being a penalty pursuing the public purpose of suppressing infringements in the field of IP among other things, is, however, a matter of private law which is based on the recognition of the equality of the civil relations participants (clause 1 of Article 1 of the Civil Code), namely the right holder and the violator of the IP exclusive right and within which the protection of the exclusive rights of the right holder shall be carried out in compliance with those arising from the constitutional principles of justice, equality and proportionality, as well as the prohibition on the exercise of human and civil rights and freedoms in violation of the rights and freedoms of others, i.e., in such a way as to ensure a balance of rights and legitimate interests of participants in civil turnover.

Compensation is subject to recovery upon proof of the fact of the offence. The right holder who applied for the protection of the right is exempt from proving the amount of damages caused to them. The court determines the sum of compensation within the limits established by the Civil Code, depending on the nature of the violation and other circumstances of the case, taking into account the requirements of reasonableness and fairness.

If one action violates the rights to several results of intellectual activity or means of individualization, the amount of compensation is determined by the court for each illegally used result. Suppose the rights to the corresponding results or means of individualization belong to one right holder. In that case, the total amount of compensation for violation of the rights, considering the nature and consequences of the violation, can be reduced by the court to below the top limit established by the Civil Code, but shall not be less than 50 per cent of the minimum amount of all compensations for the violations committed.

The right to compensation is provided, for example, in Article 1301 of the Civil Code. According to this article, if there is a violation of the exclusive right to a work, the author or another right holder can demand, at their choice, compensation payment, instead of damages, from the infringer:

1 in the amount from 10,000 rubles to 5 million rubles, determined at the discretion of the court based on the nature of the violation;
2 two times the cost of the counterfeit copies of the work;
3 two times the value of the right to use the work, determined on the basis of the price that, under comparable circumstances, is usually charged for the lawful use of the work in the manner chosen by the infringer.

In the case of a violation of the exclusive right to an invention, utility model or industrial design (Article 1406.1 of the Civil Code), the author or another right holder, along with the use of other applicable methods of protection and measures of liability established by the Civil Code, has the right to demand, at their choice, compensation payments, instead of damages, from the violator:

1 in the amount from 10,000 rubles to 5 million rubles, determined at the discretion of the court based on the nature of the violation;
2 two times the value of the right to use an invention, utility model or industrial design, determined on the basis of the price, which, under comparable circumstances, is usually charged for the lawful use of the corresponding invention, utility model or industrial design in the manner chosen by the infringer.

When filing claims for the recovery of compensation, the right holder has the right to choose one of the methods for calculating the amount of compensation specified in the relevant provisions of the Civil Code, as well as to make a decision before the court has provided its ruling, to change the chosen method of calculating the amount of compensation, insofar as the subject matter and grounds of the claim do not change. The court has no right to change the method of calculation on its own initiative.

According to the explanations given in clause 61 of Resolution of the Plenum of the Supreme Court No. 10, when claiming compensation in the amount of 10,000 to 5 million rubles, determined at the discretion of the court, the plaintiff must provide a justification for the sum of compensation to be recovered, confirming the proportionality of the required amount of compensation for the violation committed, except for the claim for the recovery of compensation in the minimum amount.

Claiming to recover the amount of compensation twice the value of the right to use the result of intellectual activity or means of individualization or two times the cost of the counterfeit copies (goods), the plaintiff shall submit a calculation and justification of the amount to be recovered, as well as the documents confirming the cost of using the right or the number of copies (goods) and their price. If it is impossible to bring the evidence, the plaintiff has the right to petition for the reclamation of such evidence from the defendant or third parties. To confirm the calculation and the cost of the violated right, the plaintiff is allowed to present data on the cost of the exclusive right, including from foreign sources.

The following regulations should also be considered important for business practice. In accordance with clause 6 of Article 1252 of the Civil Code, if various means of individualization (company name, trademark, service mark, commercial name) turn out to be identical or similar to the point of confusion and as a result of such identity or similarity consumers and (or) counterparties can be misled, the priority belongs to the means of individualization, the exclusive right to which arose earlier or in cases of establishing the convention or exhibition priority, the means of individualization that has an earlier priority. In addition, if a means of individualization and an industrial design turns out to be identical or similar to the point of confusion and, as a result of such identity or similarity, consumers and (or) counterparties can be misled, the means of individualization or the industrial design, the exclusive right to which arose earlier, has the priority, or in cases of establishing the convention, exhibition or another type of priority to which it belongs as the means of individualization or the industrial design to which an earlier priority is established.

The right holder of such an exclusive right can demand the invalidation of the legal protection to a trademark or service mark, the invalidation of the patent on an industrial design or a complete or partial prohibition of the use of the company name or commercial name. In this case, a partial prohibition of use means:

- in relation to the company name, the prohibition of its use in certain types of activities;
- in relation to a commercial name, the prohibition of its use within a certain territory and (or) in certain types of activities.

Cases related to the named regulations were considered in this book. Such a kind of equalization of IP objects is essential for Russian business practice; it allows business entities to plan their spending and initiate a particular type of activity, for example, without registering the trademark or new company name. This expands the opportunities for creativity in business. However, in business, there are cases when someone else's ideas are borrowed. This also applies to the protected results of intellectual activity. So, when absorbed in the creative process, one should not forget that a person can act in good and bad faith. Therefore, if a business entity has discovered the violation of its intellectual rights, it is advisable to consider various methods of protection, evaluate all the risks and even think about filing a suit.

As enshrined in the Civil Code of the Russian Federation (clause 2 of Article 1252), when a suit is filed in the case of a violation of an exclusive right, interim measures may be imposed that are commensurate with the size and nature of the offence and established by the procedural legislation, including the seizure of material carriers, equipment and materials, the ban on the implementation of certain actions in information and telecommunication networks, if such material carriers, equipment and materials or such actions are assumed to violate the exclusive right to the result of intellectual activity or the means of individualization. For instance, the Moscow City Court chose such an interim measure to oblige the Roskomnadzor and other entities to stop creating technical conditions that ensure the placement, distribution and other use of the audiovisual work "Marketplaces 2020" on the website infokursy.com (Ruling of the Moscow City Court of December 11, 2020, No. 2i-6077/2020).

Interim measures in cases of IP rights protection can be taken by the court at any stage of the process if there are reasonable grounds. In accordance with clause 2 of Article 139 of the Civil Procedure Code, securing a claim is allowed in any state of proceedings if the failure to take interim measures may complicate or hinder the execution of the court's decision. In accordance with Article 90 of the State Commercial Procedure Code, interim measures are applied, including if the execution of the judicial act is expected outside Russia, to prevent significant damage to the applicant. The commercial procedural legislation allows for the possibility of taking these measures, including in the event of a postponement of court proceedings to resolve the dispute.

In accordance with the explanations given in clause 13 of Resolution of the Plenum of the Supreme Commercial Court of the Russian Federation No. 11 of December 9, 2002, "On Some Issues Related to the Introduction of the State Commercial Procedure Code of the Russian Federation", state commercial courts should not take interim measures if the applicant failed to substantiate the application with specific circumstances confirming the need to take interim measures and did not provide evidence to support the arguments.

Consequently, the application for taking interim measures cannot be satisfied if those are aimed at protecting the interests of only one party to the dispute and this party has not presented evidence confirming the infliction of significant damage as a result of the failure to take interim measures.

As per the norms, the valuation of the need to apply interim measures is determined by the court according to its inner conviction, based on the study of the specific circumstances of the case.

At the same time, the application for the interim measures in the form of prohibiting the defendant and other people from performing certain actions, including the prohibition for Rospatent to consider objections to the granting of legal protection to the results of intellectual activity and means of individualization, to take actions for state registration, etc., can be satisfied if these interim measures are directly related to the subject of the stated claims and in the case of the claim satisfaction, failure to take these measures can impede or make impossible the execution of the judicial act (clause 13 of Resolution of the Plenum of the Supreme Court No. 10).

The Presidium of the Intellectual Property Court in Resolution No. SP-21/19 of August 6, 2020, explained under what conditions a preliminary interim measure[6] can be applied. This involved prohibiting Rospatent from issuing a decision on an application for trademark registration until a decision was made regarding a lawsuit on the early termination of legal protection to another person's trademarks that prevent the claimed trademark registration.

According to the court's explanation, the lawsuit for early termination of the legal protection of the trademarks compared by Rospatent to the examined sign during the examination of the application is the legal way to overcome the conclusions of the administrative authority on the presence of obstacles to the registration of the sign applied for registration as a trademark.

At the same time, the termination of the legal protection of similar trademarks by the court implies entering the corresponding information into the State Register of Trademarks and Service Marks and entails, in this case, that they shall not be compared to the signs submitted for state registration. This is, in fact, a form of judicial act enforcement. Rospatent's consideration of the submitted applications before the case hearing will actually hinder the execution of the judicial act.

The adoption of such interim measures does not violate other persons' rights and legitimate interests and does not have negative implications for them.

In order to prevent significant damage to the applicant, interim measures may be aimed at preserving the existing state of relations (status quo) between the parties: Rospatent shall make no decision on the submitted applications until the court hears the case for the early termination of the legal protection of the compared trademarks while maintaining the priority date.

At the same time, for the adoption of preliminary interim measures, confirmation of the existence of several necessary conditions is required, namely:

- the applicant (future plaintiff) filed the application with Rospatent for the state registration of a sign as a trademark;
- Rospatent sent a notice on an obstacle to the state registration of the trademark, indicating specific trademarks that prevent registration;

- the demand on the preliminary interim measures should relate to one's own applications and not affect the legal rights and interests of other persons;
- the applicant took measures to comply with the pre-trial procedure for resolving the dispute: the applicant sent the interested party's proposal to the right holder of the contrasted trademark.

It seems reasonable for the right holder or another authorized person to think also about an expert analysis, which can significantly affect the case result.

A material carrier can be deemed counterfeit solely by the court. If necessary, the court has the right to appoint an expert examination to clarify issues requiring special knowledge. Thus, the counterfeit nature of the material carrier in which an unlawfully processed computer program is expressed can be established, taking into account the opinion of the expert who established signs of such processing. At the same time, the assessment of the confusing similarity between a trademark, the exclusive right to which belongs to the right holder and the signs marking the material carrier shall not be provided by an expert, since such an assessment shall be conducted by the court from the point of view of an ordinary consumer of the goods in question, a person from the target audience of the goods for the individualization of which the trademark is registered (clause 75 of Resolution of the Plenum of the Supreme Court No. 10). In this case, the application for an expert examination will be useless.

An additional test can also be required when hearing cases of violation of the exclusive right to a work expressed in the unlawful reproduction and (or) subsequent distribution, import or rental of a copy of the work. In the absence of any disputes thereon, the court proceeds from the fact that the material carrier's actual content corresponds to that indicated by the signs used for its marking (for example, on the cover). However, if there is a dispute about the material carrier's content (for example, if the defendant objects that copies of works are expressed in the material carrier or claims that copies of other works, the rights to which belong to other people, are expressed therein), the court shall examine the evidence, including by inspecting, listening to or watching the content of the material carrier.

If necessary, an expert examination can be appointed for the inspection, watching or listening of the content. For example, if there are several performances of the same work, a test can be conducted to establish which one was used (clause 90 of Resolution of the Plenum of the Supreme Court No. 10).

An expert examination can also be appointed to establish whether the created work is a reworking of a previously created work or the result of the author's independent creative work (Resolution of the First State Commercial Court of Appeal of September 9, 2019, on case No. A43-380/2019).

When filing claims for the protection of intellectual rights in court, it should be borne in mind that, generally, measures of liability for infringement of intellectual rights are to be applied in the presence of the offender's fault, unless otherwise established by the Civil Code. It should be noted that the absence of fault is proven by the person violating intellectual rights.

However, the absence of the violator's fault does not exempt them from the obligation to stop the violation of the intellectual rights, nor does it exclude the implementation of such measures as the publication of the court decision on the violation committed, the suppression of actions that violate the exclusive right to the result of intellectual activity or means of individualization or threaten the violation of such rights and the seizure and destruction of the counterfeit material carrier. These actions shall be carried out at the offender's expense (clause 5 of Article 1250 of the Civil Code).

According to clause 4 of Article 1250 of the Civil Code, a person from whom, in the absence of their fault, damages or compensation were recovered, as well having the material carrier withdrawn, has the right to file a recourse claim against the person by whose fault they committed the violation. This claim concerns incurred damages, including the amount of money paid to third persons.

When hearing the case on the infringement of the exclusive right at the defendant's request, the court shall involve those against whom, in the defendant's opinion, the recourse claim can be submitted as third persons to the case. At the same time, failure to involve such people in the case of the exclusive right violation does not preclude the filing of a suit against them by way of recourse (clause 72 of Resolution of the Plenum of the Supreme Court No. 10).

The cases when liability arises regardless of the fault of the infringer of intellectual rights are indicated in clause 3 of Article 1250 of the Civil Code. These are the following measures of liability applied to the violation of intellectual rights committed by the violator while doing business:

- damages,
- recovery of compensation in cases where it is provided by the Civil Code.

The businessperson, being the infringer of intellectual rights, is held liable in such cases if they do not prove that the violation of intellectual rights occurred as a result of force majeure, that is, extraordinary and unavoidable circumstances.

The requirement of clause 5.1 of Article 1252 of the Civil Code is also important for business entities. If the right holder and the infringer of the exclusive right are legal entities and (or) individual entrepreneurs and the dispute is subject to hearing in the state commercial court, then prior to filing a lawsuit for damages or payment of compensation, it is necessary to send a non-judicial claim. A lawsuit for damages or payment of compensation can be filed in case of full or partial refusal to satisfy the non-judicial claim or non-receipt of an answer to it within 30 days from the date when it was sent unless another period is provided by the contract.

In conclusion, it is worth mentioning such an unconventional way of protecting intellectual rights as the liquidation of a legal entity and the termination of the activities of an individual entrepreneur in connection with the violation of the exclusive rights (Article 1253 of the Civil Code). In Russia, freedom of economic activity is established, which is guaranteed by the Constitution (Article 34) and implies the freedom to initiate business activity, its implementation and termination. Therefore, the economic entity's forced termination is not a popular and widespread sanction against a violator in Russian practice. The fact is that from the perspective of Russian law, both a legal entity and an individual entrepreneur are subjects of law. These subjects are independent and act in their own interest and have their own will (Articles 1–2 of the Civil Code).

At the same time, if a legal entity repeatedly or grossly violates exclusive rights to the results of intellectual activity and the means of individualization, if such a legal entity is found to be violating the exclusive rights, it can be liquidated by the court at the request of the prosecutor. Suppose such violations were committed while a citizen was doing business as an individual entrepreneur. In that case, the citizen's activity in this legal status can be terminated if the entrepreneur is at fault for violating the exclusive rights by the court's decision or sentence in the manner prescribed by law.

This interference in the independence of business entities is due to the need to ensure the public interests of society and the state since such an approach to business harms private entities and disrupts economic circulation and generates extra work for the courts and hampers the legality of business.

As the Constitutional Court has repeatedly pointed out in its decisions, the right to judicial protection presupposes the existence of specific guarantees that allow it to be fully implemented. Justice can be recognized as such only if it meets the requirements of fairness and reasonability and ensures an effective recovery of rights. When hearing a case, the court is obliged to investigate its actual circumstances and does not have the right to limit its actions to establishing formal conditions for the implementation of the norm; otherwise, the right to judicial protection, enshrined in Article 46 (part 1) of the Constitution, will be significantly infringed (clause 2.3 of Ruling of the Constitutional Court of October 6, 2015, No. 2317-O).

Therefore, the Russian courts' attitude to the protection of IP rights is far from formal. Practice shows that the courts pay considerable attention to the analysis of regulations and the existing practice too and the actual circumstances. In this regard, the judicial way of protecting intellectual rights seems significantly important.

Protection of legal rights and interests in the field of IP within the jurisdictional framework is possible through civil law protection methods and administrative and criminal liability. For example, part 1 of Article 14.10 of the Code on Administrative Offences establishes liability for the illegal use of the means of individualizing works or services. At the same time, the prosecution of the person who has violated the established prohibitions on the illegal use of someone else's IP does not even depend on the right holder's awareness of the violation.

Thus, the customs authority applied to the state commercial court with a claim to bring a business entity to administrative responsibility on the basis of the specified article of the Code on Administrative Offences. By the decision of the state commercial court of first instance, upheld by the decision of the court of appeal, the claims were satisfied in full, taking into account the proof of the offence provided by the customs authority and the signs of the counterfeit nature of the goods submitted for customs clearance. In its cassation appeal, the business entity referred to the argument that the foreign company (the right holder) recognized as the injured party in the administrative offence case, was not notified by the court of the place and time of the case hearing, which meant that the contested judicial acts should be cancelled. The business entity also indicated that the administrative case was initiated in violation of Article 28.1 of the Code on Administrative Offences in the absence of the right holder's claim on the violation of the exclusive rights to the trademark. Nevertheless, the Intellectual Property Court rejected these arguments and found no grounds for annulling the contested judicial acts and releasing the offender from administrative liability in view of the following. The case of an administrative offence was initiated in compliance with the requirements of Article 28.1 of the Code on Administrative Offences since the customs authority had sufficient data indicating the existence of the administrative offence. The presence of a statement by the trademark right holder is not a mandatory condition for initiating an administrative offence case mentioned in part 1, Article 14.10 of the Code of Administrative Offences. There are no grounds for the cancellation of the contested judicial acts due to the failure to notify the foreign company that owns the trademark about the place and time of the case hearing since the court of first instance did not include the right holder as the injured person either on the initiative of the business entity or on the court's own initiative. At the same time, the right holder themselves did not file either an appeal or cassation complaint on the violation of their procedural rights. Consequently, the failure of the court of first instance to involve the right holder in the case does not form grounds for cancelling the state commercial court's decision, since the adoption of the judicial act on bringing the person who committed the administrative offence to administrative liability (provided in Article 14.10 of the Code on Administrative Offences) did not and could not lead to the violation of the owner's rights (part 3 of Article 288 of the State Commercial Procedure Code). At the same time, the cancellation of this judicial act can entail a violation of the owner's rights (clause 11 of the Review of Judicial Practice, approved by the Supreme Court of the Russian Federation on December 6, 2017).

The illegal use of someone else's trademark, service mark, appellation of origin of goods or similar signs for similar goods also entails criminal liability (Article 180 of the Criminal Code of the Russian Federation No. 63-FZ of June 13, 1996; hereinafter the Criminal Code).

In particular, part 1 of Article 180 of the Criminal Code establishes that the illegal use of someone else's trademark, service mark, appellation of origin of goods or similar signs for homogeneous goods is committed repeatedly or causes major damage could be punishable by:

- a fine of 100,000–300,000 rubles or a fine worth the amount of the salary or other income of the convicted person for a period of up to 2 years,
- community service for up to 480 hours,
- corrective labour for up to 2 years,
- penal labour for up to 2 years,
- up to 2-year imprisonment with a fine worth up to 80,000 rubles or the amount of the convict's salary or other income for a period of up to 6 months.

Part 2 of the article establishes liability for the illegal use of warning markings in relation to a trademark or appellation of origin not registered in the Russian Federation if this act has been committed repeatedly or caused major damage.

Major damage is that exceeding the amount of 250,000 rubles.

There are two more parts in Article 180 of the Criminal Code providing for liability for the above offences when they are committed by a group of individuals participating in a conspiracy or an organized group.

However, by virtue of clause 3 of Article 20 of the Criminal Procedure Code of the Russian Federation No. 174-FZ of December 18, 2001, as a general rule, criminal cases of this kind are cases of private-public prosecution and are initiated only at the request of the injured person, provided that an individual entrepreneur committed them in connection with one's business and (or) management of one's property used for business or if these crimes were committed by a member of the management body of a commercial organization in connection with the exercise of one's powers to manage the organization or in connection with the commercial organization's business or other economic activities (Resolution of the Supreme Court of the Russian Federation No. 48 of November 15, 2016). Nevertheless, crimes under this article of the Criminal Code are not subject to private-public prosecution if the crime has caused harm to the interests of the state or a municipal unitary enterprise, state corporation, state company, commercial organization with the state's or a municipal formation's participation in the authorized capital (share fund) or if the subject of the crime was state or municipal property.

Thus, in Russia, there are many opportunities for the protection of IP rights. The choice of the protection method is made by the authorized person.

Due to the peculiarities, specifically the intangible nature, of IP subject matter, the right holders are limited in their ability to control observance of their exclusive rights to the results of intellectual activity and means of individualization by third parties, identify violations and establish an exact or at least an approximate value of damages incurred (especially in the form of lost profits), including if the offence was committed in the field of business.

Taking into account the above peculiarities that predetermine the need to establish special methods of protection of the violated IP exclusive rights, the

Civil Code grants the right holder the opportunity, in the cases provided in the named act for certain types of results of intellectual activity or means of individualization, to demand from the violator, instead of damages, payment of appropriate compensation and exempt the right holder from the need to prove the amount of the caused damage in court (Resolution of the Constitutional Court No. 28-P of December 13, 2016). The specified method of protection can now be considered in demand due to the above reasons. At the same time, when initiating protection, it is advisable to take into account all the regulatory provisions and the practice of their implementation.

Should anyone want to take advantage of another person's intellectual achievements, it is worth considering the likelihood of liability and prosecution, its type and possible legal measures and estimated costs, including judicial ones.

Notes

1 On this subject, see, for example, Maximov, V.A. "Security and protection of subjective civil rights, the legal nature of the right of defence" ["Okhrana i zashchita sub"ektivnykh grazhdanskikh prav, yuridicheskaya priroda prava na zashchitu"]. *Bulletin of the St. Petersburg University of the Ministry of Internal Affairs of Russia [Vestnik Sankt-Peterburgskogo universiteta MVD Rossii]*. 2016. No. 2 (70). Pp. 86–91.

2 On this subject, see, for example, Ryabinin, N.A. "The aspects of understanding the subjective right to protection of civil rights" ["Osobennosti ponimaniya sub"ektivnogo prava na zashchitu grazhdanskikh prav"]. *Legal Science and Law Enforcement Practice [Yuridicheskaya i pravookhranitel'naya praktika]*. 2018. No. 2 (44). Pp. 14–19.

3 On this subject, see Zhivikhina, I.B. "Operational method of protecting property rights" [Operativnyy sposob zashchity prava sobstvennosti]. *Russian Judge [Rossiyskiy sud'ya]*. 2006. No. 3. Pp. 16–19; Kondrakova, I.A. "Non-judicial procedure for the protection of corporate rights of shareholders" [Nesudebnyy poryadok zashchity korporativnykh prav aktsionerov]. *Juridical World [Yuridicheskiy mir]*. 2006. No. 1. Pp. 37–40

4 Matryoshka or Russian dolls ("*Матрешка*" in Russian) is a Russian wooden toy. It is a painted doll with smaller dolls like it inside.

5 In the Russian Federation, it is also possible to protect a legal entity's business reputation, but legal entities cannot make claims for compensation for moral harm.

6 Preliminary interim measures are aimed at ensuring the property interests of the applicant before filing a claim.

References

Gorbacheva, S. V. *Self-protection of Rights under Russian Legislation: A PhD Thesis in Law* [*Samozashchita prav po rossiyskomu zakonodatel'stvu: diss. na soiskanie uchenoi stepeni kand. yurid. nauk*]. Nizhny Novgorod, 2005.

Gribanov, V.P. *Exercise and Protection of Civil Rights [Gribanov V.P. Osushchestvlenie i zashchita grazhdanskikh prav.]*. Moscow, Statut, 2001. (http://civil.consultant.ru/elib/books/1/)

Intellectual Property Law: Textbook. Vol. 1: General Provisions. [Pravo intellektual'noy sobstvennosti: Uchebnik. T. 1: Obshchie polozheniya]. Edited by Novoselova, L.A. Moscow, Statut, 2017.

Ivanov, A.Yu. Myths of Legal Monopoly, or the why Russia doesn't Innovated Despite a Relentless Intellectual Property Protection Regime [Mify o legal'noy monopolii, ili skaz o tom, pochemu v Rossii ne razvivayutsya innovatsii pri upornoy okhrane intellektual'noy sobstvennosti]. *Statute [Zakon]*. 2020. No. 2. P. 86–102.

Shastitko, A.E. Protection of Competition and Intellectual Property: Pragmatic Filters in the Interdisciplinary Discourse [Zashchita konkurentsii i intellektual'noy sobstvennosti: pragmaticheskie fil'try v mezhdistsiplinarnom diskurse], in M.A. Egorova (ed.) *Actual Issues of Modern Competition Law. Collection of scientific works. Volume 2 [Aktual'nye voprosy sovremennogo konkurentnogo prava. Sbornik nauchnykh trudov. Vypusk 2*. Moscow, Yustitsinform, 2018.

12 Conclusion

Thus, intellectual property (IP) is an extremely important instrument in business activities. Despite the ongoing discussions about the content of this phenomenon, its existence and special role can hardly be questioned. In the Russian Federation, it is customary to refer to IP both as the results of intellectual activity and the means of individualization of goods, works and services and the enterprises equated to them. Moreover, the use of IP is carried out in business.

From an economic point of view, the most important will be the exclusive right, the presence of which is characteristic of all IP subject matter. However, it is irrational to diminish the non-property (moral) rights or so-called other rights, although they arise only in cases provided for by the law. They, in particular, allow the identification of the author, emphasizing his special role in the process of creating the results of intellectual activity.

Modern legislation regulates in detail the issues related to the creation, use and protection of IP. At the same time, it should be noted that the combination of dispositive and mandatory norms allows us to choose the most appropriate set of behaviour, taking into account the binding rules with which failure to comply will entail negative consequences.

In addition, the sphere of IP is a vivid illustration of the combination of three principles of regulation (competition, monopoly and cooperation), enabling a reasonable balance both in relations between private entities and the implementation of private and public interests.

However, while recognizing the value of IP, it should not be overestimated. The mere existence of IP is not an unambiguous condition leading to a positive effect. Incompetent management, lack of proper attention to various aspects of its use and indifference to its protection can neutralize all possible advantages. Moreover, unjustified expectations can lead to disastrous consequences for the business.

In this book, an attempt was made to highlight the most significant issues related to IP in business, based on Russian practice. Certainly, there are more aspects that could be covered, but within the framework of this book, the task was set to give an overview of IP in business. We hope that this material will arouse the interest of readers and encourage them to continue their research in the sphere of IP.

Glossary of terms

Administrative liability (*administrativnaya otvetstvennost'*) – responsibility arising in connection with the recognition of a person guilty of committing an administrative offence, which is understood as an unlawful, guilty act (inaction) of an individual or legal entity, for which the Code on Administrative Offences or the laws of the subjects of the Russian Federation on administrative offences established administrative liability (Article 2.1 of the Code on Administrative Offences).

Author of the result of intellectual activity (*avtor rezul'tata intellektual'noy deyatel'nosti*) – a natural person that created a result of intellectual activity.

Commercial legal entity (*kommercheskoe yuridicheskoe litso*) – a legal entity that is established for making profit. The forms of commercial legal entities are: a business partnership (*khozyaystvennoe tovarishchestvo*), business company (*hozjajstvennoe obshhestvo*), peasant farm enterprise (*krest'yanskoe (fermerskoe) khozyaystvo*), production cooperative (*proizvodstvennyy kooperativ*), economic partnership (*khozyaystvennoe partnerstvo*) and unitary state (municipal) enterprises (*gosudarstvennye i munitsipal'nye unitarnye predpriyatiya*) (Article 50 of the Civil Code).

Corporate legal entity (*korporativnoe yuridicheskoe litso*) – a legal entity, the founders (participants) of which have the right of participation (*uchastie*)/membership (*chlenstvo*) in it and form the supreme governing body of the corporation. They are a business partnership (*khozyaystvennoe tovarishchestvo*), business company (*hozyajstvennoe obshhestvo*), peasant farm enterprise (*krest'yanskoe (fermerskoe) khozyaystvo*)), production cooperative (*proizvodstvennyy kooperativ*), economic partnership (*khozyaystvennoe partnerstvo*), consumer cooperatives (*potrebitel'skie kooperativy*), public organizations (*obshchestvennye organizatsii*), social movements (*obshchestvennye dvizheniya*), associations (unions) (*assotsiatsii (soyuzy)*), chambers of notaries (*notarial'nye palaty*), real estate owners associations (*tovarishchestva sobstvennikov nedvizhimosti*), Cossack societies entered in the State Register of Cossack Societies in the Russian Federation (*kazach'i obshchestva, vnesennye v gosudarstvennyy reestr kazach'ikh obshchestv v Rossiyskoy Federatsii*), communities of indigenous peoples of the Russian Federation (*obshchiny korennykh malochislennykh narodov Rossiyskoy Federatsii*), etc. (clause 1 of Article 65.1 of the Civil Code).

Courts of general jurisdiction (*sudy obshhey yurisdikcii*) – federal courts of general jurisdiction and courts of general jurisdiction of the constituent entities of the Russian Federation. Courts of general jurisdiction consider all civil and administrative cases on the protection of violated or disputed rights, freedoms and interests protected by law, with the exception of cases that are considered by other courts in accordance with the legislation of the Russian Federation; all criminal cases; other cases referred by the Constitution of the Russian Federation, federal constitutional laws and federal laws to their jurisdiction. Federal courts of general jurisdiction include cassation courts of general jurisdiction; courts of appeal of general jurisdiction; the supreme courts of the republics, territorial and regional courts, courts of cities of federal significance, the court of an autonomous region, courts of autonomous regions; district courts, city courts, inter-district courts (district courts); military courts, the powers, procedure for the formation and activity of which are established by federal constitutional law; specialized courts, the powers, procedure of formation and activity of which are established by federal constitutional law. The courts of general jurisdiction of the constituent entities of the Russian Federation include justices of the peace.

Criminal liability (*ugolovnaya otvetstvennost'*) – liability, the basis of which is the committing of an act containing all the signs of a crime provided for by the Criminal Code of the Russian Federation.

Essential terms of contract (*sushchestvennye usloviya dogovora*) – the terms of the contract, in the absence of which the contract is considered non-concluded. Inconsistency of conditions can be regarded as their absence.

Good faith (*dobrosovestnost'*) – behaviour expected of any participant in civil turnover, taking into account the rights and legitimate interests of the other party (clause 1 of Resolution of the Plenum of the Supreme Court No. 25). The Civil Code provides for the presumption of good faith and the principle of good faith. The principle of reasonableness (*printsip razumnosti*) is associated with good faith. It implies the validity and appropriateness of the decision made.

Joint stock company (JSC) (*aktsionernoe obshchestvo*) – a corporate commercial legal entity, the authorized capital of which is divided into shares of stock certifying the rights and obligations of the participants (shareholders) to the company. Shareholders are not liable for obligations of the legal entity and bear a risk of losses related to the entity's activity within the value of shares of stock owned by them (clause 1 of Article 96 of the Civil Code .

Individual entrepreneur (*individual'nyy predprinimatel'*) – a physical person registered as an individual entrepreneur by tax authorities. As a rule, the person has the right to engage in entrepreneurial activity without forming a legal entity from the moment of state registration as an individual entrepreneur. The rules of the Civil Code that regulate the activities of commercial legal entities are accordingly applied to the entrepreneurs unless otherwise follows from the law, other legal acts or the essence of the legal relationship (Article 23 of the Civil Code).

Intellectual property rights (*intellektual'nye prava*) – rights that arise in respect of the results of intellectual activity and means of individualization of legal entities, goods, works, services and enterprises equated to them. The Civil Code provides for exclusive right, personal non-property (moral) rights and other rights.

Legal entity (*yuridicheskoe litso*) – an organization that has separate property and is responsible for its obligations with it and, on its own behalf, may acquire and exercise civil rights and bear civil obligations and be a plaintiff and defendant in court (Article 48 of the Civil Code). The law provides for different types of legal entities, namely, corporate and non-corporate (unitary), commercial and non-commercial, private and public, etc.

Limited liability company (LLC) (*obshchestvo s ogranichennoy otvetsvennost'yu*) – a corporate commercial legal entity, the authorized capital of which is divided into participatory shares. An LLC can be set up by one or several persons. Participants of LLCs are not liable for the obligations of the legal entity and bear the risk of losses related to the entity's activity within the value of the participatory shares. The legal status of an LLC is regulated by the Civil Code and the Law on LLCs. This form of commercial legal entity is the most widespread in the Russian Federation. The legal status of an LLC is regulated by the Civil Code of the Russian Federation and the Law on LLC.

Non-commercial legal entity (*nekommercheskoe yuridicheskoe litso*) – a legal entity that is established to achieve different goals except for making profit. Non-commercial organizations may carry out income-generating activities if provided for by their statutes, only insofar as it serves the achievement of the goals for which they were created and if it is consistent with those goals. They do not distribute the received profit among the participants. They can be created in the form of consumer cooperatives (*potrebitel'skie kooperativy*), public organizations (*obshchestvennye organizatsii*), social movements (*obshchestvennye dvizheniya*), associations (unions) (*assotsiatsii (soyuzy)*), chambers of notaries (*notarial'nye palaty*), real estate owners associations (*tovarishchestva sobstvennikov nedvizhimosti*), Cossack societies entered in the State Register of Cossack Societies in the Russian Federation (*kazach'i obshchestva, vnesennye v gosudarstvennyy reestr kazach'ikh obshchestv v Rossiyskoy Federatsii*), communities of indigenous peoples of the Russian Federation (*obshchiny korennykh malochislennykh narodov Rossiyskoy Federatsii*), funds (*fondy*), institutions (*uchrezhdeniya*), autonomous non-profit organizations (*avtonomnye nekommercheskie organizatsii*), religious organizations (*religioznye organizatsii*), state corporations (*gosudarstvennye korporatsii*) and public companies (*publichno-pravovye kompanii*) (Article 50 of the Civil Code).

Non-corporate legal entity (*unitarnoe yuridicheskoe litso*) – a legal entity, the founders of which have no right of participation (*uchastie*) or membership (*chlenstvo*). They are unitary state (municipal) enterprises (*gosudarstvennye i munitsipal'nye unitarnye predpriyatiya*), funds (*fondy*), institutions (*uchrezhdeniya*), autonomous non-profit organizations (*avtonomnye nekommercheskie organizatsii*), religious organizations (*religioznye organizatsii*), state corporations (*gosudarstvennye korporatsii*) and public companies (*publichno-pravovye kompanii*) (clause 2 of Article 65.1 of the Civil Code).

Patent attorneys (*patentnyy poverennyy*) – citizens who have received the status of a patent attorney in accordance with the law and established procedure and carry out activities related to the legal security of the results of intellectual activity and means of individualization, the protection of intellectual rights, the acquisition of exclusive rights to the results of intellectual activity and means of individualization, and the disposal of such rights.

Plenum of the Supreme Court of the Russian Federation (Plenary Session of the Supreme Court, *Plenum Verhovnogo Suda Rossijskoj Federacii*) – formed in the Supreme Court of the Russian Federation. It is composed of the Chairman of the Supreme Court of the Russian Federation, the First Deputy Chairman of the Supreme Court of the Russian Federation and Deputy Chairmen of the Supreme Court of the Russian Federation – chairmen of the judicial Collegia of the Supreme Court of the Russian Federation and judges of the Supreme Court of the Russian Federation. Among its other functions, it considers materials of analysis and generalization of judicial practice and gives explanations to the courts on issues of judicial practice in order to ensure the uniform application of the legislation of the Russian Federation.

Presidium of the Intellectual Property Court (*Prezidium Suda po intellektual'nym pravam*) –composed of the Chairman of the Intellectual Property Court, his deputies, chairmen of the judicial panels and judges who are members of the Presidium of the Intellectual Property Court. The Presidium of the Intellectual Property Court carries out, as cassation instance, an examination of the legality of the judicial acts of the Intellectual Property Court that have entered into legal force, adopted by it in the first instance and considers issues of judicial practice, etc. (Articles 43.5 and 43.6 of Federal Constitutional Law No. 1-FKZ of April 28, 1995, "On State Commercial Courts in the Russian Federation").

Procedure codes (*protsessual'nye kodeksy*) – codes that regulate court procedures.

Right of prior use (*pravo prezhdepol'zovaniya*) – the right of a person who had been exploiting, in good faith, a solution identical to the invention or a solution that differs from it only in some comparable features, created regardless of the author, within the territory of the Russian Federation before the priority date of the invention, utility model or industrial design, had made necessary preparations for it, such a person retains the right to further non-compensated use of said identical solution without the extension of the scope of use. It is called the right to prior use (Article 1361 of the Civil Code).

Right of subsequent use (*pravo poslepol'zovaniya*) – right of a person, who began to use an invention, utility model or industrial design, or made the necessary preparations between the date of termination of a patent for an invention, utility model or industrial design and the date of publication in the official bulletin of the federal executive body for intellectual property of information on the restoration of the patent, to use it free of charge without expanding the scope of such use (Article 1400 of the Civil Code).

Self-regulatory organizations (*samoreguliruemye organizatsii*) – non-profit organizations created for the purposes provided for by the Law on Self-Regulatory Organizations and other federal laws, based on membership, combining subjects of entrepreneurial activity according to the unity of the industry of production of goods (works, services) or the market of manufactured goods (works, services) or subjects of professional activity of a certain type (Federal Law No. 315-FZ of August 3, 2018, "On Self-Regulatory Organizations").

State commercial courts (*arbitrazhnye sudy*) – federal courts that are part of the judicial system of the Russian Federation. They resolve economic disputes. The main tasks of the state commercial courts when considering disputes within their competence are the protection of violated or disputed rights and legitimate interests of enterprises, institutions, organizations and citizens in the field of business and other economic activity and assistance in strengthening the rule of law and prevention of violations in the field of entrepreneurial and other economic activities. The system of state commercial courts consists of the first instance courts (state commercial courts of regions and cities of federal importance), appeal courts (state commercial courts of appeal), and cassation courts (state commercial courts of circuits) special courts (IP Court) (Federal Constitutional Law No. 1-FKZ of April 28, 1995, "On State Commercial Courts in the Russian Federation"). State commercial courts should be distinguished from non-state arbitral courts (*treteyskie study*) (Federal Law No. 382-FZ of December 29, 2015, "On Arbitration in the Russian Federation").

Unified State Register for Legal Entities (USRLE) (*Edinyy gosudarstvennyy reestr juridicheskih lits*) – state register containing information on registered legal entities in the territory of the Russian Federation. The register is maintained by the Federal Tax Service and its territorial bodies.

Unified State Register for Individual Entrepreneurs (USRIE) (*Edinyy gosudarstvennyy reestr individual'nyh predprinimateley*) – state register containing information on individually registered entrepreneurs in the territory of the Russian Federation. The register is maintained by the Federal Tax Service and its territorial bodies.

Index

Taylor & Francis Group
an informa business

Taylor & Francis eBooks

www.taylorfrancis.com

A single destination for eBooks from Taylor & Francis with increased functionality and an improved user experience to meet the needs of our customers.

90,000+ eBooks of award-winning academic content in Humanities, Social Science, Science, Technology, Engineering, and Medical written by a global network of editors and authors.

TAYLOR & FRANCIS EBOOKS OFFERS:

- A streamlined experience for our library customers
- A single point of discovery for all of our eBook content
- Improved search and discovery of content at both book and chapter level

REQUEST A FREE TRIAL

support@taylorfrancis.com

Routledge
Taylor & Francis Group

CRC Press
Taylor & Francis Group